High Count

By F

High Country of Central Oregon takes the reader into one of the most scenic parts of the state. Here are glacial-clad volcanoes, secluded alpine meadows, sparkling lakes, crystal-clear streams and extensive pine forests. The book describes the major volcanoes and mountain passes of the Cascades from spire-like Mt. Jefferson to Fuji-shaped Bachelor Butte, incorporating historical events into their geographical setting, with accounts of early-day explorers and trail blazers through the region.

The author traces the development of winter sports in the Cascades from the early 1920's, when Scandinavians, seeking snow courses in the McKenzie Pass area, introduced ski jumping and cross-country skiing and tobogganing. Later, in 1927, they helped create the Bend Skyliners, still an active organization dedicated to ski competition and instruction. Today, Bachelor's powdery slopes host well over a quarter-million skiers each season.

The Deschutes River—Oregon's famous "River of the Falls"—is followed downstream from its quiet beginnings at Little Lava Lake, past large reservoirs, through roaring rapids and peaceful meadows to Bend. The Sunriver story is included in the Deschutes River chapter—a uniquely planned community that has attained nationwide reputation for excellence in design. The book takes the motorist, or armchair traveler, along the Cascade Lakes Highway—a favorite for recreationists visiting Central Oregon—with "stops" being made at many recreational and scenic places such as Todd, Elk, and Cultus Lakes.

One chapter explores the Newberry Volcano Country, with visits to Newberry Crater. Another focuses on the history of logging, with accounts of the early scramble for the pine forests, the interesting story of those who lived in the Shevlin-Hixon and Brooks-Scanlon logging camps, and contemporary logging practices. *High Country* recounts the early history of the main north-south route through Central Oregon and the development of the small but bustling communities of La Pine, Gilchrist, and Crescent. A final chapter explores the Sisters Country. All chapters include many photos of Central Oregon's scenic High Country.

HIGH

COUNTRY

of CENTRAL OREGON

Raymond R. Hatton

Binford & Mort Publishing
Portland, Oregon

To Phil F. Brogan
whose half century of journalism in Bend
is reflected in *High Country
of Central Oregon*

High Country of Central Oregon
Copyright © 1980, 1987 by Binford & Mort Publishing
All rights reserved. No part of this book may be reproduced in any form or by any electronic or mechanical means including information storage and retrieval systems without permission in writing from the publishers, except by a reviewer who may quote brief passages in review.
Printed in the United States of America
Library of Congress Catalog Card Number: 80-7801
ISBN: 0-8323-0458-1 (softcover)
First Edition 1980
Second Edition 1987

Foreword to the Second Edition

Several years have passed since the printing of the first edition of the *High Country of Central Oregon*, and in that time cultural landscape changes have occurred in the region. The expansion at the Mt. Bachelor Ski Resort during the 1980's included the construction of two new chairlifts, including a lift to the summit, and replacement of older chairlifts by more modern faster lifts. A new Nordic Center, with an attractive lodge and new groomed trails, have made Mt. Bachelor a major ski resort for both Alpine and Nordic skiers. During the 1986-87 season, Mt. Bachelor Ski Resort estimated the number of skier-days to have exceeded 600,000.

Recreational activities in the High Country in recent years have included a greater participation in whitewater rafting on the Deschutes River, the staging of the Cascade Lakes Triathalon, and the Cascade Cycling Classic which has events at Lava Butte, Mt. Bachelor, and in downtown Bend. At Elk Lake, windsurfing has become a popular summertime activity.

During the 1980's, major developments took place at the three large destination resorts located in the High Country. A paved highway, open all year, was constructed to provide a more direct link between Sunriver and Mt. Bachelor Ski Resort. The Sunriver Mall was greatly expanded in the mid 1980's. Retail stores and professional offices, which front a brick-paved "Town Square" provide additional attractive shopping and service facilities. The opening of the North Golf Course and adjacent swimming pool, plus the construction of a new access (Cottonwood Road) to Highway 97 have helped develop the northern section of the Sunriver properties. By 1987 some 1,000 people called Sunriver "home."

At the Inn of the Seventh Mountain, construction of an 18-hole golf course was commenced in 1986. Expanded recreational and dining facilities were completed during the 1980's. In April, 1987, the assets of the Black Butte Ranch Corporation ($5.2 million) were transferred from Brooks Resources, Inc. to the resort's homeowners. Commercial expansion occurred in the city of Sisters during the 1980's with the opening of several new businesses and the construction of motel and convention facilities just west of the city.

The eruption of Mt. St. Helens in 1980 has alerted geologists (and, perhaps the lay person) to keep an eye on the volcanic Cascades in Central Oregon. The moraine-impounded Carver Lake, located at the northern foot of South Sister, was, in 1986, designated a natural hazard by Corps of Engineers geologists with, should the moraine suddenly give way, the potential for causing flood damage in parts of the City of Sisters.

Despite the above-mentioned changes, the High Country has largely remained unchanged and the beauty of the region continues to beckon visitors.

CONTENTS

Introduction xi
1. GEOGRAPHIC SETTING 1
   Volcanic Landscapes 5
   Glaciation 6
   Weather and Climate 7
   Vegetation 11
   Wilderness Areas 13

2. THE CASCADES 15
   Naming the Cascades 16
   The Cascades Create Two Oregons 18
   Weather and Climate 19
   Mount Jefferson 23
   Three Fingered Jack 27
   Santiam Pass 29
   McKenzie Pass Highway 34
   The Three Sisters 43
   Three Sisters Reveal Their Ages 45
   North Sister 46
   Middle Sister 47
   South Sister 47
   Green Lakes 48
   Wickiup Plains and Rock Mesa 50
   Pacific Crest National Scenic Trail 52
   Broken Top 54
   Mt. Bachelor 57

3. WINTER SPORTS 60
   McKenzie Pass Site Selected 60
   New Ski Area Developed 66
   Mt. Bachelor Ski Resort 69

4. THE DESCHUTES RIVER 73
   Source of the Deschutes 76
   Crane Prairie Reservoir 77
   Wickiup Reservoir 79
   Pringle Falls 82
   La Pine State Recreation Area 83
   Fall River 83
   Little Deschutes River 85
   Spring River 87
   Sunriver 88
   Benham Falls 97
   Ryan Meadow and Dillon Falls 100
   Lava Island Falls 102

5. CASCADE LAKES HIGHWAY 105
    Building of the Highway 105
    Inn of the Seventh Mountain 107
    Dutchman Flat and Tumalo Mountain 109
    Todd Lake 110
    Sparks Lake 113
    Devils Garden 115
    Devils Lake 115
    Elk Lake and Hosmer Lake 116
    Mink Lake Basin 118
    Lava Lakes 118
    Cultus Lakes 118
    Twin Lakes 119
    Pringle Falls Experiment Forest 120
6. NEWBERRY VOLCANO 122
    Lava Butte... 130
    Lava Cast Forest..................................... 138
    Lava Caves 141
    The Devils Garden 147
7. LOGGING THE HIGH COUNTRY 149
    Giant Lumber Mills Come to Bend 150
    Logging and Living in the High Country 155
    Economic Impact of the Lumber Mills 161
8. COMMUNITIES ALONG HIGHWAY 97 168
    Highway 97 168
    La Pine.. 170
    Gilchrist... 175
    Crescent... 176
9. THE SISTERS COUNTRY 179
    Sisters... 179
    Indian Ford Ranch 185
    Black Butte 186
    Black Butte Ranch 189
    Metolius River Valley................................ 192
    Head of the Metolius River 198
    Camp Sherman 202
    Wizard Falls Fish Hatchery 204
    Head of Jack Creek 205
    Suttle Lake—Blue Lake Area 206
    Camp Tamarack....................................... 210
    Epilogue 211
Notes 213
Bibliography... 215
Index 218

viii

ACKNOWLEDGMENTS

I wish to express my gratitude to the following: Dr. Bruce O. Nolf, Professor of Geology, Central Oregon Community College, gave of his time for consultation and advice on the geology of the High Country. To the several employees of the Deschutes National Forest Service, including the Silviculture Laboratory, Bend, for help with various aspects of the manuscript including historical photographs. Edith Kostol verified the story of early-day winter sports. Alice Bishop and Rosanna Duberow for recounting their early years living in logging camps. Leo Bishop, Brooks-Scanlon employee for 47 years, and Professor Ward S. Tonsfeldt, Central Oregon Community College, who helped with details on early-day logging. James L. Crowell and Tom Turner, Brooks-Scanlon, respectively helped organize and conduct a field visitation to study logging operations.

Assistance with the research or with reviewing short sections of the manuscript was provided by Eleanor Bechen, Roblay McMullin, Betty and Laurence Dyer, Oscar Spliid, Kitty Warner, Luther Metke, Mary Lou Loar (Metolius River Valley), Ken Lovegren (Blue Lake), Bill Smith (Black Butte Ranch), Dick Patterson, Tillie Wilson, Linda Smith (Sisters), Fred Arpke (Indian Ford Ranch), and Donna Gill (Camp Tamarack). The chapter on Highway 97 was read by Dean Hollinshead, Charlie Shotts and Kay Nelson. Jay Bowerman reviewed the section on Sunriver, and Chuck Cleveland, Bend, recalled the early history of the Elk Lake Resort.

Thanks are extended to the many other Central Oregonians who directly or indirectly contributed to the compilation of the High Country.

Special thanks are extended to Carol Reynolds for her drafting of the map and to Doris Trueax for her patience and persistence in the typing of the manuscript. The Central Oregon Community College Foundation provided financial assistance for the reproduction of many of the photographs. Photographs used in the book, other than my own, came from several different sources; each is identified.

The entire manuscript was read by Phil F. Brogan, long time Bend resident and author of *East of the Cascades*, and by Professor R. Keith Clark, co-author of *The Terrible Trail, The Meek Party Cutoff*. Their helpful suggestions and corrections are appreciated.

In addition, the author is grateful for the work performed by Thomas Binford, publisher, and Laura K. Phillips, editor, of Binford & Mort, who helped create the book from the manuscript.

R.R.H.

INTRODUCTION

My first views of the High Country of Central Oregon were while traveling along Highway 97 periodically during the summer months in the late 1950's and early 1960's. Like many others who use Highway 97 to travel between northern Idaho or Washington and California, I became deeply fascinated, even curious, about the attractive snow-capped volcanoes and undulating forested hills west of Bend.

Some of the more distinctive landscape features of the area soon became known by name, shape and location. For example, I would look for Mt. Jefferson's spire-like peak standing aloof in its isolation and seemingly defying access to those who try to approach it by road. Black Butte was remembered for its somber-looking, conical-shaped bulk rising abruptly above the forested foothills of the Cascades.

The Three Sisters, Broken Top and Bachelor Butte are mountains that dominate the skyline to the west of Bend. When seen from Bend, the peaks line up one after another from north to south and are quite easily named. However, when you approach Bend from the north or the south, these same peaks seem grouped together and are less easily identified. While traveling through the juniper lands north of Bend early on a June morning, one impressionistic view of the Three Sisters was when the first rays of the sun brought life to the snow-covered peaks, tinting them with a pinkish glow while, at the same time, the lower slopes still slept in semi-darkness.

During my first journeys through Central Oregon, I became familiar with the topography of the Cascade peaks, but I knew nothing of the hidden beauty tucked away in the mountains and forests. The scenic Pacific Crest Trail, the quiet beauty of alpine meadows, the recreational opportunities on the many lakes of the High Country, and the aesthetic appeal of the Deschutes River were all kept secluded by the vast forest lands which stretch westward from Bend. In my early visits to Central Oregon I had noted the rather foreboding bulk of Newberry Volcano south of Bend. However, travel time did not allow glimpses inside the brooding mass. The fascinating geological story associated with Newberry Volcano was, at that time, unknown to me.

It was several years ago that I drove the spiral road to the summit of Lava Butte, the 500-foot-high cinder cone that lies adjacent to Highway 97, some ten miles south of Bend. The 360-degree panorama as seen from Lava Butte is as impressive today as it was twenty years ago. Extensive pine forests spread out from the edge of the apron of lava—which had gushed forth from the base of the butte—then climb the slopes of Newberry Volcano and claw the lower reaches of the Cascades. These forests have formed the basis for the lumber industry, a major economic activity for Bend since 1916. The scars created by early-day logging are largely healed by nature's restorative powers. But as I viewed the green landscape at that time, I had never heard of the mobile logging camps operated by the Shevlin-Hixon and Brooks-Scanlon companies.

Twenty-five years ago, recreational land sales in Central Oregon were in their infancy compared to today. Most privately owned forest lands and river meadows still awaited the developers and the subdividers. The peaceful meadow along the banks of the Deschutes River, a few miles south of Lava Butte, was the Hudspeth cattle ranch. These attractive lands awaited the arrival of John Gray, the master-mind behind the Sunriver concept.

Several years after my early introduction to Central Oregon, I was to become acquainted with many parts of the High Country through travel and research. In recent years, since living in Bend, I have hiked many of the mountain trails, climbed many of the Cascade peaks, and explored forests, lakes, lava flows, lava caves, and cinder cones. I have followed the course of the Deschutes River and seen its various moods and settings. Cross-country skiing, a sport that I had never participated in prior to living in Bend, has enabled me to see the High Country in its winter splendor. I have researched the various impacts that tourism and recreation have had on the lands and the economy of the Bend area.

The intent of this book is to acquaint the reader with the High Country of Central Oregon. It includes an examination of the structure of the Cascades, along with the physical and psychological impacts of the mountains. The reader is taken to alpine meadows where summer flowers add to the already picturesque settings. The story of winter sports in the Cascades of Central Oregon is traced from the time Scandinavians migrated to Bend to work in the logging and lumber industry. We follow the course of the Deschutes River from its source in the high lakes, through man-created reservoirs, down white-water rapids, past peaceful meadows and beautiful pine forests, into Bend.

I have included a guided tour of the Cascade Lakes Highway, a 100-mile scenic journey deep into the Deschutes National Forest, to within a few miles of the Three Sisters and Broken Top. The character and unique charm of the Sisters country is described along with historical developments which have helped shape the landscape of the area. Here recreational land sales, tourism, and the revival of frontier western-style architecture in the town of Sisters have revitalized the economy of the old community.

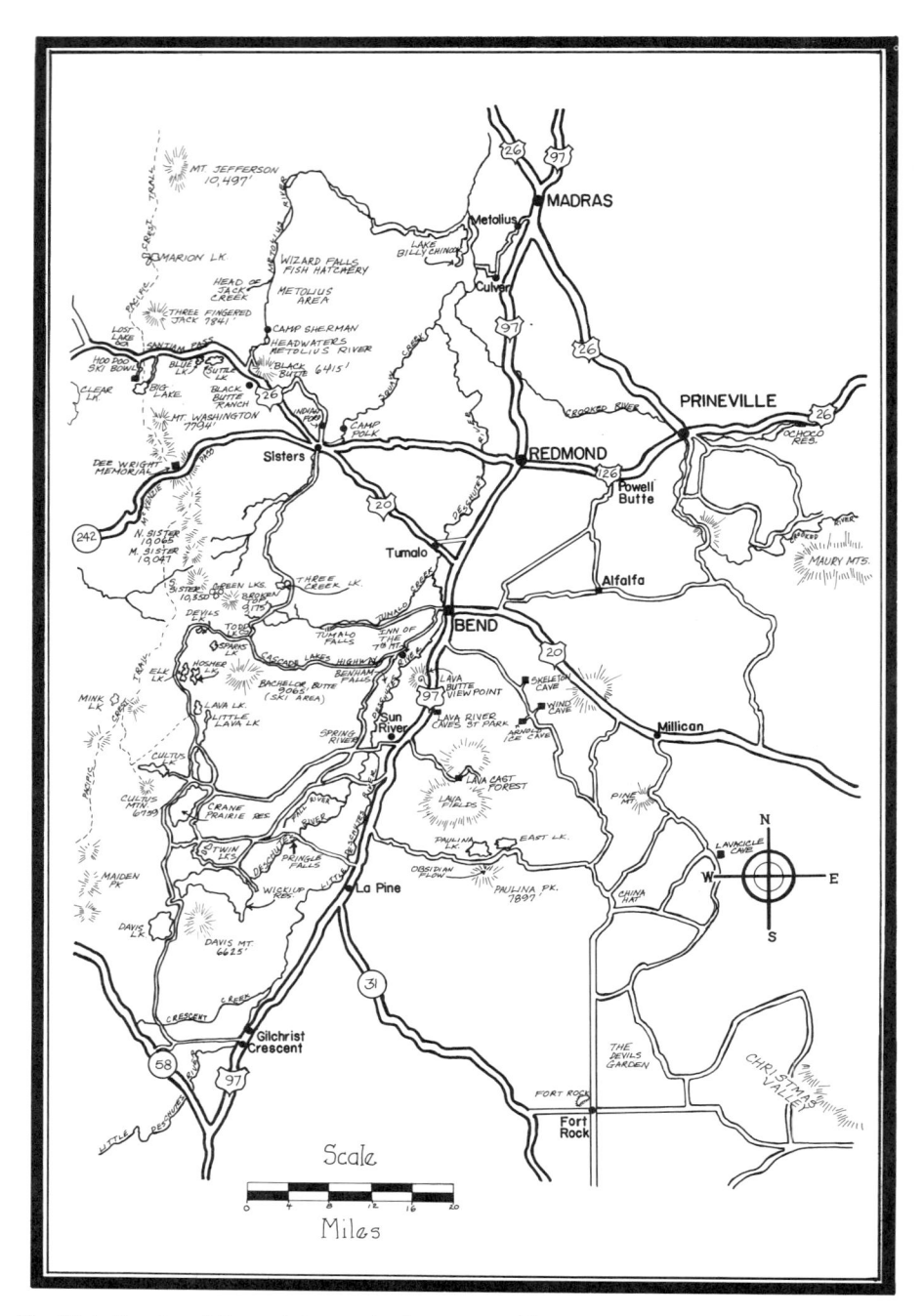

The High Country of Central Oregon is characterized by numerous volcanoes, alpine lakes, clear streams and vast pine forests. Most of the region lies within the Deschutes National Forest.

1.
Geographical Setting

The High Country of Central Oregon is one of the most aesthetic areas of the state, and, in recent years, a sought-after place to establish permanent residence or a vacation home. Towering volcanoes, part of the Cascade Range, rise like islands above an undulating sea of blue-green forests. Snow, clinging to the upper mountain slopes even in late summer, reminds one (using a geologist's calendar) of "yesterday" when snow and ice buried the fire-born mountains, and icy fringes protruded down toward the lowlands.

Nestled within the vast forests are countless lakes. These lakes, locked in by nature's icy key during the long High Country winter, sparkle like jewels in bright summer sun. Cold, crystal-clear streams that emerge from springs or lakes, slice through forests, cut and roar past jagged lava flows and meander quietly across lush, green meadows. Here and there, partly secluded within the forests or conspicuous on the riverine meadows, man has carved roads, platted homesites, and established his domain, either year-round or seasonal. Within the region, recreationists seek out their favorite pastime, whether it be summer or winter. Giant log trucks, bearing capacity loads, scurry toward the mill that will cut and shape the timber.

This, then, is the High Country, a region which was partly explored by 1850, first settled in the late nineteenth century, but whose resources have been tapped only in relatively recent years. The High Country is a distinctive part of Central Oregon. While most of the mid-state area is cursed

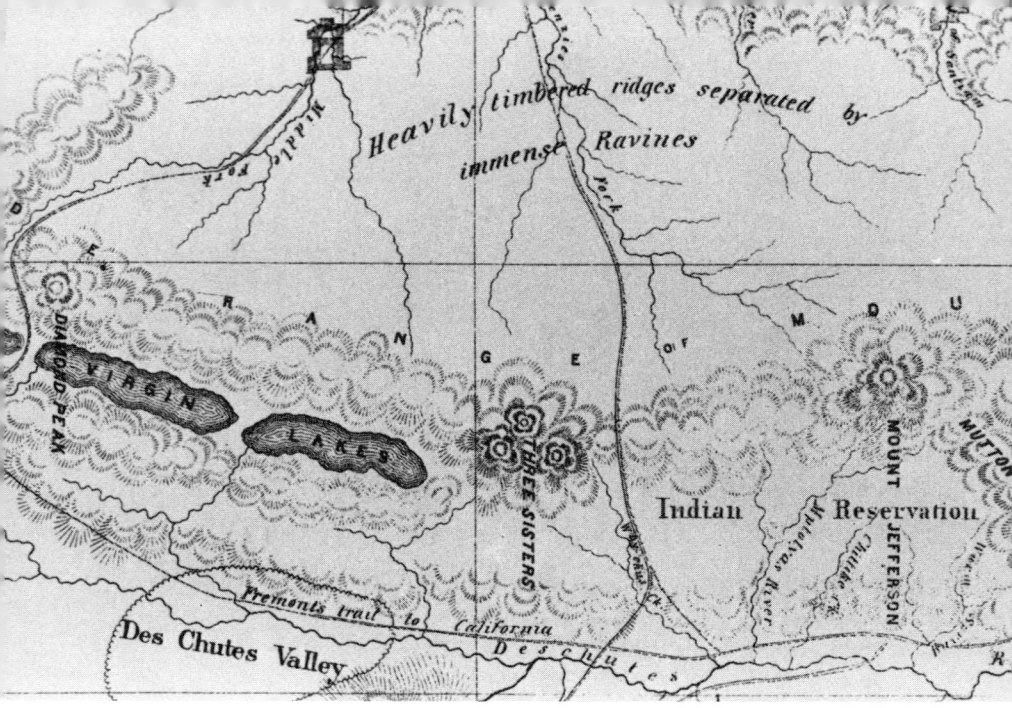

Map of part of the High Country in 1863. At that time, Central Oregon was barely explored and mapped. The map shows the Fremont Trail through the Upper Deschutes Valley and one trail across the Cascades. Note the absence of settlements. *(Early Oregon Atlas)*

The High Country sleeps under winter's blanket of snow. Cascade volcanoes shown include The Three Sisters, Broken Top (right) and, in distance, Mt. Jefferson and Mt. Hood. Frozen lakes are Elk (left), Hosmer (right), and, to the north, Sparks Lake. The "white ribbon" cutting through the forested lands is the Cascade Lakes Highway *(Oregon Dept. of Transportation)*

by aridity and characterized by juniper trees and sagebrush, greater moisture in the High Country is reflected by the vast forests of pine and fir.

The landscapes of the windswept lava plains of Central Oregon are brown and gray, except where irrigation waters have quenched the thirsty lands. Old rounded shield volcanoes rise above the lava plains and, to the north, the plains are deeply incised by spectacular vertical canyons. In the Basin and Range country to the southeast, the parched lands are tilted by great fault scarps. Within the High Country, except for the snow-capped peaks and exposed volcanic rock of the Cascades, the landscapes are predominantly a subdued green and blue. In places, volcanic activity is "recent" and the especially "younger" features have not yet been modified by agents of weathering.

The resources of the High Country are mainly timber and scenery. The industrial and commercial districts of Bend, located on the eastern edge of the region, reflect the utilization of these resources. Agriculture, except for grazing on scattered meadows and pastures, is of minor significance. Where precious water has reached the desert and juniper lands of Central Oregon, agriculture has assumed great importance. Here, irrigated pastures, mint, potatoes, alfalfa and other crops have created swatches of green within the brown plains. Urban areas, small as they are, reflect the agrarian economy of the area.

In winter, heavy snowfall settles on the High Country, creating a landscape that typifies the region's name. From the snowpack comes water for the dry lowlands to the east. Energetic Scandinavians, migrating to jobs created by the lumber industry, sought recreational outlets, and it was natural that such men would bring winter sports to the snow-covered slopes of the Cascades. Today, the High Country hosts thousands of winter sports enthusiasts and has helped balance what was previously a seasonal tourism and recreation economy.

For many Oregonians and residents of other states, the High Country has become the mecca for summer recreation. Indeed, residents of Central Oregon experience a weekly Friday evening "invasion." This armada, consisting of autos, pickups, campers, and motor homes, originating in the Portland metropolitan area and the urban centers in the Willamette Valley, converge on the region's campgrounds, summer homes, and recreation resorts. A host of recreational activities—fishing, hiking, mountain climbing, water skiing, sailing, canoeing—an exhilarating climate, and magnificent scenery await the visitor.

As tourism has increased, so has the desire by many to live within the forested lands of Central Oregon. Most of the territory within the High Country is in public domain, largely under the jurisdiction of the U.S. Forest Service. It is not surprising, then, that the relatively modest amount of privately owned land is in great demand. Land developments are now significant; also, controversial aspects of the land-use issues. However, for the most part, the High Country is sparsely populated. The author estimates that in the region (2000 plus square miles) there is a year-round population of approximately 8000, of whom 6,000 live in the La Pine area.

The name "High Country" is no more an official name of a distinct region of Central Oregon than is the "High Desert." Yet, over the years, common usage of unofficial geographical names leaves almost indelible imprints, if not by the map-makers, at least in the minds of those familiar with the region. Thus, historically, the High Country has been a place where cattlemen and sheepherders have grazed their livestock on forest lands and alpine meadows, and where loggers have cut wide swaths through the pine forests. Bend Skyliners established winter sports in the High Country in the 1920's. Today, both Nordic and alpine skiers converge on the region. Weather forecasts made by the meteorologist on Bend-based KTVZ television station includes specific weekend forecasts for High Country sportsmen. Some Central Oregon businessmen, seeking titles for their operations, have adopted the name "High Country."

In brief, the High Country of Central Oregon, for the purposes of this book, encompasses the Cascade Range from Mount Jefferson in the north to Davis Mountain in the south, and the adjacent forested foothills to the east of the Cascades. It also includes the upper Deschutes Basin, with its attractive natural and man-made lakes, the beautiful Sisters Country, and bulky Newberry Volcano. It approximates many of the boundaries of the Deschutes National Forest. Virtually all of the lands are above 3,500 feet in elevation and many are higher than 5,000 feet.

Volcanic Landscapes

Residents of Central Oregon may take for granted that, for the most part, they live on volcanic rock and that the Cascade skyline to the west is a visible result of volcanism. In clear weather, an observer on Pilot Butte in Bend can see at least ten major volcanoes, many dozen cinder cones, and miles of level land that were created by extensive lava flows thousands of years ago. What a pyrotechnic spectacle it would have been as seen from Pilot Butte!

It has been at least 1000 years since volcanic activity in the way of lava flows or the creation of cinder cones occurred in the High Country. It may have been 600,000 years, since avalanches of glowing volcanic fragments were hurled toward Bend from the Broken Top area or from some other source. Residents of Central Oregon and visitors can take comfort that they will not likely be threatened by the wrath of Vulcan.

Except by special permit issued by the U.S. Forest Service, the taking of volcanic rocks and cinders for private use is not permitted. Commercial use of the volcanic materials is quite widespread. Many of the unpaved roads in Central Oregon have an attractive red-cinder base. Cinders are used extensively to combat slick highways in winter; also for driveways and pathways. Red cinders, mixed with asphalt, have provided the attractive red highways found here and there in Central Oregon. Such highways have been attributed to W. E. Chandler, an early-day engineer with the Oregon State Highway Department, who in the 1950's advocated mixing the brilliantly colored scoria from cinder cones with oil.

Stone masons commonly use rough and porous lava rock for constructing walls and building fireplaces. Extensive pumice mines provide the raw material for pumice blocks and as aggregate for concrete. Volcanoes affect the water supply of most of Central Oregon. The porous rock is a notorious absorber of water flowing down from the Cascades, both in streams and in the miles of canals. The potential for geothermal energy has not gone unnoticed, and explorations in the volcanic lands are attempting to find such energy. Today, skiers, builders, road builders, and tourists recognize and appreciate the legacy of volcanism in the High Country. In 1964, space engineers and astronauts tested the mobility of moon-suited work on the rugged terrain in the Newberry Crater and McKenzie Pass areas.

Glaciation

Volcanic fires have created many of the landform features in the High Country. Moving rivers of ice, the glaciers, have, over a period of thousands of years, attacked the volcanoes, cutting into their flanks and carrying material down the mountains. Today, the volcanoes of Central Oregon host no less than 20 glaciers. The largest in the area are on the north and northeast sides, hidden from the glaciers' enemy, the sun. Central Oregonians are accustomed to seeing glistening ice on their nearby peaks even on the hottest summer days.

Glaciers occur when masses of snow are frozen and compacted, forcing the air out and forming dense layers of ice crystals. Throughout the Cascades, glaciers have created many landform features. As a glacier moves down a valley, it polishes bedrock and leaves scratches (striations). It plucks rocks from both beneath and along the sides of the glaciers, carrying them downslope, and it deposits the gathered debris in narrow ridges, called moraines. These moraines may be near the sides of the glaciers (lateral moraines) or near the end (terminal moraines). These gray, elongated ridges are quite common sights throughout the slopes of the Cascades. Morainal material is found in and near Black Butte Ranch, and it created Suttle Lake, west of Sisters. Higher in the Cascades, a number of picturesque small lakes, often a pretty aqua color, were formed by the work of glaciers.

When glaciers fall over a steep slope, the ice becomes brittle under tensile stress, and potentially dangerous crevasses appear on the surface of the glacier. These crevasses may temporarily be covered by mud or late summer snowstorms, thereby making travel across the glaciers even more hazardous. The melting of the glaciers in the High Country contributes to the hydrology of Central Oregon. For example, Squaw Creek, Fall Creek, and Soda Creek are some of the streams which get considerable discharge from melting snow and ice. The presence or absence of glacial material in the Cascades strongly influences the type of vegetation found in a particular area. In summary, the work of glaciers within the High Country has played a significant role in shaping the landscapes of the region.

Weather and Climate

The climate of an area is of great importance to residents and visitors. Travel, house construction, heating costs, the growing season, recreational opportunities, and even the general livability of an area are but some of the major climatic considerations. In brief, the High Cascades divide Oregon into two dissimilar climatic regions. West of the Cascades is the stereotype of what Oregon's climate is like, with considerable cloudiness throughout the winter and abundant, but often exaggerated, amounts of precipitation (New York and Miami each gets more precipitation than Portland, Oregon). West of the Cascades, the winters are mild. Summers are warm, and the growing season is moderately long for the latitude.

Within and east of the Cascades, the climate creates different worlds. The Cascades are buried by enormous snowfalls—up to 500 inches in one year. To the east of the mountain range, precipitation drops off sharply, and although Santiam Pass records about 90 inches of precipitation, Sisters, just 20 miles to the east, receives only about one sixth that amount.

For a greater part of the year, much of the High Country is snow covered, and residents of the area must adapt to living, working, and driving in snow. Also, roofs of houses must be designed and built to withstand the weight of snow, or more precisely, the water equivalent of the snow. Each

This photo reveals several geographical aspects of the High Country. The Cascades are effectively blocking moist, marine air from the Pacific Ocean. Hayden Glacier, between North Sister (right) and Middle Sister, is deeply crevassed on the upper reaches. The snow-covered ridges extending down from Middle Sister are moraines, materials deposited by glaciers. *(Oregon Dept. of Transportation)*

Left: The ponderosa pine forests of Central Oregon have an aesthetic appeal in all seasons. The ponderosa, or yellow pine, has long provided a resource for the lumber industry of the region. *(USFS)* Right: Tumalo Falls, located deep in the forests 13 miles west of Bend, is a favorite visiting spot for summer vacationers and winter cross-country skiers. A devastating man-caused fire in July, 1979, despoiled much of nature's creation around the falls. *(Oregon Dept. of Transportation)*

inch of snow depth, or water equivalent, extends a pressure of 5.2 pounds per square foot at the bottom of the snowpack. For example, a water equivalent of 14 inches would create a pressure on the roof of 72.8 pounds per square foot. Remote, unplowed roads within the High Country are likely to become impassable during times of prolonged snow. Even plowed highways may require frequent use of chains. No wonder this is considered four-wheel drive country!

Winter landscapes typically portray snow bearing down heavy on evergreens and smothering buildings. With clearing weather, the scene is typical of that found on Christmas cards that portray life in snowy rural areas of long ago. It is, of course, the total depth and duration of snow in the higher elevation that enables winter sports to begin early (often in November) and last until enthusiasts tire of their winter recreation (usually in May). Campgrounds along the upper Deschutes and Metolius rivers are usually free of snow by April, although campgrounds in Newberry Crater and at Elk, Sparks, and Devils Lake may not be free of snow until May. Impatient hikers and backpackers often have to wait until June and sometimes July before high elevation trails are open.

Winter temperatures within the High Country are similar to those found throughout most of Central and Eastern Oregon. In January, the average monthly temperatures for the region is within a few degrees of Bend's January average of 30° F. Daytime maximum temperatures peak at just above freezing, allowing for some thawing of snow even in winter. As the air is usually dry, the cool temperatures are not disagreeable for human comfort. On rare occasions, extreme maximums of 50° F and even 60° F may be experienced—even in the coldest months.

Extreme minimum temperatures for January are all of the bone-chilling type, down to -30° F on rare occasions. Of greater significance to residents of the area is the duration of low temperatures. Small wonder that wood stoves are popular in the region and that most residents have wood piles near their houses. Not unexpectedly, the growing season in the High Country is extremely limited. Freezing temperatures can be expected any month of the year.

Spring comes late to the High Country. There are those who would even contend that there is no spring, just a sudden transition from a long winter to a summer which comes and goes all too quickly. For example, at Sisters, temperatures average a meager 42° F in April, but by June the monthly average has spurted to a comfortable 57° F. Throughout the summer, there is a succession of clear blue skies, abundant sunshine, warm days but cool nights. Temperatures usually climb to over 80° F by 3 or 4 p.m. but extreme maximums very rarely reach 100° F and more likely climax to the mid-90's. After sunset, the dry, clear Central Oregon air is conducive to rapid radiational cooling and the mercury quickly plunges from whatever maximum had been recorded. By early morning, even following a day with 90° F, the air can be quite chilly. Extreme summer minimums for Sisters are 20° F for June, 24° F for July and 26° F for August. Things have not changed in over 125 years! Lieutenant Henry L. Abbot, in his journeys through Central Oregon in 1855, noted in his diary, August 29, while camping at Rosland (just north of La Pine): "During the night, ice of considerable thickness formed on the water vessels, and just before sunrise the thermometer stood at 15° F."[1]

Visitors to Central Oregon, seeking relief from the warm, humid nights typical of the Midwest or parts of the South, certainly find it. Campers especially note the cool nights and a campfire is a real comfort. Residents of the region, well accustomed to such cool temperatures, frequently take the chill off with a late evening lighting of the fire or wood stove. Summer precipitation in Central Oregon is usually low and likely to be confined to late spring weather fronts moving in from the Pacific Ocean or to periodic moist air intruding from Arizona or California, spreading along the Cascades and over Newberry Volcano. The latter often brings thunderstorm activity and needed moisture for tree growth and for dampening the woods to help combat fires. On the negative side, the thunderstorms may trigger forest fires and would certainly dampen the spirits of recreationists.

Fall months in the High Country are often delightful. High pressure usually lingers over the Pacific Northwest, bringing Indian summer, successive clear days with pleasant temperatures in the 60-70° F range, and crisp, invigorating mornings. Most of the tourists have returned home and the campgrounds and lakes and trails are almost deserted. The leaves of the vine maple in the Cascades and the aspens in damp spots and willows along streams are nipped by fall frosts. The western larch turns a light yellow before cooling winds whirl the soft needles to the ground. Throughout this time period, the evergreens sharply contrast with coloring provided by autumn.

Often, even by early fall, the first snow of "winter" has freshened the Cascade peaks. As suddenly as it ended, winter now suddenly sweeps over the High Country. Moisture-laden clouds shroud the Cascades and chilling winds suddenly replace the warmth of Indian summer. Ice begins to cover the shallow high lakes, and the coats of domestic pets and livestock begin to thicken. Residents of the area have long since checked their wood piles. Winter woolies are dusted and snow tires are mounted on vehicles. Conversation includes discussion on how severe the forthcoming winter will be and nature's weather-lore signs are noted.

Vegetation

Vast areas of the High Country are covered by forests of pine or fir. Ponderosa pine and lodgepole pine are the most widespread. These forests provide a valuable watershed, helping retain or delay snowmelt until spring or early summer when ranchers, farmers and others critically need water in the semi-arid lands of Central Oregon. Obviously, the forests also contribute to a major segment of the economy in Central Oregon. Logging operations and the manufacture of lumber and the wood products alone account for about 20 percent of the employment in Crook, Deschutes, and Jefferson Counties. Prineville and Gilchrist are decidedly "mill towns," and La Pine, Bend, and Redmond depend on the nearby forests for part of their economy.

The ponderosa pine *(Pinus ponderosa)*, formerly known as western yellow pine, is not only the most widespread tree of the High Country but, for many residents and visitors, it is the best known and an aesthetic favorite. It is found mainly in elevations of 3500 to 6000 feet where there is an average annual precipitation of 14 to 30 inches, mostly in the form of snow. Despite the modest precipitation and the porous, pumice soils of parts of the region, ponderosa pine survives drought because of its deep tap roots.

The tree grows in mixture with other species, especially at higher elevations, but it is the pure stands, often creating a park-like setting, that make the forest so attractive. Early-day descriptions and photographs of ponderosa pine forests near Bend indicate that little undergrowth allowed inspection by auto without even roads. Historically, small, unsuppressed blazes a few inches high have swept through the forest, burning the flammable organic debris, pine needles, and pine beetles—thereby keeping the forest floor clear of undergrowth. Even two-to-three-foot ponderosa pine can survive the periodic light fires. Giant, overly mature pines frequently bear the scars of fires, but the tree is quite fire resistant, the thick bark of mature trees offering effective protection. On the other hand, competing trees in the same area, such as the grand fir and Douglas fir, are much less fire resistant. Since man has logged the ponderosa pine and exposed the floor of the forest lands, young pine seedlings, grasses such as Idaho fescue, the thorny bitterbrush, the familiar bright green manzanita, and the snowbrush have occupied the land.

Motorists traveling the Fremont Highway (Highway 31) toward La Pine from Silver Lake, or the stretch of Highway 20 between Sisters and Black Butte Ranch, cannot help noticing the stands of mature ponderosa pine with their light yellowish-brown or orange-red bark. The bark of older pine is divided into large plates, four, six, or eight inches wide. The needles are a distinctive bright green and glisten in sunlight. In the fall, clusters of golden needles are swept to the ground and the turpentine in these fallen needles holds down heavy underbrush. On sunny days, light is able to penetrate the pine forest. It literally sparkles on the light pumice soils, and the glow from fallen needles and the coppery trunks creates a warm feeling. Add to this, the fragrant pine-scented air, and the sound of wind stirring the tops of the pines and you have a magnificent landscape setting.

After the ponderosa pine, the lodgepole pine *(Pinus contorta)* covers the next largest area in the coniferous forest lands of the High Country. This tree, with its slim straight trunks—sometimes 100 feet tall—has a wide ecological range. It thrives on wet, poorly drained soils—where ponderosa will not grow—and on coarse-textured soils. Lodgepole grows at different elevations and slopes, including depressions where cold-air drainage and lower nighttime temperatures kill ponderosa pine seedlings. At higher elevations, it takes on a different form, in part because of the competition with mountain hemlock, and in part because of the isolation and different climatic zone. The higher altitude lodgepole pine has a thicker trunk with a softer, thicker bark than its cousin in the "jackpine" forests below.

Early settlers found the straight, uniform trunks ideal for building log cabins, corrals, sheds, and stables. Later, the lodgepole pine was found suitable for making fruit boxes, telegraph poles, bridges, and when treated with creosote, mine props and railroad ties. In 1906, a *Bulletin* article stated, "Although the jackpine is worthless for lumber, it is said to make good railroad ties and recent tests have showed that an excellent grade of paper pulp can be made from it."[2] Samples of lodgepole pine were sent to Lebanon, Oregon, paper mill to test the wood for paper qualities. A report from the mill showed that tests indicated a "high quality pulp, whiter than average with a very good fiber."[3]

Today, a revival of interest in log cabins is again focussing interest on the lodgepole pine. With specially designed harvesting and mill equipment, small log mills (such as at Brooks-Scanlon) are easily handling the tree. Lodgepole pine makes for easy-to-get firewood and is a favorite for part-time and "professional" wood cutters in Central Oregon.

Wilderness Areas

Three wilderness areas, Jefferson, Three Sisters and Washington, totaling 346,226 acres, straddle the Cascades within the High Country. These are special areas where the earth and its communities of life are untrammeled by man, and where man himself is a visitor. In recent years these wilderness areas have experienced sharply increased use. Indeed, some areas, such as Green Lakes and Jefferson Park, are threatened by overuse and the U.S. Forest Service is imposing more controls on their use. The U.S. Forest Service estimated that 84,700 visitors entered the three wilderness areas within the High Country in 1986, about 74,700 of whom used the Three Sisters Wilderness Area.[4]

Cutting through the wilderness areas of the High Country is the Pacific Crest Trail. The idea of such a trail, to be constructed from Canada to Mexico, was proposed to the U.S. Forest Service and National Park Service by Clinton C. Clark of Pasadena, California, in 1932. Considerable trail work was performed on the John Muir Trail and Oregon Skyline Trail by Civilian Conservation Corps crews. The Pacific Crest Trail System Conference, established to manage the trail, had three objectives—to preserve wilderness, to encourage public use, and to promote appreciation of the outdoors.

The trail route, laid out in 1935, incorporated several connecting trails. In 1968 the National Trails System Act established national scenic trails, with the Appalachian Trail and the Pacific Crest Trail the first two. The Pacific Crest Trail traverses 17 degrees of latitude, but winds 2,400 miles. Elevations on the trail range from sea level to over 13,000 feet. It passes through a variety of climatic zones and different vegetative types, but for the most part is located on public lands. Within the High Country, the Pacific Crest Trail is clearly marked on wilderness maps put out by the U.S. Forest Service.

In this chapter, the geographical setting of the High Country has been reviewed. However, the various components of the natural environment—geology, climate, vegetation, soils—are experienced in their relationships one with another. Visitors to the High Country will undoubtedly find that it is the total experience with the landscape that is memorable.

2.
The Cascades

The Cascades are part of the horseshoe of volcanic mountains that edge the Pacific Ocean. Within North America, they extend from Southern British Columbia to Northern California, a distance of 1000 miles. Perhaps the most striking feature of the Cascades is their succession of isolated peaks rising one mile or more above their surrounding terrain and visible on clear days from over 100 miles. Within the State of Oregon, these towering volcanoes are possessive landmarks for residents of some cities. Portlanders and residents of The Dalles and Hood River cherish their views of nearby Mt. Hood. Central Oregonians, likewise, lay claims to the aesthetic appeal of Mt. Jefferson and the Three Sisters.

The geology of the Cascades is complex, but, in brief, the major peaks in Oregon—Hood, Jefferson, the Three Sisters—were born during the Pleistocene period, within the last million years. These prominent, youthful peaks are representative of the High Cascades, in contrast with the older (5 to 40 million years) time-worn western Cascades. Although some of the jagged peaks of Central Oregon—Three Fingered Jack, Mt. Washington, North Sister, and others—are said to be extinct, other peaks may only be dormant.

Historically, several peaks within the Cascade Range have shown signs of volcanic activity since 1800. Lassen Peak, in Northern California, erupted intermittently from 1914 to 1921. In 1915, a spectacular eruption sent columns of ash skyward and masses of steam and fiery rock fragments sweeping down the northwest slopes of Lassen Peak. Mt. Baker, in Northern Washington, in recent years has been monitored for seismic activity. In 1980, the devastating explosion of Mt. St. Helens demonstrated the potential energy that the Cascade Volcanoes can unleash.

Within the High Country, "hot spots," where snow melts in midwinter, have been noted on Mt. Bachelor by skiers. In 1948, U.S. Forest Service crews reported wisps of vapor drifting from the north slope of snow-blanketed Garrison Butte, located 7 miles north of the town of Sisters. Other buttes where fumaroles have been reported include Poly Top Butte, located on the flanks of Newberry Volcano, Bates Butte (5 miles south of Sunriver) and Lava Butte. It may be that other buttes within the High Country are sleeping volcanoes. However, while the giant volcanoes are "resting," geologists are hesitant to say how long the period of dormancy would last.

While fire has created the Cascades, three periods of glaciation have shaped the volcanoes. The last major glacial period ended about 2,500 years ago (the Little Ice Age). Huge ice fields accumulated in the Cascades, and glaciers extended down the slopes as low as 3600 feet. For example, glaciers reached from Mt. Washington as far as the Suttle Lake area. Fingers of ice that still cling to the High Cascade peaks glisten and sparkle in the summer sun, contrasting sharply with nearby barren ridges. Today, observant hikers in the Cascades can note moraines, gray unsorted deposits of rock particles which accumulated at the margins of melting glaciers. Striations are to be seen on exposed lava rocks, testimony to the days when deep snows and ice covered the High Country.

Naming the Cascades

The Cascade Range has endured a succession of names. In 1790, a Spaniard, Manuel Quimper, mapped the mountains, "Sierras Nevadas de S. Antonio." Two years later, the English explorer George Vancouver referred to the mountains as the "Snowy Range." In 1805, Lewis and Clark reported on the snow-capped peaks, calling them the

"Western Mountains." "Cascades" was used by botanist David Douglas in the 1820's. This name had previously been applied to the narrows of the Columbia River where the river divides the Oregon and Washington mountain range.

In 1839, Hall J. Kelley sought to change the name to the Presidents' Range. Thomas Jefferson Farnham, writing of Oregon in 1843, used this name in describing the distant mountains. Had the change from Cascades to Presidents' Range occurred, the Three Sisters would have become Madison. In 1844, Robert Greenhow's *History of Oregon and California* included maps which showed the name "Far West Mountains." George Wilkes' *History of Oregon*, in 1845, used Cascade Range. Nathaniel J. Wyeth, in his memoirs, 1839, also used the name Cascades. According to Lewis McArthur, only one tribe of Indians, the Klamaths, had a name for the Cascade Range. To them, the mountains were "Yamakiasham Yaina," meaning "mountains of the northern people."[5]

To the Indians, the Cascade peaks had religious significance. Captain John Fremont, in his explorations of Central Oregon in 1843, wrote in his diary (November 27, 1843): "The Indian superstition has peopled these lofty peaks with evil spirits, and they have never yet known the tread of a human foot. Sternly drawn against the sky, they look so high and steep, so snowy and rocky, that it appears almost impossible to climb them. . . ."[6]

Many of the major peaks of the Cascades had special meanings to different Indian tribes and it is not surprising that legends about individual peaks have survived. For example, in Indian mythology, giant canoes rest on Mt. Baker and Mt. Jefferson. The canoes saved people from Puyallup flood waters. Evidence of the canoes, some Indians say, can still be seen near the summits of these two peaks.[7] Farfetched as the canoe part of the legend is, it is a geological fact that tremendous flows of meltwater from Mt. Rainier have at different times created extensive floods around the giant volcano.

The Cascades have always been impediments to east-west travel across the range. Before precise elevations were made, some early-day estimates of the highest peaks put their heights at 12,000 to 18,000 feet. Between the Columbia River and the Californian border, a distance of nearly 300 miles, only seven all-season highways cross the Cascade divide. In 1921, there were only three passes open all year.

The Cascades Create Two Oregons

The Cascades divide Oregon into two different regions; anyone who has traveled across the Santiam Pass has experienced both. Western Oregon is characterized by green forests that may include the ever-present Douglas fir, a variety of deciduous trees, and lush, thick, green undergrowth. Moisture seems to cling to and drip from all forms of vegetation throughout the long winter months. For extended periods of time, moisture-laden skies are dull grey, and the landscapes, often seen through mists or through hazy atmosphere, are subdued. Geological events, time, and erosion have combined to help smooth landforms. Come spring and summer, however, the landscapes of Western Oregon provide a pleasing diversity, especially where areas of cultivation are blended with islands of "natural" forests.

But cross the divide and you enter a different world, where skies are usually lighter or clear. The air is noticeably drier and visibility is often over 100 miles. In the clear air, the more youthful landforms stand out sharply. In Central Oregon, there are broad areas with similar landscapes. For example, the ponderosa pine country is characterized by miles of tall trees with coppery trunks and little undergrowth to impede both vistas and movement. Within the High Country, much of the winter precipitation is in the form of snow, resulting in a picture-book landscape of blue skies, green foliage, brown-trunked pine trees, and a snow-covered forest floor. Farther east, the region is characterized by the unique juniper tree, scattered in lands of sagebrush. Where irrigation waters have reached parched soils, patches of green are in marked contrast to the gray or brown desert-like lands.

Weather and Climate

The Cascades create their own weather, establish a distinctive "highland climatic region, and help make the landscapes of Central Oregon what they are today. The Cascade Range forces the westerly air-flow from the Pacific to rise abruptly, cool, and deposit moisture on the windward slopes. Air sweeping down the east slopes of the mountains is warmed by compression (5.5° F 1000'). As temperatures are increased, the air mass's ability to hold more moisture is increased. Thus, while the Cascade peaks may be shrouded in clouds, just a few miles east the clouds begin to break up and patches of blue sky and rays of sunlight peak through. In Bend and Redmond it is likely that the sun is shining through cloudless skies. The consequences of these meteorological events are well known to most Oregonians. The annual precipitation for Eugene (airport), in the Willamette Valley, averages 39 inches; Detroit, located in the western foothills of the Cascades, is drenched in 71 inches, while Bend and Redmond average a scant 12 inches and 8 inches respectively.

Weather stations within the Cascades are few and far apart. Santiam Summit is one of the few locations in the entire Cascade range with temperature and precipitation data. An analysis of the weather readings for Santiam Pass for the period 1965-78 shows an average seasonal (July 1— June 30) snowfall of 488 inches. In the same period, Sisters averaged 40 inches and Bend 34 inches. Extreme seasonal totals at Santiam Pass ranged from a 689-inch snow blitz (1970-71) to a paltry 227 inches in the dry winter of 1976-77. At times during the winter season, which starts in September or October in the Cascades and often runs into May, prodigious snowfalls accumulate. For example, on January 10, 1950, 36 inches of snow piled up in one night at Santiam Pass.

The dramatic effect of the Cascades on storms is best seen when examining precipitation totals for the entire storm. Between January 17 and 26, in 1972, Santiam Pass accumulated 10.85 inches of precipitation (rain or water equivalent of melted snow). During the same storm period, Sisters received 3.80 inches, Bend 1.90 inches, and Brothers, on the High Desert, 0.57 inches.

During exceptionally heavy snows, highway department crews have a hard time keeping the Santiam Pass open, and periodic traffic snarls are part of the winter scene in the High Country. Despite any inconveniences to motorists, the heavy Cascade snowpack is welcomed by many who live in Central Oregon. Skiers, those in the tourist business, ranchers, power company officials and others, whose livelihood directly depends on the snows or on the spring and summer runoff, anxiously monitor snow-depth reports.

In beautiful weather, the alpine environment of the High Country is invigorating. The scenery is spectacular and for those hiking, climbing, or cross-country skiing, the experience is exhilarating. However, aesthetic as the Cascades may be in good weather, tragedy has occasionally struck. Weather changes in the mountains can be sudden, dramatic, and devastating for those ill prepared.

Winter storms are to be expected, but out-of-season storms surprise many outdoor enthusiasts. Winter-type storms sweep in from the Pacific often around Labor Day. Such was the case early September, 1927, when the first breath of winter was felt in the High Country. On Monday, September 5, a savage snowstorm broke loose, blanketing the higher Cascade slopes and peaks with 10 inches of snow. Two climbers, Guy Ferry, Tygh Valley High School principal, and Henry Cramer, University of Oregon student, had planned to scale North Sister that Labor Day. When the climbers failed to return to their car, fear was expressed for their safety. Search parties were quickly organized. A brief let-up in the storm made temperatures plunge to near zero Fahrenheit, and by Thursday, September 8, blizzard conditions once again prevailed in the Cascades. Expert alpinists from Bend—Nels Skjersaa, Emil Nordeen, Nels Wolfsberg, and Chris Kostol—braved the elements, scouring the North and Middle Sister for the whereabouts of Ferry and Cramer. The first clue was found on Middle Sister. A note dated September 5 and left on the summit read: "We left Frog Camp about 11 am. Reached the summit at

3:35 pm. We were up here yesterday in such a blizzard that we could not find the register box. Stormy and cold. (signed) Guy Ferry. Henry Cramer." The discovery of the note prompted renewed searches, all futile. Then, almost two years to the day that they were reported missing, hikers discovered their bodies near the Cascade divide.

Each year tragedy in one form or another strikes in the Cascades. Of all the searches and rescues conducted in the State of Oregon, one fifth are in Deschutes County. In Bend, the Continuing Education Division of Central Oregon Community College conducts several classes on wilderness survival, backpacking skills, climbing, cross-country skiing, and other outdoor-related subjects.

The changing of the seasons brings many landscape changes. Winter is the predominant season in the Cascades. Periodic storms envelope the mountains, sometimes for several days at a time. The clearing weather that follows heavy snowstorms is like the opening of a heavy curtain, for suddenly, the majesty of the Cascades, completely mantled in a new white coat, is unveiled. At times strong westerly winds, whipping across the higher Cascade peaks, pick up streamers of snow and carry the plumes eastward over the High Country. Those in Central Oregon unaccustomed to the sight may, at first, believe that the volcanoes have suddenly come alive—so realistic is the phenomenon.

During spring, the major change in the landscape is the receding snowline, with dark spots appearing on the south slopes where melting snows expose volcanic rocks. For the most part, summers in Central Oregon are dry and warm. In the Cascades, rapidly melting snows transform what were small, timid streams in the morning into raging rivers by afternoon. As summer advances, the once pristine Cascade skyline is soiled by rockfalls and swirling pumice dust. At times, you wonder if the snowfields can even survive until their fall revival.

The advent of fall in the Cascades and throughout the High Country is appreciated by many. Phil Brogan, Bend, who has keenly observed the arrival of fall, commented on the season and its special meaning to Central Oregonians:

Nature is ritualistic in its annual presentation of the Autumn season in Central Oregon. Dates vary from year to year. First rehearsals may be as early as fading August when snow robes the Three Sisters with white, changes high Bachelor into an inverted ice cream cone and brushes with frost the old ribs of a Pliocene volcano early-day stockmen named Broken Top. But the first snow doesn't last long. It merely serves as a warning that the great production of Autumn is about to begin. . . .

As the rehearsals for Autumn progress, a haze creeps into Central Oregon to dim distant horizons, tint Smith Rock with a bluish-purple and provide a screen on which the Sisters cast their long shadows at sunset. The rehearsals for Fall eventually near their conclusion. Frosts chill basin air, to wilt tender vegetables, summer flowers and potatoes. . . .

Finally, rehearsals are completed and nature starts its big show—the arrival of Autumn. Ice clouds and evanescent altocumulus give way to low clouds that massively roll in from the ocean. High Cascade peaks disappear. Winds shifts to the southwest, and there is the aroma in the air of burning slash in the distant, damp, western Oregon hills. Welcomed by hunters, ranchers and foresters, the heavy clouds, not fully dehydrated by the high Cascades, drop moisture in the inland country. Rains patter on roofs briefly. Dust is settled. The first heavy snow of the Fall, with its gusty southwest winds, passes, and the Three Sisters and attendant peaks stand out in all their glory, white and ready for winter. That will be the finale of nature's grand show—the annual presentation of the Autumn season in the high country east of the Three Sisters.[8]

By late September or early October, frost in the Cascades has "turned" the vine-maple leaves. Many motorists, armed with cameras, take the triangular loop from Sisters over the McKenzie Highway and return via the Santiam Pass to Sisters. As the colorful leaves flutter to the ground and chill winds replace the warmth of early fall days, the familiar face of winter appears.

Mount Jefferson

Mount Jefferson, located on the northern edge of the High Country of Central Oregon, stands aloof, defying approach to all except those traveling on foot or by horse. The mountain rises nearly one mile higher than the surrounding terrain and looks all of its elevation of 10,495 feet. Within the State of Oregon, only Mt. Hood, 11,235 feet, towers higher. Mt. Jefferson was named after President Thomas Jefferson by explorers Lewis and Clark, who spotted the peak from near the mouth of the Willamette River (Portland) on March 30, 1806. Although most nineteenth-century maps of Oregon show an absence of landmarks in the High Country, Mt. Jefferson is one of the exceptions.

Early explorers' accounts of Mt. Jefferson mention the untamed beauty and inaccessibility of the mountain. For example, Abbot in his journal, September 27, 1855, wrote:

> This morning it rained. After following a westerly course through the wet bushes for about a quarter of a mile, we suddenly saw the light breaking through the dense forest before us, and, hoping that we were approaching another prairie, pressed eagerly forward. We soon stopped in blank amazement on the verge of an immense cañon, which was found by subsequent measurement to be 1,945 feet deep. Far below us we heard the roar of a mountain torrent. Opposite rose, steep and black, and hitherto unseen by civilized man, the naked base of Mount Jefferson, while around it clustered gloomy, fir-covered mountains, whose tops were hidden in rolling masses of clouds. . . .It had ceased raining, and the heavy clouds which shrouded the opposite mountains rose slowly until a noble panorama lay outspread before us.[9]

Rugged as the Mt. Jefferson country is, Indians evidently traversed the area and their trails provided rough but passable travel for Abbot. The explorer noted that at one place along the trail there were "a few rude pictures of men and animals scratched on the rocks."[10]

Left: The Three Sisters as seen from the juniper lands near Redmond. Much of the water for the thirsty lands east of the Cascades is stored in deep winter snows and released in summer. Deschutes River (shown here) is used to serve several major irrigation districts in Central Oregon. *(Oregon Dept. of Transportation).* Right: Mt. Jefferson as seen from the south. The volcano, Oregon's second highest peak at 10,497 feet (Mt. Hood is the highest), hosts 4 glaciers. Mt. Jefferson is part of the 99,600-acre Mt. Jefferson Wilderness Area. *(Oregon Dept. of Transportation)*

The Cache Creek Toll Station, about 1935. The station, located around 5 miles west of Black Butte Ranch, was built in 1896 for collecting tolls from travelers using the Santiam Wagon Road. Rates included $2 for a two-horse team, 75 cents for a horse and rider, 10 cents for each head of cattle, 3 cents for sheep. The building is now collapsed, but a marker tells the significance of the site. *(USFS)*

The Mt. Jefferson Wilderness Area covers 99,600 acres, extending from just south of Breitenbush Lake in the north to within a half mile of the Santiam Pass Highway on the south. Most of the Wilderness Area has a vegetative cover and nearly two thirds is covered with timber—mainly Douglas fir, subalpine fir, mountain hemlock, lodgepole pine, ponderosa pine, and several species of cedar. There are some 150 lakes in the area, about 60 of them with fish.

There is not space in this volume to do justice to all the interesting and scenic places in the Mt. Jefferson Wilderness Area. However, two places should be singled out—Hole-in-the-Wall and Jefferson Park. Hole-in-the-Wall is reached by the undulating Cabot Lake Trail. The trail climbs through dense forests from an elevation of 4,500 feet, then past a series of small alpine lakes, Cabot, Shirley, and Carl. In this stretch of the trail, views of Mt. Jefferson are mostly limited to periodic, teasing glimpses of just the top pyramid spire of the peak. North of Carl Lake, the trail switchbacks and climbs sharply from 5200 feet to 6000 feet elevation, then twists and turns through the edge of a jagged lava field southwest of Forked Butte, a prominent cinder cone. Suddenly, as the trail crests a ridge, the whole southern slope of Mt. Jefferson, only 4 miles distant, towers on the skyline—a magnificent spectacle.

Hole-in-the-Wall Park is now only 4 miles away. The trail drops sharply from the ridge, past Patsy Lake, skirts the base of The Table (an extensive plateau with excellent views of Mt. Jefferson), then climbs from Table Lake through dense stands of mountain hemlock. Hole-in-the-Wall Park is a gap in a volcanic ridge overlooking small but turbulent Jefferson Creek, incised some 600 feet in a canyon. Beyond this canyon, the huge pinnacle of Mt. Jefferson rises skyward one mile above the timberline. Waldo glacier, with its crevasses opening in late summer, sweeps down the southern slopes of the volcano, only to end abruptly at a giant terminal moraine. The majestic spectacle created by the work of fire and ice, the roar of Jefferson Creek, and the fragrant pine-scented air combine to make Hole-in-the-Wall Park one of the most spectacular viewpoints in all of the High Country.

The rugged landscapes of Hole-in-the-Wall Park contrast with those at Jefferson Park, one of the most popular places in the area. Jefferson Park, nestled in a flat, two-square-mile valley on the northwest side of Mt. Jefferson, is a prime example of the beauty of an alpine meadow. Here, a myriad of small and modest-sized pools reflect the nearby peak and separate a series of lush, deep-sodded meadows that, in turn, host clusters of blue lupines, crimson and orange Indian paintbrush, red heather, and pink shooting stars, Quiet streams meander through the lush meadows, their water rippling over small pebbles. Here and there, outcrops of glaciated andesite boulders and alpine firs add diversity to the valley. The whole is park like.

The erratic behavior of glaciers, whose work helped shape the valley and surrounding landforms, is evident. Outcrops of solid rocks bear glacial striations. The countless pools in Jefferson Park and the irregular drainage reflect what happens when glacial action scours out depressions and moves sediments and morainic material to block drainage channels. Rock cliffs that hem in the east side of Jefferson Park are the result of the plucking action of moving ice that has pulled away blocks of rocks. The work of glaciers, however, is not all just historical. High above the "park," Russell, Jefferson Park, and part of Whitewater glaciers continue the work of gnawing away at the upper slopes of Mt. Jefferson. Blue ice, heavily crevassed and pinnacled, gives warning to potential climbers.

Although Mt. Jefferson was first believed to have been climbed in 1888, there was no actual proof of the feat. A party of Bend Skyliners, on scaling Mt. Jefferson in September, 1930, found evidence of a climb by the Mazamas that took them near the summit on July 13, 1895.[11] The Mazamas were taking part in an experiment to flash messages, using large mirrors, from one Cascade peak to another, hoping to send messages from Mexico to Canada. However, credit for the first climb to the top pinnacle is debated. Several groups of climbers have reported scaling what they thought was the highest pinnacle—including one group led by guide, George "Lem" Gates, in 1897. It is the crumbling summit pinnacle that climbers report to be one of the most difficult parts of the climb. Mt. Jefferson is a beautiful peak but at times it has brought tragedy to the unwary and inexperienced climber.

Three Fingered Jack

All that is left of what once was a shield volcano are skeletal remains which, when seen from different positions, take on a variety of shapes and forms. From a distance, details of the crumbling pinnacles are lost. When seen from Highway 20, traveling west down the Santiam Pass, motorists catch a brief glimpse of Three Fingered Jack which, from this point, looks like a single spire towering nearly 3000 feet above the highway. From the plateau lands east of Sisters, Three Fingered Jack seems to resemble its name, with one prominent finger flanked by two smaller satellites.

Origin of the name of the mountain is uncertain. Early explorers seemingly ignored the mountain in their journals. In the 1870's, it was called Mount Marion, but the present name, Three Fingered Jack, came into use about 1900. According to McArthur (1974), the name originated not from its shape but because of a three-fingered trapper named Jack who lived in the area.

The elevation of Three Fingered Jack, a little over 7,800 feet, is modest but, as with the other isolated Cascade peaks, the volcano is distinctive and imposing. Close up, Three Fingered Jack takes on a different character, revealing its age. The three "fingers" or spires that are noted at a distance prove to be innumerable rocky pinnacles, each seemingly ready to crumble and fall. Volcanic tuff intermingles with more resistant material, giving the once-interior of the volcano a multi-layered structure similar to that of Broken Top. Viewed close up in the morning from the east side, the various colors—greys, tans, yellows, reds, and blacks—are easily visible. Dikes—long, narrow fissures filled with volcanic rock—cut diagonally across the colored strata.

A small snowfield clings to the precipitous northeast slope. In summer, meltwater from the snowfield thunders down the mountain from underneath the snowfield, discharging into a small ice-blue lake, or tarn. A moraine—a ridge of glacially deposited material—contains the lake except where water has eroded part of the glacial debris. Here cascades of water hurtle and roar down the rocky slopes of the volcano, only to be tamed in Canyon Creek Meadow, half a mile to the east.

Canyon Creek Meadow is a small but picturesque area secluded by serrated ridges and by Three Fingered Jack, whose pinnacles rise 2200 feet above the alpine meadow. Hikers who time their visit to Canyon Creek Meadow when the alpine flowers are bursting into color are indeed fortunate. The meadow is like a colorful carpet with a bright green background that supports clusters of blue subalpine lupines, yellow arrowleaf groundsel, white grays monksflowers, fluorescent red Indian paintbrush, and a variety of other species. Water from the Three Fingered Jack snowfield gurgles quietly through the meadow in small separate channels that have incised themselves two or three feet into the meadow.

The stark, rocky ridges that tower 1000 feet above the meadow make the valley even more attractive. While distant views within the meadow area are restricted, individuals who have time and energy can secure magnificent views of nearby Mt. Jefferson to the north and the Three Sisters to the south by climbing any of the ridges. In addition, a panorama of forests and lakes of the High Country and the parched juniper lands to the east reward the energetic.

Three Fingered Jack is a mountain to be climbed only by experienced alpinists. For many years groups of climbers attempted and failed to scale the volcano. Climbers in 1910 and 1917 almost scaled it, but it was six young Bend climbers who made alpine history when, on September 3, 1923, they conquered the highest part of Three Fingered Jack.[12] The summit area, barely large enough to support the six boys, consisted of a 15-foot-long ridge whose knife-like edge vibrated in gusts of wind. The youths had conquered Mt. Washington's slender spire for the first time only a week previously. People in Bend and elsewhere wildly acclaimed the climb of Mt. Washington but enthusiasm for the more difficult climb of Three Fingered Jack was much more subdued.

Large-scale maps of the Three Fingered Jack and Mt. Jefferson areas show Minto Pass, a name that is not as well known as Santiam or McKenzie Pass. Nonetheless, Minto Pass, named after John Minto, has an interesting history. In 1874, Minto, while searching for a pass to link Salem with Central Oregon, followed an old Indian trail that led up the North Santiam River and Marion Creek over the Cascades north of Three Fingered Jack, then traveled the eastern slopes of the mountains down to the head of the Metolius.[13]

The Indian trail that Minto investigated had been used by the Molalla Indians for many years. These Indians had twice unsuccessfully engaged in battle with the Cayuse from east of the Cascades, both battles being fought along the trail near the Cascade divide north of Three Fingered Jack. According to Indian legend, spirits of the dead warriors haunt the spot where they died, and the Molallas abandoned the trail. In 1873 and 1874, Minto examined the deeply worn trail up the North Fork of the Santiam and over the Cascades. Although his route was known as the Marion and Wasco Stock and Wagon Road and the trail was used for horse travel, no wagon road was ever constructed. Interest in the Minto Pass route faded, once surveys of the Santiam Pass route revealed that it was some 600 feet lower in elevation.

The Minto Trail was improved by the Forest Service and part of it crosses the Cascades within the Mt. Jefferson Wilderness Area. A short hike from Jack Lake to Wasco Lake leads to Minto Pass and the site of the legendary Indian battles. Along the trail route, many geographical names originate from people who were part of the Minto party. Perhaps the best known is Pamelia Lake, named after Pamelia Ann Berry, the cook for the Minto survey team.

Santiam Pass

Only two mountain passes, the Santiam and McKenzie, cross the Cascades in the High Country of Central Oregon. Farther north, Government Camp crosses the Cascade divide south of Mount Hood. Willamette Pass connects Eugene with Klamath Falls just south of the High Country.

Both Santiam and McKenzie have interesting historical and geological stories, but the two passes have dissimilar landscapes, and only Santiam is kept open throughout the winter months.

Santiam Pass has long been a place to cross the Cascades, having been used by Indians for centuries. Hudson's Bay Co. trappers, including Peter Skene Ogden, traveled through the pass in 1825. However, Central Oregon historians quickly point out that migrant wagon trains such as the Elliot Cut-off Party (1853) and the Macy Party (1854) crossed the Cascades by the Willamette Pass. The eastern slopes of the High Cascades are quite steep and even today, with a modern highway, the road cut into the hillside north of Suttle Lake requires a steep climb, ascending 1,400 feet in 5 miles. Despite the climb, Santiam Pass, at an elevation of 4,817 feet, is a low spot in the Cascade Range and, geographically, a logical crossing.

It was in the mid-nineteenth century that Andrew Wiley, a hunter, repeatedly penetrated an old Indian trail up the South Santiam River and, in 1859, assisted by two fellow hunters, crossed the Cascades near Hogg Rock. Wiley subsequently assisted the Willamette Valley and Cascade Mountain Company, which was building roads up the McKenzie and the South Santiam valleys. The road up the South Santiam from Linn County, cut through dense forests, was completed in 1866, allowing livestock and teams to move into Central Oregon from the Willamette Valley during the summer months.

The Santiam Wagon Road, as it was called, was located 3 miles south of the existing highway (US 20), but at about the same elevation. The old route, still traceable in places, is marked on the "Three Fingered Jack" U.S. Geological Survey Quadrangle. This map shows that the road passed north of Sand Mountain and Big Lake, then headed east down Cache Creek and on to where Camp Polk was located (3 miles northeast of Sisters). From Camp Polk, the road continued east, crossing the Deschutes River at Tetherow Bridge (north of Redmond). This Old Santiam Wagon Road played a significant role in the settlement of lands in Central Oregon. Along Cache Creek, a toll station was built by J. W. Jordan in 1896 for the purpose of collecting tolls from travelers using the Old Santiam Wagon Road. The tollstation ruins withstood time and the elements until they were blown down by high winds in the 1960's.

Within the same low divide through the Cascades (all termed Santiam Pass on USGS maps) but 3 miles to the north of the Old Santiam Wagon Road, another attempt to provide transportation from Western Oregon to the vast territory east of the Cascades took place late in the nineteenth century. Most travelers using the Santiam Pass today probably drive by the Oregon Historical marker sign (located one mile west of the Santiam Pass summit), probably unaware of the story behind "Hogg Rock," the large vertical-faced remnant of a volcano that towers over the highway.

Colonel T. Egenton Hogg—who had obtained control of the Corvallis Valley and Eastern Railroad and the road and land grants that went with the wagon road—started a vast rail project. From Yaquina Bay (Newport), 143 miles of track were completed to within 12 miles of Santiam Pass, and trains moved over parts of the lines carrying passengers from Corvallis to Yaquina (1885) and from Corvallis to Albany (1887). Even combined rail and sea excursions from Corvallis to San Francisco (cost $14) were arranged. To meet contractual agreements that called for operating a train over the Santiam Pass (or Hogg Pass as it was originally called), Chinese laborers, under Hogg's direction, cut a grade into the hard andesite rock and constructed about 300 feet of track. A boxcar was then hauled up in pieces, assembled, and pulled back and forth along the tracks by mules.

Despite financial backing by Eastern investors, Hogg's vision of a rail crossing at Hogg Pass was doomed to failure. Yaquina Bay proved too shallow for large ocean-going vessels. Portland became the terminus for both the Northern Pacific (1883) and the Southern Pacific (1887). Furthermore, the lands in Central or Eastern Oregon were never settled to any great extent until the twentieth century. It was not long before the railroad venture ran out of funds and the company was forced to foreclose. Parts of the old railroad grade on Hogg Rock and on the east side of Santiam Pass are still to be seen.

One outcome of the rail project was the land grants involving thousands of acres of farm range and forest land

Left: A trail guide leads a pack trip into the Mt. Jefferson Wilderness Area. *(Oregon Dept. of Transportation)* Right: View looking north from the Hoodoo Ski Area near the Santiam Pass. The Santiam Highway sweeps around Hogg Rock. Mountains shown include the spires of Three Fingered Jack and (beyond) Mt. Jefferson *(Oregon Dept. of Transportation)*

Clearing charred trunks from within the Airstrip Burn fire near Hoodoo Ski Bowl. This lightning-caused fire, one of the most damaging in the High Country, occurred in August, 1967. The fire burned 8000 acres of forest, was fought by 2000 men and cost over $2 million in fire-fighting expenses and lost timber. Hayrick Butte is in the background. *(USFS)*

that were received by the Oregon and Western Colonization Company. Today, between Suttle Lake and Sisters south of US 20, the ownership of lands reflects a checkerboard pattern with sections alternately in private ownership and under U.S. Forest Service jurisdiction. Land use and management plans in this area must work around the discontinuous nature of the land-ownership pattern.

The Santiam Pass area has much to offer geologists, hikers, campers, winter sports enthusiasts, and photographers. Spectacular views of many of the Cascade peaks are possible from different parts of the Santiam Pass area. Motorists climbing the grade from Sisters get a bird's-eye view of elongated Suttle Lake and circular Blue Lake, and a fine exposure of Mt. Washington's slender spire.

At the Santiam Pass summit, a short side road heads south to the Hoodoo Ski Area, Hayrick Butte, and Big Lake. Hoodoo Butte is a recent cinder cone whose fascinating name origin is uncertain. McArthur states that the name "may come from the word that indicates a run of bad luck or a Jonah. On the other hand, throughout the western part of the United States the word is used to refer to natural rock piles or pinnacles of fantastic shapes. The name Hoodoo may have been applied during the days of the Santiam Toll Road because of difficulties in construction or travel. . . ."[14] Although Hoodoo Butte cannot compare in size with Bachelor Butte as a ski area, some good shorter runs can be groomed on the slopes. Further discussion of the Hoodoo Ski Area is included in the section on "Winter Sports."

Near Hoodoo is Hayrick Butte (elevation 5523 feet). Hayrick Butte reminds the author of Sir Conan Doyle's story on the "Lost World," where those who ascended the precipitous slopes of a previously unexplored plateau (in Brazil) discovered the live world of prehistoric animals. It is unlikely the plateau of Hayrick Butte would house animals of any kind. The mass of basaltic andesite (the same platy-jointed basaltic andesite that is seen in the cliffs of Hogg Rock) were, at one time, covered with glacial ice, as was Hogg Rock.

Appropriately named Big Lake—a mile long—is an extensive body of water located in a glacially carved basin called Hidden Valley on U.S.G.S. maps. Forests surround

Big Lake but fine views of Mt. Washington are obtained from the lakeshore. Camping and water sports are popular recreational activities at Big Lake in the summer months.

The Santiam Pass area is a focal point for hikers. The Pacific Crest Trail slices north - south through forested lands near the summit. The trail can be reached by following signs to an off-road parking area north of the highway at the crest of the pass. Trails lead north to the Three Fingered Jack country with side trails to many lakes located on the upper slopes of the Cascades. Those hiking south pass through the dusty soils in the Airstrip Burn and on to the Mt. Washington Wilderness Area.

McKenzie Pass Highway

McKenzie Pass Highway has long been recognized as one of the most scenic in Oregon. There are both similarities and differences between the Santiam and McKenzie Pass routes. For example, the Santiam Highway, at the summit, is flanked by tall, thick stands of conifers. McKenzie Pass is exposed, and its windswept summit area is largely devoid of trees; the few trees scattered amidst the rugged lava are stunted and pathetic looking. At and near the Santiam summit, travelers get only fleeting glimpses of the High Cascade peaks, but McKenzie Pass provides travelers with far-reaching views north and south across some of the most recent lava flows in the continental United States. McKenzie Pass is used by motorists only during the summer months. Santiam Pass, despite periodic heavy winter snows, is a year-round highway.

Pioneer crossings of the McKenzie Pass area took place about the same time as the discovery and crossing of Santiam Pass. In 1862, Felix and Marion Scott, following the McKenzie River to Salt Springs (Belknap Springs), traveled east to the north of Deer Butte, past what is now Scott Lake. They then climbed up a trail long used by Indians, crossing lava fields just north of Yapoah Crater. From that point, Scott and his party of 50 to 60 men, 9 wagons of supplies, and 900 head of cattle, headed north toward Matthieu Lakes, crossing the divide south of the present-day Mc-

Kenzie Pass route, at an elevation of about 6000 feet. The Scott Party spent the 1862-63 winter on Trout Creek before continuing to Boise.

Those familiar with the steepness of the climb from Scott Lake (elevation 4800 feet) to where the Scott Trail crosses the Cascades can well believe the report that Scott used 26 oxen to pull one wagon. A later recollection of the Scott Trail described how it wound over jagged lava beds, and that it was necessary to throw rocks into lava fissures to allow wagons to be drawn across.[15] Today, a forest-service trail from Scott Lake heads east to Yapoah Crater, north to South Matthieu Lake, then east to Trout Creek, following the Scott Trail.

In the mid-1860's and the 1870's, there were different attempts to incorporate wagon roads over the McKenzie Pass area. Scott had proved that a new route from the Willamette Valley to Central and Eastern Oregon was possible. In 1863, the "McKenzie Wagon Road Company" was formed with the intent to develop a route over the Cascades near the Three Sisters to the Deschutes River where it was forded (Tetherow Crossing north of Redmond). Two years later, another corporation, the "McKenzie Valley and Deschutes Wagon Road Company," was formed.

In 1866, another route over the Cascades was discovered. John Latta blazed a trail up Lost Creek Canyon, up what is now called Dead Horse Hill and over McKenzie Pass lava beds, 1000 feet lower in elevation than the Scott Trail. Work on the trail was done by John Craig who, earlier, was part of the Felix Scott party. In 1871, John Craig was president of the "McKenzie Salt Springs and Deschutes Wagon Road Company," another of the several wagon road companies formed in the 1860's and 1870's.

During the period 1871 to 1894, the McKenzie Salt Springs and Deschutes Wagon Road Company collected tolls, first at McKenzie Bridge (previously Craig's Bridge) then at Blue River. Toll rates included $2 for a wagon drawn by two horses, $1 for a horseman, 10 cents a head for cattle and horses and 5 cents a head for sheep. The pay for a toll keeper was $150 for a season's duty. Tolls amounting to $17,969.50 were collected in a 22-year period.[16]

Following the establishment of the Camp Polk post office, and the opening of the McKenzie road, the road company secured a contract to deliver mail between Eugene and Prineville by way of Camp Polk. In December, 1877, John Craig, working for the wagon company, started eastward from McKenzie Bridge, a pair of skiis over his shoulders and a mail sack over his back. When he failed to return to McKenzie Bridge on schedule, there was fear that something had happened to him. At that time there was no way of getting directly in touch with Camp Polk to find out whether the carrier had arrived. A letter was sent to Camp Polk by way of Portland, up the Columbia River by boat to The Dalles, south by pony carrier to Prineville, then west to Camp Polk. The answer—Craig had never reached Camp Polk.

Early in 1878, a search party discovered Craig's body in a shelter cabin located just west of the McKenzie Pass summit. Craig had apparently entered the cabin by way of the "Santa Claus" (wide) chimney and managed to start a fire. However, the fire extinguished itself while he slept. Unable to relight the fire, he froze to death in the dying embers. John Craig was buried near the cabin in which he died.

On July 12, 1930, John Craig's efforts to carry the mail across the wintry McKenzie Pass were honored by the Oregon rural mail carriers. In a ceremony attended by 400, men with bared heads stood in brilliant July sunshine around the tomb, while various speakers traced the history of the beginnings of the mountain road which nearly half a century later evolved into the McKenzie highway.

Travel across McKenzie Pass in the early years of the twentieth century was an adventure. Reports on the road noted the presence of large rocks, small rocks, high centers and stumps, and sandy spots trapping light-powered vehicles. At one time, motorists, approaching the summit from the east, traveled over wooden planks laid across the jagged lava. In 1917, McKenzie Pass was designated a state highway. Two years later, work began on grading a 15-mile section of the highway. At Windy Point, now a deep cut in the lava just east of the summit, 6 tons of TNT were exploded in an attempt to blast through a mass of rock 200 feet long, 30 feet high, and 30 feet wide. So stubborn was the

A 1921 motorist negotiates thick dust along the McKenzie Highway near Sisters. The photo shows the cutting of ponderosa pine adjacent to the scenic highway, a practice no longer permitted. *(USFS)*

Early-day motorists pause on the journey across the McKenzie Highway lava beds. The McKenzie Pass route was designated a state highway in 1917, but it never became a year-round route. For many years, travel across the summit was an adventure, with reports of top speeds of 5 mph over the lava beds. *(USFS)*

lava that the rock rose into the air and promptly settled back into place.

Work on the highway continued for several years, but travel across the summit area was still difficult. In September, 1924, a motorist traveling over the Pass reported that he was unable to travel at a speed of more than 5 miles per hour for several miles over the lava beds. An auto stage, operating daily along the pass, had to purchase new tires every 15 days![17] One party, traveling west from Central Oregon, returned via The Dalles, refusing to travel over the lava beds again.

At that time, Linn County residents were promoting development of the Santiam Pass route, pointing out that such a route was more scenic and did not have to negotiate "hell's half acre." In 1925, motorists took up to 12 hours to travel from Corvallis to Sisters via the McKenzie Pass. By September, 1925, McKenzie Pass Highway was deemed "completed" and was accepted by the U.S. Bureau of Public Roads. Travel over the pass increased following completion of the road and publicity on the scenic qualities of the High Country. In 1926, Oregon Stages carried 2227 passengers. The ride was described as a "cool, clear ride over the McKenzie Pass and down along the beautiful McKenzie River, past interesting lava beds on the summit, with marvelous views of the mountains." The fare from Bend to Eugene was $6; round trip was $10.

Heavy snows block the McKenzie Pass throughout the winter. In relatively dry autumns, it has remained open into the winter. In the 1939-40 winter, it was not closed until January 10, 1940. In 1926, it opened as early as April 29. In the 1925-26 winter, venturesome motorists used the road throughout the season. Each spring, many motorists eagerly await word on the opening of the pass. However, nature is unpredictable in the High Country and the pass is ordinarily not opened until late June or early July.

In June, 1935, *The Bulletin*, reporting on the Pass, reprinted a Eugene *Register Guard* editorial which aptly sized up the feelings of many Oregonians:

The opening of the pass is always a joyous event. It means that people on this side can get through to the beautiful lakes and streams of the high desert country, and it means that people on the other side can get to the "green country" and the rhododendrons of the coast. The change is always exhilarating though one is always glad to get back.[18]

Prior to the completion of the Clear Lake cutoff, in 1962, there were several suggestions that the McKenzie Pass be made a year-round highway. In 1922, district engineers had contemplated making the McKenzie Pass an all-year route by using snow sleds during the winter months. However, the cost of $25,000 was considered prohibitive. In September, 1923, the people of Sisters voiced complaints that a closed highway was an economic hardship for their community. By May, 1949, an estimated cost of making the McKenzie Pass a year-round highway was put at $6 million. However, an opened pass would have given direct access to an area for winter sports.

Throughout the winter months, Nordic skiers now venture to the McKenzie Pass summit to experience the beauty of the area. Lava beds are transformed into a great white prairie, and the rugged outlines of North Sister and Mt. Washington are obliterated by heavy snows. Each year, in April, the John Craig Memorial ski race is held. The race and ski tour commemorate the efforts of John Templeton Craig to deliver mail across the McKenzie Pass in December 1877. Mail, stamped especially for the occasion, is carried by skiers. Today, motorists use McKenzie Pass as a scenic route to view close-up some remarkable geological landscapes. Hikers and climbers, wanting access into the Three Sisters and Mt. Washington wilderness areas, can use trailheads that are adjacent to the McKenzie Highway.

Sisters, elevation 3184 feet, is the High Country gateway to the McKenzie Pass area. Just west of town, Highway 20 splits: the main route goes northwest toward Black Butte and Santiam Pass and the McKenzie Pass route (State Highway 242) continues west, past the Patterson Arabian Horse and Llama Ranch. A panorama of Tam McArthur Rim, Broken Top, and the Three Sisters is visible from this point.

A marker giving a brief history of the McKenzie Pass is located on the north side of the highway, opposite the Patterson Ranch.

The highway slices through tall ponderosa pines and passes Cold Springs campground, where the edge of a lava formation releases pent-up water. The road cuts into the base of a terminal moraine that dates back to the Wisconsin Ice Age. North of the highway, several cinder cones rise above the glacial deposits. The highway then climbs sharply through dense stands of mixed ponderosa pine, lodgepole pine, fir, and an increasing density of undergrowth.

Suddenly, at Windy Point, the highway emerges from its corridor of trees to enter a world of volcanic vistas. Miles of black lava and jagged piles of burned-out rock extend west and north toward the horizon. Beyond, Mt. Washington and Mt. Jefferson rise over the lava. Few motorists passing at Windy Point realize that over half a century ago, the area was the scene of a "gold rush."

In September, 1927, the cry of "gold" spread throughout the West. Hundreds of men, most from Eugene and Corvallis, converged on Windy Point. Over 500 claims were filed, many of them scattered in the lava fields on both sides of the McKenzie Pass summit. The people of Bend, perhaps more knowledgeable about the mineral content of lava rock, remained curious but skeptical. An assay office was set up near Windy Point and an "imported" assayer, checking samples of the suspected rock, reported that the gold in the Windy Point rocky promontory was in the proportion of $75 to $80 a ton. The assayer noted, ". . . .the entire dike which issues from the mountainside, ending far out in the black, burned lava flow, is made up of stone which is permeated with gold."[19]

Two Bend men, taking rock quarried from just south of Bend, had their samples tested and found them to contain gold flakes. However, a second testing of the rock revealed its true nature. The Windy Point rock was soon properly proved to be hyperseane andesite—chunks of unequaled road-building material—with fragments of silica, iron oxide, aluminum oxide, calcium oxide, magnesium oxide and moisture—but no gold.[20] Bend heaved a sigh of relief that the impossible could not be so and settled back into its business of producing lumber. Overnight, the assay office closed, the assayers disappeared, and disappointed gold seekers abandoned the windswept lava fields, but not before some claimants lost up to $1000 to the Windy Point assayer and his associates!

South of the highway opposite the lava fields at Windy Point is the trailhead to the summit of Black Crater (7251 feet). The trail, 4 miles long, climbs 2300 feet through dense forests and past small meadows. The red-cindered summit, once the site of a fire lookout tower, offers spectacular views of the nearby Three Sisters, Broken Top and, to the north, a line of Cascade peaks extending from Mt. Washington to Mt. Hood. The "crater" at the summit of the volcano is actually a glacial cirque, open to the northeast. West of Windy Point, McKenzie Pass Highway skirts the edges of the lava fields. In places, lava towers above the motorist. A short side road on the south leads to Lava Camp Lake and to a Pacific Crest trailhead for hikers venturing south to Matthieu Lakes, Yapoah Crater, and beyond, skirting the western flanks of the Three Sisters.

Just east of the McKenzie Pass Summit is the Dee Wright Observatory, a conspicuous round tower built of lava rock and reached from the highway by climbing stone steps. Most motorists traveling the McKenzie Pass Highway stop at the Dee Wright Observatory, if only to view the volcanic landscape from road level. Those who climb up to the observing "room" are rewarded by a 360-degree panorama that is one of the most spectacular in the High Country. The observatory commemorates the work done by Dee Wright in constructing the Pacific Crest National Scenic Trail (formerly the Skyline Trail) between the McKenzie Pass and Sunshine Meadow (west of North Sister). Dee Wright was also foreman of a Civilian Conservation Corps team working on the observatory in the 1930's. Wright died before completion of the observatory.

Perhaps one of the most interesting of the many landscape features of the McKenzie Pass summit area is Belknap Crater, the large summit cone located northwest of the observatory. More than 70 square miles of treeless wilderness of basalt confront the visitor. The two main vents that gave birth to the formation of the lava fields were Belknap Crater

The McKenzie Pass summit area has considerable history and scenic geology to offer motorists. The old "highway" across the lava beds can still be seen in places (foreground). A short, paved trail within the lava fields has interpretive signs explaining a variety of volcanic features. The Dee Wright Observatory provides a 360-degree panorama of many of the Cascade peaks. Lava flow (background)—from Little Belknap Crater (not shown)—is less than 3000 years old, leaving a scoria cone as an island. Volcano on the skyline is Belknap Crater (elevation 6872 feet).

The Three Sisters are mirrored in Scott Lake. Early fall storm and chill bring light snow to the peaks and bright colors to the broad-leaved bushes and trees bordering the lake. Scott Lake and nearby Scott Mountain were named for Felix Scott, pioneer builder of the McKenzie Wagon Road which passed by the lake in 1862. *(Oregon Dept. of Transportation)*

(6872 feet) and Little Belknap (6305 feet). The volcanoes were named after J. H. Belknap, who was involved in the operations of the toll road that crossed McKenzie Pass in the 1870's.

Just west of the Dee Wright Observatory, the highway crosses the McKenzie Pass summit at an elevation of 5324 feet. North of the highway at the summit, the Pacific Crest National Trail is embedded in an undulating sea of frozen lava; it takes hikers into the Mt. Washington Wilderness Area and into the midst of the source of volcanic activity.

Mt. Washington, elevation 7802 feet, is the skeletal remnant of what was once a volcano that may well have rivaled in size those of the other major Cascade peaks. Following extensive glaciation, only the more resistant volcanic neck and radial dikes remain of the volcano. The pinnacle-tipped mountain looks difficult to climb. It is, and although several unsuccessful attemps had been made, the mountain finally yielded to six Bend youths on August 19, 1923. Although parties of climbers scale the crumbling pinnacle each summer, experts warn that only qualified climbers with the proper equipment should attempt the climb. The final ascent to the summit of Mt. Washington is through rock chimneys and up sheer rock.

Just under 2 miles west of the McKenzie Pass summit, the highway passes the John Craig Memorial (on the south side of the highway), then descends through an arboreal tunnel into dense vegetation typical of the western Cascades. During the early fall, many motorists set aside one weekend to photograph or simply view the beautiful coloring of the vine maple. Periodic views of the Three Sisters, short hikes to scenic lakes (such as Scott or Linton), and a visit to beautiful Proxy Falls are some of the many attractions for those who travel the historical McKenzie Highway.

The Three Sisters

The Three Sisters are the best known of all the landform features in Central Oregon. This trio of volcanoes dominates the western skyline from many different parts of the region. Travelers arriving from the north, see the glacial-clad peaks seemingly supported by an indistinct aura of blue-green forests. Seen from the High Desert near Millican or even as far away as Brothers, 70 miles distant, the Three Sisters and other Cascade peaks line up in formation along the western skyline. From the La Pine country, the Sisters appear clustered together.

If Newberry Volcano, which to the writer appears as a large, brooding volcano, then the Three Sisters are friendly looking mountains. Perhaps it is the sun sparkling on the snowfields, rather than being absorbed by the dark green forests or by black lava, that makes the Sisters more attractive than Newberry. From a distance it is difficult to get an impressionistic photo of Newberry. The Three Sisters, on the other hand, have frequently posed for photographers and painters. Not that there is but one mood of the peaks! Far from it! Ray Eyerly, renowned painter of landscapes and resident of the Sisters area, has included the Three Sisters in no less than eight of his paintings. In each, he has found totally different perspectives.

Their moods change throughout the day and seasonally, even when seen from the same place. For a moment, early morning sunlight casts pinkish glows on the snow-clad peaks, even when the High Lava plains remain in semi-darkness. On clear mornings they stand out in sharp contrast to the blue skyline, their glaciers and snowfields glistening. By midday, the sun—having "moved" to the south —begins to cast shadows across the north-facing slopes. Details that were seen in the early morning are lost, especially in summer when afternoon haze masks even the higher peaks. At sunset, the Three Sisters and the other Cascade peaks once again stand out clearly as they are silhouetted by a setting sun.

Depending on the season, the position of the setting sun changes from winter to summer. When viewed from Pilot Butte at the time of the summer solstice, the sun sets behind Mt. Washington's slender spire. As the days shorten, the setting sun "creeps" along the Cascade skyline, selecting one peak after another as its departure point. By early fall, the sun, seen from Bend, disappears behind the Sisters, casting long shadows across the midstate plateau.

Throughout the winter months, the Three Sisters are frequently shrouded in storm clouds. As weather systems hurdle the Cascades, the peaks trigger prodigious snowfalls from the air masses. With the advent of higher pressure, the skies clear, revealing the winter majesty of these mountains robed in the freshly fallen snow. Periodically in the winter months, cold, heavier air lingers in the valleys of the High Country, trapping low-lying fog blankets. At the same time, the Sisters and Broken Top may rise dramatically above the fog, their heights seemingly magnified by the clear air and by their bulk. Whatever the season or time of day, the Three Sisters are barometers and landmarks to the residents of large parts of Central Oregon.

Midway through the nineteenth century, maps of Oregon which included the central part of the state were characterized by an absence of place names—both physical and cultural. A Bureau of Topographical Engineers map (1859) showed only three physical landmarks in Central Oregon: Mt. Jefferson, Three Sisters, and Fall River (Deschutes River). According to McArthur, the Three Sisters were mentioned but not named by David Douglas on October 5, 1826.[21] However, Douglas noted but two peaks, a situation not surprising as the Three Sisters appear as one, two, or three mountains, depending on the position from which they are viewed.

Origin of the name "Three Sisters" is not clear. In the 1840's the Methodist Mission at Salem had individual names for the peaks, calling them Mount Faith (North Sister), Mount Hope (Middle Sister), and Mount Charity (South Sister). Today, in addition to the Three Sisters, lesser peaks have been included in the family and large-scale maps of the area show Little Brother, The Wife, and The Husband.

Three Sisters Reveal Their Ages

The Three Sisters are by no means triplets. Indeed, their years of birth are far apart and their respective ages show different signs of wear and tear. However, in 1925, Dr. Edwin T. Hodge, professor of Economic Geology, University of Oregon, published his theory that the Three Sisters were remnants of what was once one large volcano. However, another professor, Howel Williams, who had studied Crater Lake and large calderas in the Pacific region, concluded that most calderas were formed by collapse of the volcanic peak and not by explosion. Williams, following his geological research in the Three Sisters area in 1940, concluded that each peak was a separate volcano, although some of the lesser peaks may have been parasitic to a major one.

North Sister

North Sister is the second highest of the Three Sisters, and the oldest of the trio. The peak may have been built up in three stages. First, a broad basaltic shield, 15 to 20 miles wide, rose to a height of 8,000 feet by "quiet eruptions." More violent activity then built up a 3,000-foot pyroclastic cone on top of the shield. The last stages of growth included volcanic activity, including a large number of dikes which may have helped hold the mountain together and which have resisted erosion. Today, many of these dikes on North Sister are visible close up. Indeed, where glacial erosion has gnawed into the sides of the peak, the internal organs of the volcano are exposed. Precipitous cliffs have multilayers of yellow and brown tuff, red, gray, and black scoria, and where volcanic gases have oxidized the rocks, layers of orange and red are seen. Despite the kaleidoscope of colors, climbers rate North Sister as a difficult peak to scale. In the fall of 1978, when a light plane flying in dense clouds slammed into the upper western slopes of North Sister, killing all three on board, experienced climbers reported that rescue attempts were beset with extreme danger.

At the time of greatest glaciation, North Sister was covered by glaciers, and ice reached down to the 4000-foot elevation on both the northern and eastern flanks. On the west, glaciers 15 miles long extended their icy fingers as low as the 1000-foot elevation. Today, three glaciers, Linn, Thayer and Villard, cradle the slopes of North Sister. In addition, Collier Glacier is shared with Middle Sister.

Middle Sister

Middle Sister is the smallest of the Three Sisters and the least impressive. It does not have the summit pinnacles nor the ruggedness of North Sister, nor the bulk of South Sister. Yet Middle Sister is a more perfect cone and does host four glaciers. Collier Glacier, which originates on the upper western slopes of the mountain, extends for one and a half miles. In 1925, Hodge reported that Collier Glacier covered 442 acres. By way of comparison, Zig Zag Glacier, the largest glacier on Mt. Hood, spread over 354 acres. Collier Glacier—named after Professor George H. Collier, pioneer instructor at the University of Oregon—has shrunk measurably during the twentieth century. There is photographic evidence that just prior to the turn of the century it extended to the base of Collier Glacier viewpoint, nearly one mile from the snout of the glacier. Much of the recession occurred in the 1930's, a decade of above-normal temperatures in Central Oregon. In recent decades there is evidence that the glacier has stabilized, although in the dry summer of 1977, a scientific study of the glacier by a University of Oregon graduate student revealed that the glacier shrank by 16 feet that summer.[22] In 1979, Collier Glacier covered less than 200 acres. Prouty Glacier, which has melted more slowly, is now larger than Collier.

South Sister

The youngest and highest (10,358 feet) of the Three Sisters is South Sister. From the Bend area it is easily identified by its bulk and its long south slope. Only South Sister, of the trio of mountains, has a summit crater. A half-mile-diameter crater is cradled within the rocky edges that form the summit perimeter. Most of the year all of the crater is mantled in ice and snow, but given sufficient warming, a small aqua-colored lake, the highest lake in Oregon, appears in the northwest corner.

The views from South Sister are spectacular. On clear days, Mount Rainier in Washington State, 180 miles distant, is visible. From South Sister, the role of the Cascades in separating two dissimilar Oregons is quite evident. To the west, a sea of hazy blue-green forests extends roller-coaster fashion over the smoother Western Cascades. To the east, the level lands of the mid-state plateau are brown and parched. At the northern foot of South Sister the landscape is predominantly gray and decidedly inhospitable where glaciers have left countless moraines. Secluded amongst the morainic debris is a host of small green and icy-blue lakes, collectively known as Chambers Lakes. Those brave enough to peak over the abrupt edge at the top of South Sister note how precipitous and crevasse strewn are the northern and eastern slopes of Prouty, Eugene, and Carver glaciers.

South Sister is a favorite peak for climbers. Expert alpinists find the above-mentioned north and east slopes challenging. Beginners will find the southern route nothing more than a long hike. Two possible approaches to the southern slope are from Moraine Lake or from Green Lakes. Either way, climbers skirt the southern edge of Lewis Glacier, then ascend the moderately steep but seemingly interminable trail up the cindery slope on the south side of the mountain. Hikers not acclimatized to high altitudes should take into consideration that, at 10,000 feet, there is less than 70 percent of the oxygen pressure experienced at sea level.

Green Lakes

The Green Lakes area is one of the most popular destinations for hikers in the Three Sisters Wilderness Area. It is frequently used by backpackers, by day hikers, and as a base for alpinists wishing to scale Broken Top or South Sister. Many organizations and clubs have set up camp close to Green Lakes. In winter, a few advanced Nordic skiers snow-camp in the Green Lakes area.

Green Lakes consist of two tiny and one modest-sized lakes, all nestled at 6,500 feet in a valley between Broken Top and South Sister. An extensive lava field, the Newberry Flow on the lower southeast slope of South Sister, temporarily blocked drainage from snow meltwater. Today, two streams roar and tumble water down precipitous slopes into the largest of Green Lakes. Fall Creek has cut a channel around the east side of the lava flow, then drops 1000 feet in 5 miles before discharging into Sparks Lake.

Around the lakes are extensive areas of white pumice supporting very fragile vegetation consisting of sparse grasses and a scattering of alpine flowers. Higher morainic ridges and hummocks contain clusters of mountain hemlock and fir. In summer, the bright orange, blue or red backpack tents scattered around the lakes sharply contrast with the natural coloring of the landscape. On calm days, the crystal-clear waters of Green Lakes mirror the adjacent peaks; many visitors have photographed South Sister reflected in the quiet waters.

Those who have camped at Green Lakes at the time of a late-summer full moon may well have experienced the rising of the "Broken Top moon," a phenomenon vividly described by Phil Brogan on the occasion of a Boy Scout camp:

> It was a beautiful cloudless evening. Not even a wisp of cloud was draped around the peak of South Sister far above the (scouts') campfire and the reflecting lake. . . .suddenly, a pulsating fire appeared on the steep south slope of Broken Top, like a volcano fire rekindled. It was the rising moon at its full phase. Magnified by contrast with the sheltered peaks that were so near the camp, the moon appeared immense as its golden disc cut across a lava crag that was once a part of a stately mountain. Below on the Broken Top slope were grotesquely gnarled trees, like gnomes of the night caught in a mountain raid.
>
> The phenomenon of the mountain moonrise was over in a moment, but as the scouts turned to their camp duties they were amazed to see the South Sister radiant and distinct in the moonlight. Glaciers, lava flows, waterfalls could be clearly seen.[23]

Few people realize that in 1915 Green Lakes were investigated as a possible source of irrigation water to be used on the parched lands around Lower Bridge and Plainview, east of Sisters. Tentative plans called for a tunnel to be cut through the divide north of Green Lakes and for water to be diverted into Pole Creek and Squaw Creek. A dam, 20 feet high, would have stored 7,500 acre feet of water. At that time, the estimated cost of the dam and the tunnel was set at $80,000.[24] Then, in 1922, when Bend was looking for alternate water sources, Mayor R. H. Fox suggested that the city file a claim on Green Lakes as a "reserve source of pure water." Fortunately for lovers of wilderness areas, nothing came of either plan.

Wickiup Plains and Rock Mesa

Rock Mesa is a sizable mass of obsidian that seems to have spilled out from the south base of South Sister and flowed like thick syrup, wrinkling and buckling as it cooled. From the air, Rock Mesa stands out dramatically, its ridges and pinnacles spread out concentrically in successive waves, from some hidden vent. Part of the flow cooled to obsidian —shiny black glass that for centuries was used for the making of arrowheads.

For several years Rock Mesa has caused controversy. In January, 1963, a Los Angeles-based firm, the U.S. Pumice Company, filed ten claims (totaling 1460 acres) for mining pumice. Commercial block pumice has a variety of uses, including polishing material, grill stones, skin softeners, etc. The thought of strip mining in the Three Sisters Wilderness Area disturbed many Oregonians, and newspaper stories and editorials focused on the Rock Mesa issue. In May, 1971, Oregon Senators Bob Packwood and Mark Hatfield introduced bills in Congress to restrict mining the area. The Bend Chamber of Commerce passed a resolution opposing mining there, and in a fund-raising drive, paid for transporting Bend attorney, Owen Panner, and retired Forest Service engineer, C. E. "Slim" Hein, to testify in Washington D.C. for passage of the bills. At that time the mining company had at least a 10-years' supply of block pumice left at their mine in the Inyo National Forest near Lee Vining, California.

Part of the controversy at Rock Mesa revolved around potential damage to the environment. Access to Rock Mesa would have involved building a road from Devils Lake, following an existing hiking trail.

In 1975, the U.S. Pumice Company notified the Forest Service of its intent to begin mining. The validity of the U.S. Pumice Company claims was then challenged by the U.S. Forest Service, the Bureau of Land Management, and OSPIRG (Oregon Students Public Interest Research Group). The challenges were based on the way the claims were located and staked on unsurveyed land, on the poor commercial value of the block pumice, and the fact that mining operations would violate Oregon Department of Environmental Quality dust and noise standards for wilderness areas. A court hearing on the validity of the claims was held in Portland in October, 1978. The claim was declared valid. However, the Federal Government purchased the land from the U.S. Pumice Co. in 1983 and withdrew the land from open entry.

On the edge of Rock Mesa is a geological oddity, Le Conte Crater, named after a pioneer Californian geologist, Joseph Le Conte, one of the first scientists to study the Columbia River lava flows. Le Conte Crater is also an excellent vantage point for viewing Rock Mesa and the rugged slopes of South Sister. The perfectly preserved 200-foot-high cone of basaltic scoria cradles a 100-foot-deep crater that, for a short time following late spring snowmelt, supports a small lake. Mountain hemlock tops the rim and the northern-facing slope. The unusual geologic mystery of the Le Conte Crater is that the cone is strewn not only with fire-formed debris—pumice, obsidian and dacite of recent (geological) origin—but also with older lavas which bear glacial striations. Had Le Conte Crater been subjected to glaciation it would not have maintained its perfect shape. Dr. Howel Williams, geologist, contended that fire rocks and glacial debris that cover Le Conte Crater were blown from a nearby volcanic vent which was subsequently buried by later lava flows.

Pacific Crest National Scenic Trail

The Three Sisters Wilderness Area covers nearly 200,000 acres and includes within its span the Three Sisters and adjacent peaks. First established as a Primitive Area in 1937, it was reclassified a Wilderness in 1957 and included in the Congressionally established National Wilderness Preservation System in 1964. Numerous trails lead hikers to a variety of places around the base of Three Sisters.

The Pacific Crest National Scenic Trail passes just west of the Three Sisters. Hikers can sample part of the trail on day trips in the Matthieu Lake or Wickiup Plains areas or they can leisurely backpack from Devils Lake on the Cascade Lakes Highway to McKenzie Pass, a distance of 25 miles. Along the way there is some spectacular scenery as well as many interesting geological features.

Starting at Lava Camp near the McKenzie Pass, the Pacific Crest Trail heads south, skirts the eastern flank of an extensive lava flow, climbing nearly 600 feet in 2 miles to North Matthieu Lake. The lake—named by Professor Edwin T. Hodge after Francis Xavier Matthieu, early-day Willamette Valley pioneer—is small but scenic. The trail then climbs to Scott Pass, site of the old wagon road blazed by Felix Scott. Lieutenant Williamson and other members of the Abbot party explored the Scott Pass area in 1855. Williamson's journal for September 6, 1855, noted the snow on the trail, the steep ascent of the divide at that point, and the impracticality for a railroad. Williamson, however, did note that to the north a lower pass (McKenzie Pass) offered better prospects for a railroad.[25]

From Scott Pass, the trail then crosses a rugged lava flow before contouring around Yapoah Crater. Continuing south, it climbs past Minnie Scott Springs, an extensive alpine meadow area that makes a good campsite, then switchbacks up and over Oppie Dildock Pass (elevation 6890 feet). Oppie Dildock Pass, a ridge of twisted lava and clinkery cinders, was named by Dee Wright and U.S. Forest Service Ranger Ralph Engels after an early twentieth-century comic strip character who seemingly always got out of difficult predicaments.

Aerial view of Rock Mesa and Le Conte Crater (left). The Rock Mesa flow, consisting of obsidian mantled by pumice, can be reached by a trail from Devils Lake. Le Conte Crater is the circular cone on the lower left. *(The Bulletin)*

Left: Yapoah Crater, a 500-foot-high cinder cone, towers over the Pacific Crest Trail in the Three Sisters Wilderness Area. The crater is one of several scoria cones that erupted within the last 3000 years along fractures which extended north from Collier Cone. The McKenzie Highway, just east of the summit, cuts through thick aa-type lava which flowed north 4 miles from Yapoah Crater. Right: Broken Top, the remnant of a composite cone that once rose well above its present elevation of 9175 feet. The cone was built of tephra (ash) flows and injected sills and dikes upon the flanks of the Tam McArthur shield volcano. Because Broken Top was deeply dissected by glaciation, it makes an excellent outdoor laboratory for geology students. The multi-colored crater walls, lingering snowfields, alpine meadows, and clear streams provide a favorite subject for photographers. *(Oregon Dept. of Transportation)*

Just south of the pass, a short side trail leads to Collier Glacier viewpoint where there is an excellent view of Collier Glacier. Nearby, horseshoe-shaped Collier Cone (7534 feet) erupted within the last 1000 years, its lava spreading west 13 miles down the valley of White Branch Creek, then spilling into the valley of Linton Creek and damming the drainage, forming Linton Lake. The view from Collier Cone is interesting. In addition to the familiar succession of Cascade peaks, a vast, barren black-and-red cinder field, the Ahalapam Cinder Field, smothers an area over two miles long and nearly one mile wide north of the cone.

The Pacific Crest Trail finally leaves the rugged lava flows, descending to Sunshine Shelter, a favorite camp area for climbers scaling Middle or North Sister. A bronze tablet, the Prouty Memorial, located in Sunshine Meadow, honors Harley H. Prouty, president of the Mazama Club, Portland —believed to have been the first man to climb North Sister. South of Sunshine Meadow, the trail climbs sharply and passes refreshing Obsidian Falls. Excellent close-up views of North and Middle Sister are obtained from the trail south of the falls.

Along the trail, the beauty of the High Country is ever present. So are the forces of nature, with the work of ice evident where striations or tell-tale grooves on rocks give evidence of past glaciation. On the western flanks of the Three Sisters, few streams cut across the trail. However, just north of Rock Mesa, a few spring-fed creeks provide water along an otherwise dry trail. The trail finally climbs sharply from Mesa Creek up to the pumice desert at Wickiup Plains. The Pacific Crest Trail is but one of many trails for exploring the Three Sisters Wilderness Area.

Broken Top

It would be difficult to think up a name more appropriate than that applied to Broken Top. Even when seen from Bend, 20 miles away, the mountain has a distinctive shape quickly recognized by visitors. Close up, it is, perhaps, more impressive than its 9175-foot elevation suggests. The volcano's jagged spires, like a series of castle turrets, are impressive whether mantled by deep-winter snows or exposed by scorching summer sun. The white apron of the Bend snowfield, nestled in the glacial cirque, contrasts sharply with the surrounding rocky fortress. A torrent of water, run-off from melting snow, has cut into and through a grey moraine near the base of the snowfield. From there, rivulets of clear, icy-cold water, pulled by gravity, tumble over rocks and boulders, providing moisture for small alpine meadows. Considerable water discharges from springs emerging from the eastern slopes of the Broken Top Country. These springs, with their clear, cold water, drain into Tumalo Creek, furnishing the volume of water for scenic Tumalo Falls. One of the creeks, Bridge Creek, supplies part of the water used by the City of Bend.

Geologists from many parts of the Pacific Northwest make field visits to the Broken Top country to study, close up and first hand, both volcanism and glaciation. Broken Top's semi-circular crater walls, long exposed by glaciation and weathering, reveal the inner structure of a volcano, with layers of ash, pumice and lava flows. "Bands of red, purple, and black scoria alternate with yellow, brown, and orange lapilli tuffs and tuff breccias.[26]"

In 1905, Broken Top was the scene of a gold rush when specimens of soft porphyritic rock were discovered in a gulch at its base. Laidlaw (formerly Tumalo) people stampeded for "Old Broken Top" and claims were soon staked out. In 1911, another gold strike near Broken Top was reported. News of it reached Bend on August 8, 1911, and attracted so many residents that, according to *The Bulletin*, the town was almost deserted by evening, as scores of residents rushed to secure their claims. Territory adjacent to the strike on Tumalo Creek, near the headgates on the Columbia Southern ditch, was "literally plastered with location papers and boundary markings." Other claims were reported in the Broken Top area. One nugget worth $17 had been found the year before. On August 16, another gold field, near the head of the west fork of Tumalo Creek, was reported. Several tunnel shafts, one to a depth of 100 feet,

A moraine created by glacial deposition, tenuously holds back water in an alpine lake at the foot of Crook Glacier on Broken Top. On October 7, 1966, part of this moraine broke, sending an estimated 50 million gallons of water down Soda Creek. The flood deposited large boulders along Soda Creek and up to 20,000 tons of sediment near Sparks Lake. *(Oregon Dept. of Transportation)*

Aerial view of Bachelor Butte. The mountain has been developed as a ski resort since 1959. In 1979, Mt. Bachelor Ski Resort operated seven chairlifts. The nearby area is popular for Nordic skiing. *(Don Peters)*

were dug, but the gold content of the rock proved to be too low for extraction.

Broken Top Country today includes some of the most spectacular scenery of the High Country. It is a favorite place for intermediate and advanced Nordic skiers, who find miles of excellent terrain for skiing, along with the beauty and the solitude they seek. Because Broken Top Volcano is in the Three Sisters Wilderness area, summer hikers can obtain the wilderness experience there. This part of the High Country is remote and parts are rarely visited by people.

In December, 1969, a 21-pound female wolverine was accidentally trapped in the Broken Top area.[27] The wolverine, a ferocious animal if cornered, was believed extinct in Oregon until one was killed by a deer hunter near Three Fingered Jack in September, 1965. That was the first recorded wolverine in Oregon since 1912, when one was reported killed in the Three Sisters area.

Bachelor Butte

Standing alone and aloof from the family of Sisters clustered together to the north, is an almost symmetrical volcano, Bachelor Butte. Bachelor looks higher than its elevation (9065 feet) suggests. Its isolation, its size, its 3000-foot relief over Dutchman Flat and the surrounding forest combine to bolster the butte's image.

During the winter months, given favorable atmospheric conditions—principally cloud formations—Bachelor Butte, seen from Bend, silhouettes some spectacular sunsets. At times, throughout the summer, puffy cumulus clouds hover over the butte, casting moving shadows across lingering snowfields on the northern slopes. During the buildup of thunderstorms, Bachelor sulks behind menacing thunderheads. It is a mountain with a personality of its own.

Ardent alpine skiers strongly favor Bachelor Butte. They know that powdery snow falling on its northern slopes provides several long, thrilling downhill runs. So possessive is the ski fraternity that they have even changed the name of the volcano! In June, 1978, the U.S. Forest Service asked the Oregon Geographic Names Board to change the name to Mount Bachelor, from Bachelor Butte, citing that it is the ninth highest point in Oregon, towering over two nearby mountains (Tumalo, 7,775 feet, and Sheridan, 6,890 feet), also that many local residents referred to it as Mount Bachelor. Curiously enough, Mt. Bachelor at one time was named "Brother Jonathan," then simply "The Bachelor" by early pioneers. On some early twentieth-century maps, it was called "Old Baldy" and even "Snow Mountain." By 1920, however, U.S. Forest Service maps bore the name, Bachelor Butte.

Geologically, Mt. Bachelor is one of the most recent active volcanoes of the Cascades. Howel Williams, in 1944, wrote, "the symmetry of the volcano is quite unmarred [by extensive glaciation]. It may be judged, therefore, that whether or not the volcano began its growth during the Pleistocene, it has continued to erupt within very recent times. No one who sees the barren flows of basalt which poured from fissures on the northern flank and spread in branching tongues into Sparks Lake can doubt that they must have escaped only a few centuries ago."[28]

The volcanoe's youthful appearance is deceptive, for the volcano predates the Mazama eruption (6600 years ago) that created Crater Lake. A topographic map of the Bachelor area reveals that the mountain is located at the north end of an alignment of volcanic buttes. Extending to the south of Bachelor are Tot Mountain, Kwolh Butte, Siah Butte, Lumrun Butte, Lolah Butte, Sheridan Mountain, Three Trappers Butte and countless unnamed buttes. Bachelor and these other volcanic landforms may well have been formed along a zone of weakness in the earth's crust. Indeed, perhaps the volcanic activity is only dormant. Skiers today report "hot spots" on Bachelor's northern slopes. In May, 1946, two Bend residents noticed smoke curling in puffs from such a hot spot. Watching from different places, the observers could pick out the location of a possible "fumarole" near a glacier-gouged lake halfway up the mountain.

The volcanic activity that formed Bachelor must have lasted many years; parasitic cinder cones which often build up on a large volcano are to be found on its slopes. One well-known cone, Red Hill—or the Cinder Cone—is a favorite mini ski slope for show-off skiers to indent zigzag patterns on pristine snow. Lava from the butte probably changed drainage patterns in the area. Sparks, Hosmer, and Lava lakes were formed by the damming effect of its lava flows.

Mt. Bachelor, along with many other isolated peaks in the Central Oregon High Country, was once used by the U.S. Forest Service as a vantage point for a fire lookout tower. The tower was completed in August, 1922. Lumber for the building was carried to the summit over a jagged trail of lava by a pack string of five horses. Pack horses were also used to carry supplies and food to the guard manning the lookout tower throughout the summer months. In 1928, the Forest Service guard "complained" that the trail to the summit was becoming too popular when he noted that two girls took a moonlight climb to the summit.

One of the problems hampering operations was the heavy snowfall. In 1930, as late as July, the door of the lookout was jammed with ice and deep snow. That "summer," heavy snow had fallen in the Cascades the last week in June. In September, the lookout was crushed by ice. What a summer 1930 must have been in the High Country! Because clouds frequently socked in the fire observers, the tower was eventually abandoned. Today, the scattered remains of weathered wood and wire litter one of the small summit depressions, which is all that was left of the crater after lava retreated following the dying gasps of the volcano.

Climbing Mt. Bachelor is not difficult, nor is it a long distance from the parking lot. In early summer, indeed anytime there is sufficient snow, skiers climb to the summit in two hours and ski down in ten minutes. During the summer months Mt. Bachelor Resort operates a chairlift to the summit for sightseers. The 360-degree panorama from the summit justifies the climb or the ride. In one sweep the view encompasses most of the High Country. It is breathtaking — windy or not!

3.
Winter Sports

Snow sports were started in Central Oregon by a group of energetic Scandinavians employed in the local lumber companies. As early as 1919—just three years after the Brooks-Scanlon and the Shevlin-Hixon mills opened—Chris Kostol, a Norwegian by birth, began skiing alone in the Bend area, mostly on Lava Butte. Three years later, in January, the Bend Commercial Club was making plans for a winter sports club. The expertise of the Scandinavians living in Bend was recognized as the nucleus of a club which would "make Bend the winter sports center of the Northwest."[29]

McKenzie Pass Site Selected

By February, 1922, an outdoor club had been formed, with Shevlin Park the site for toboggan slides, ice skating, and snowshoeing. The enthusiasm and persistence of skiers such as Emil Nordeen, Nels Skjersaa, Chris Kostol and Nels Wulfsberg was evident in their attempt to seek out and use many different locations for their winter sports activities. A good ski course was made on the north slope of Lava Butte in 1922, but access from Bend was sometimes next to impossible. That same year, a newly constructed road on Pilot Butte was used for skiing, but here the slope was not considered steep enough. Ski courses were also tried on the slopes of Black Butte, but the McKenzie Pass road became the most attractive and promising site for the club. At first, skiing was in the Cold Springs area just west of Sisters, but snow conditions higher in the Cascades eventually proved better for longer winter sports activities.

Turning the calendar back sixty years, it is not difficult to imagine the scene as described in *The Bulletin:* "A crystal frost lay on the old snow, glistening sharply in the cold sunlight. Mt. Jefferson and Mt. Washington seemed but a stone's throw away in their nearness. Cheery shouts of derision or encouragement flew back and forth among the group as they sailed down the ski track among the pines, or toiled laboriously back up the hill, skiis over their shoulders."[30]

A satisfactory course was found on the McKenzie Highway midway between Windy Point and the lava cut, where the old road crossed the highway. A sharp descent approaching and leaving the highway made good ski coasting, and the grade of the highway created a challenge to the expert. Cars were used to transport skiers, or to pull others up at the end of ropes trailing behind the car. At the top, people piled out—or dropped the ropes—and coasted down the grade to where coffee, hot dogs and doughnuts awaited.

The Scandinavians, with skiing evidently in their blood, went so far as to drive from Bend to within one mile of Broken Top Crater in August of 1926, using the snowfield of the Crater Bowl for some mid-summertime skiing. In February, 1927, three members of the "Bend Ski Club," Emil Nordeen, Nels Wulfsberg, and Nels Skjersaa, competed with 21 other runners in the first long-distance ski contest in Oregon, a 42-mile race from Fort Klamath to Crater Lake lodge (an elevation gain of 4000 feet) and return. Because of the impassable highway conditions south of Bend, the three skiers journeyed to The Dalles, Portland, Roseburg, Medford, and Klamath Falls—a distance of 662 miles—to reach the start. Travel time was 30 hours, and the skiers lived on "candy and crackers." Nels Skjersaa took third in the race. Emil Nordeen, then 37 years of age, had not skied for 19 years but he completed the course.

Nordeen subsequently won the "Fort Klamath—Crater Lake and return" race in 1929 and 1931. The 38-inch-high trophy, solid silver and trimmed with gold, was donated by Nordeen to the Swedish Ski Association in 1960 at the

Oxen struggle to pull up wagons over jagged lava on Bachelor's northern slope in the filming of "The Way West." This movie, starring Kirk Douglas, Richard Widmark and Robert Mitchum, was filmed almost entirely in Central Oregon.

The Skyliner ski cabin and jump near the McKenzie Highway. This site was used by the Skyliners in the early 1930's for ski jumping, sledding and Nordic skiing. *(Grace Skjersaa)*

Squaw Valley Olympics, to promote international long-distance ski races.

In a speech to the Bend Chamber of Commerce in May, 1927, Nels Wulfsberg pointed out the potential for developing the nearby High Country for skiing:

> Here are hills and timber and snow abundant. From the Metolius Country, over the Sisters region, Broken Top, Bachelor, extending westward and southward, is a skier's paradise. If this country had been somewhere in Norway, that territory would have been covered with small cabins which the owners would have visited every possible opportunity during the winter, as well as in the summertime. It would have been furnished with restaurants and hotels, making it possible for the sportsmen to reach farther out in the territory, enabling them to stay for days at a time.
>
> Bend would become a center of ski carnivals, attracting people from all Oregon and neighboring states. Winter resorts would develop in the area. The name of Bend would be brought before large crowds on days of contests and before tourists throughout the winter. Nothing is more invigorating than fresh, cold winter air—air which brings the blood into circulation, stimulating energy, courage and initiative.[31]

In November, 1927, the Tumalo Ranger Station cabin was used by club skiers entering the Broken Top country for weekend ski parties. In December, the name "Skyliner," suggested by Paul Hosmer, Bend amateur naturalist, was officially used for the club which had been variously known as the Outdoor Club, Ski Club, or Alpine Club.[32] The decision to use the name "Skyliners" was not unnoticed by the local newspaper. In an editorial, *The Bulletin* noted:

> Skyliners is a word of action, a word descriptive of those of the outdoors who would peer over distant hills, a word which pictures the presence of mountains and trails that touch the heavens.
>
> It covers well the activities of the organization it denotes, the recently formed Bend outdoor club. Skiing, skating, tobogganing, hiking, geologizing, mountain climbing, botanizing—what more desirable name

than Skyliners could be chosen to cover these varied activites. Always there is present to persons taking part in these outdoor activities a skyline—skyline serrated by the Cascade peaks, that gently broken by the Paulinas, that made picturesque by the Smith Rock formation, that of the distant Ochocos.

The snow which extends into the eastern foothills from the Three Sisters skyline makes possible a great variety of winter sports. The chill born in cold regions beyond the north skyline congeals water into icy surfaces for skating. The lakes hidden away near the western skyline hold recreation and rest for the camper, the angler, the swimmer. The skylines to the west, the south, the east and the north, softly colored by distant pines and junipers, invite the motorist, the hiker, the geologist, the botanist.

Also there are in Central Oregon skylines of the distant past—skylines known to the geologist as horizons. Here, in innumerable strata exposed by stream and wind, are horizons which once teemed with strange and now extinct forms of life. There, in sedimentary layers, are horizons over which great oceans once slept, leaving in their wake mineralized shells. And over yonder is a horizon which held forests of giant conifers. Skyliners, Bend greets you. Go your varied ways realizing you are significantly named.[33]

Winter recreational activities in the 1920's and 1930's also included ice skating when conditions were right. One of the favorite "rinks" was at Tumalo Reservoir, located northwest of Bend, where the pines merge with the junipers. Here, throngs of people drove from Bend to skate by the light from huge bonfires. In January, 1926, Central Oregon's first ice hockey game was staged when the "Polars" and the "Arctics," teams consisting of men who had played in Europe, Alaska, Canada, and the Mid-west, faced-off before an enthusiastic crowd of 1500 spectators. Bonfires lined the shores of the frozen reservoir—and there were hot-dog stands for the hungry skaters. On other occasions at the Tumalo Reservoir, people skated to music from a radio which, using a juniper tree as an aerial stand, picked up a broadcast from the San Francisco Hotel.

Winter Sports

A novel ice-skating rink was prepared in November, 1926, when water from the Little Deschutes River was pumped over part of the William Vandevert Ranch meadow (south of the site of Sunriver). A rink 170 feet by 65 feet was formed, using earth embankments. People skated at night with light from huge bonfires and from lanterns.

The Skyliners staged an ice carnival at the Tumalo Fish Hatchery near Shevlin Park in December, 1931. Some 300 people went to the new rink to watch or participate in races. Prizes were awarded by Bend merchants. In one event, the one-mile, Olaf Skjersaa sped to a 3 minutes 4/5 second victory. In recent years, the old Tumalo Fish Hatchery site has been restored for skating by the Bend Metro Parks and Recreation District.

In the late 1930's, ice skating was staged at the Skyliners' area, near the Tumalo Creek Lodge. Water for the rink came from the Bend City Water mains, and artificial light was provided by a "Little Bonneville" made by the Bend High School manual training class, in collaboration with the Shevlin-Hixon Company. Charges were 15 cents for adults and 10 cents for children. Seats were placed around the edge of the rink and sandwiches and coffee were served. Bonfires at rinkside provided some warmth. Popular as skating was, though, periodic heavy snowfalls covered the rinks, making skating impossible without considerable work in clearing the snow.

By 1928, the activities of the Skyliners had expanded from winter sports to mountain climbing and hiking throughout the summer months. Expeditions to climb Broken Top, North Sister, and Bachelor Butte were organized. Even a walking race from Bend to Redmond was staged. However, the main interests and activities of the Skyliners were in winter sports. They constructed a ski area adjacent to the McKenzie Pass Highway on land owned by Louis W. Hill, railroad and timberman. Permission was granted with the payment of a nominal lease fee of one dollar a year.

Although the winter playground adjacent to the McKenzie Pass Highway had been in operation for only one season, in 1929 the Skyliners urged the State Highway Department to plow the road to Blue Lake from the Jefferson County line (near Black Butte Ranch) to open up the Santiam Pass area to winter sports. It was several years later (1938) that Hoodoo Ski Bowl was ready for skiing.

Meanwhile, the Skyliners combined competition with fun at the McKenzie Pass ski area. In February, 1930, 2000 spectators watched the first ski carnival. Competition included a 25-mile cross-country race and ski jumping. The following year, the carnival included a baseball game on skis, with Hood River challenging the Skyliners. Prior to the game Paul Hosmer said, "This is going to be some game. None of the ski artists from Scandinavia can play baseball and few of the Americans can ski."

For several years in the 1930's the Skyliners used the site along the McKenzie Highway, although the 1934 ski carnival was cancelled because of lack of snow. Indeed, in 1934 only Crater Lake boasted sufficient snow for skiing. Even there, a scant six feet of snow remained by March. Both The McKenzie Pass and Paulina Lake were opened to traffic by March 4, 1934.

New Ski Area Developed

Skyliner officials, for some time, had been discussing the possibility of a ski area 10 miles west of Bend near the Anderson Mill. By late 1935, the decision was made to build a new playground on the Anderson Mill Road along Tumalo Creek. Several factors made the area suitable. The fir- and spruce-covered banks of Tumalo Creek, only 100 yards from the city of Bend water main, provided an excellent site for a winter cabin. The nearby 900-foot-high hill sheltered a northern slope from the melting rays of the winter sun. And, the area was only ten miles from Bend, much nearer than the McKenzie Pass ski area. The latter was abandoned in the fall of 1935.

Work on the Tumalo ski area (later known as the "Skyliners") was commenced in August, 1935, by Civilian Conservation Corps (C.C.C.) boys and 35 men from local relief rolls, working for the U.S. Forest Service. By November, the facility was beginning to take shape. The main cabin, 44 by 64 feet, was constructed with the finest spruce logs that could be found. Plans called for three fireplaces, a furnace, city water, electric lights, a large modern kitchen, and a dancing room. A full concrete basement for ski waxing and upstairs living quarters were also in the plans.

Trails from the Skyliners led to Tumalo Falls, Tumalo Lake, Swampy Lakes, and to the Broken Top country. At times while the road to the Skyliners was being completed, a heavy snowfall isolated the ski area. Once, not to be denied their skiing, several dozen Bend residents—aided by starlit skies, a big bonfire, and gasoline lanterns—used the snow-covered volcanic slopes of Lava Butte. In February, 1936, a Bend High School ski team was organized and taken to Lava Butte to learn ski fundamentals from the Skyliners.

At the same time, the Skyliner lodge and ski hill along Tumalo Creek was dedicated before a crowd of 1500. The problem of clearing the road from Bend to the Skyliners' hill often made access difficult and snow removal costly. A road tax of 25 cents was charged, with proceeds going toward the cost of snow removal. At times, a team of horses and caterpillar tractors were used to help skiers reach the area.

During 1938, a new ski area was developed on the Santiam Pass Recreation Area with the help of the C.C.C. boys. On the following January 29, Hoodoo Ski Bowl was dedicated before about 400 people who braved a near blizzard. A ski lodge was added at Hoodoo and dedicated February 4, 1940. However, future plans, which included a ski jump on the slopes of Three Fingered Jack, never materialized.

Despite the development of the Skyliners' playground along Tumalo Creek, late spring and early summer skiing was held on the northern slopes of Bachelor Butte. In late May, 1941, the Skyliners staged Class A competition on Bachelor which included a downhill event, starting on the top of the mountain at 9000-feet elevation and ending at timberline, 6500-feet elevation. The winner, Olaf Skjersaa, took only one minute, nineteen seconds for the run of over one mile.

During World War II, little use was made of the Central Oregon ski areas, but immediately after the war, the Skyliners' club was reorganized. Interest in winter sports was renewed with serious consideration given to using the slopes of both Broken Top and Bachelor Butte. Although the Bend Chamber of Commerce favored paving Century Drive to

Hoodoo Ski Bowl, near the Santiam Pass, is within easy driving distance of major population centers in the Willamette Valley. The bowl was dedicated in January, 1939. Facilities include chair lifts, rope tows, ski school, ski shop and lights for night skiing. *(Oregon Dept. of Transportation)*

Left: The Three Sisters provide a scenic background for alpine skiers at Mt. Bachelor. A long ski season and powder snow help make the area popular. *(Oregon Dept. of Transportation)*
Right: A cross-country skier pauses on the banks of Soda Creek near the Cascade Lakes Highway. The High Country has many areas where the Nordic skier can find beauty and solitude. *(The Bulletin)*

Dutchman Flat in 1947, no development was to take place at Bachelor Butte for over a decade. Meanwhile, for a period of several years, Skyliners, the Bend City Recreation Department, and the Bend High School ski team, worked on the abandoned tow rope, ski jump, and slopes of the Skyliners' hill. The restored ski area, accessible by a paved road from Bend, was opened for use and dedicated on January 8, 1955, by Bend mayor, Hans Slagsvold.

The first winter carnival with ski racing and jumps was staged at the Skyliners, March 3, 1956, with 1000 spectators in attendance. Despite 7000 skiers using the ski tow during the 1955-1956 season, the area, at 4700-feet elevation, was able to average only three months of operation. Throughout the 1956-1957 winter season, lack of snow reduced use of the runs to only five weeks. This situation prompted the Skyliners to take "inventory" of the Mt. Bachelor area.

Mt. Bachelor Ski Resort

An earlier "inventory" of the Mt. Bachelor area was taken by the Union Pacific Railroad. A Skyliner, Chris Kostol, guided the railroad representatives. Although the possibilities of a developed ski area were acknowledged, the expense of a railroad into the area was not considered advisable.[34] On February 26, 1956, the "inventory" proved favorable — "good ski slopes for both beginning and expert skiing amongst beautiful scenery." That momentous day for winter sports in Central Oregon started proceedings for U.S. Forest Service permission to develop Mt. Bachelor.[35] This was granted and, by September, 1958, construction of the access road, a warming hut, and a pomalift tow (from Fontaine, France) was completed. Not completely resolved, however, was state approval of the clearing of the highway from Bend to Bachelor in the wintertime. During the first year of operation, Mt. Bachelor Ski Area, as it was then called, attracted approximately 10,000 skiers.

In the early 1960's, a thousand or more students "invaded" Bend for an intercollegiate ski carnival. In late spring, 1963, Bachelor was the stage for a ski Mardis Gras with the "cast" dressed in colorful costumes. U.S. Olympic skiers first trained at Mt. Bachelor in August, 1963, and have returned to the high snowfields many successive summers. In 1964, 6000 were on hand at Bachelor for a ski carnival staged by Portland State University. Local newspapers reported that in Bend summer-like weather prevailed, but crisp hard-packed snow on the Bachelor ski runs greeted competitors from 40 colleges and universities. Ski jumping was held at the Skyliners' jump west of Bend.[36]

Since the 1960's, Mt. Bachelor has expanded its facilities considerably. In 1976-77, the main lodge was completely remodeled and additional parking areas were added. By 1979, Mt. Bachelor operated ten chair lifts and boasted over 40 runs. The highest lift, the summit, has a vertical rise of 1,700 feet and takes skiers to an elevation of 9,065 feet, which is above the timberline. The outback lift gives expert skiers the chance to tackle unpacked runs.

The expanded facilities at Bachelor and the increased popularity of alpine skiing have attracted an increasing number of skiers. In the 1960-61 season, some 26,700 skiers used the resort. This number had increased to over 600,000 during the 1986-87 season. Each season, Mt. Bachelor, Inc., hosts competition for high schools, colleges, and ski associations. Central Oregon Community College ski teams, U.S. National Community College Champions in 1977, use the Bachelor ski area as training grounds. Bachelor is usually open for the impatient skier by Thanksgiving, sometimes even sooner, and invariably sufficient snow covers the slopes for ardent skiers to get a suntan and spring-type skiing into July.

Beginning in 1977, Mt. Bachelor, Inc., groomed trails near the lodge and extending into Dutchman Flat for Nordic skiers to tour or practice technique. During the 1970's, cross-country skiing grew in popularity in the High Country as it has throughout the nation. Some of the popular cross-country ski trails for beginners (and others) include the three-mile trail to Tumalo Falls from the Skyliner Lodge, the short Swampy Lakes trail from the Cascade Lakes Highway, and the Todd Lake tour from Dutchman Flat. Intermediate and advanced Nordic skiers can virtually make

Mt. Bachelor as viewed from Tumalo Mountain. The mountain has been developed as a major ski resort, operating ten chair lifts and over 40 runs. (Mt. Bachelor, Inc. Photo.)

their own trails and tours, with perhaps the best cross-country skiing in the Broken Top-Tam McArthur Rim country. The Santiam Pass area also has some scenic trails both north and south of Highway 20.

Snowmobiling also has grown in popularity, since the early 1970's. Snowmobilers have their own parking and play areas along the Cascade Lakes Highway, about 15 miles west of Bend. Other popular snowmobile areas include Newberry Crater, McKenzie Pass, and Three Creeks Lakes, south of Sisters.

It has been over 60 years since Scandinavians brought winter sports to the High Country. Since those early years, new equipment, modern technology, and a more affluent society have combined to popularize these sports. Today, the tourist industry of the Bend area has, as prophesied in 1926, become of year-round importance.

4.
The Deschutes River

> The Deschutes is a river of many roles; it roars and rushes in white-water cascades, it sparkles gently in a myriad rippling rapids, it is sedate as a mill pond, sometimes its banks are fields flanked with flowers, sometimes steep slopes with black pools below and great trees above, sometimes lined with alders or with needle-carpeted forest marching out to the very water's edge. . . . If there are any more beautiful or varied [rivers] than Oregon's "River of Falls," I have yet to make their acquaintance.[37]

This description of the Deschutes, written in 1918, still applies to the river in the 100 miles from its source to Bend. One of the most important rivers in Oregon, it is unique, scenic and useful. Geologists have long noted its remarkably even flow—perhaps more uniform than any other river in the United States of comparable size. In 1905, geologist Israel C. Russell, before any dams or reservoirs were constructed on the Deschutes, noted:

> From the mouth of the Crooked River upstream to Benham Falls, near Lava Butte, a distance of about 50 miles, the variation in the height of the [Deschutes] river throughout the year is not more than 8 or 10 inches where the width is abnormally restricted. Wooden bridges that cross the river in this part of its course are placed only 2 or 3 feet above its summer-stage surface, and even the amount of space thus afforded beneath their floors is determined by the height of the approaches and not by fluctuations in the level of the water.[38]

The reason for the nearly constant volume of water, especially between Benham Falls and the confluence of the Crooked River, is mainly because the Deschutes passes over and through porous lava which is able to absorb excess water. Thus, even with heavy rains and rapid snow run-off, the Deschutes River rarely creates a flood. In Bend, homes that line the river just a few feet higher than its banks are seldom bothered by high water flooding basements.

The Deschutes is a remarkably clear and clean stream, but concern over pollution goes back many years. An editorial in *The Bulletin* in 1903 called for a special statute to prevent pollution of the Deschutes.[39] Reference was made to throwing kitchen wastes, animal carcasses, tin cans, and even old stoves into the river. Eight years later, the Oregon legislature made it unlawful to "deposit in the Deschutes River, or any tributary thereof, or artificial canal or ditch in which the waters of said Deschutes River run, any sewage, refuse, waste or polluted matter, or any dead animal carcass or part thereof, or any matter which either by itself or in connection with any other substance, will corrupt or impair the quality of the water of said river for domestic or municipal purposes."

The Deschutes provided cool waters for immigrant trains, and it has supplied irrigation water for 100,000 thirsty acres in three Central Oregon counties. Stockmen 100 years ago were attracted to the grassy banks of the stream. Here they established homesteads, built cabins, and grazed their livestock on lush pastures in otherwise dry lands. The river has also long provided recreation not only for Central Oregonians but for thousands of visitors. In 1903, *The Bulletin* noted that "both banks of the river were on Sunday lined with anglers of both sexes. Not less than 1000 trout were taken from their home that day. At this rate, in a few years the Deschutes will have a well-deserved reputation of being a celebrated has-been trout stream."[40] The stream's fishing fame spread far and wide. Notables who came to fish its clear waters included former President Herbert Hoover and author, Irvin S. Cobb. For a number of years, Hoover had a cabin at South Twin Lake.

The name of the river, Deschutes, goes back to the early days of fur trading when the river was called the Riviere des

Left: The Deschutes and the Little Deschutes River, along with the many lakes of the High Country, are invaded by thousands of anglers each season. Right: The Little Deschutes River meanders across its flood plain near La Pine. This aerial view reveals many meander scars, indicating that, in years past, the stream has flooded then carved near courses. Wickiup Reservoir is the water body in the background. *(USFS)*

The severe drought of 1977 left the source of the Deschutes River dry as no overspill occurred from a shrunken Little Lava Lake. Springs fed the Deschutes River just downstream from its usual source.

Chutes, meaning River of the Falls.[41] However, although the Deschutes has many falls in its journey to the Columbia, the falls referred to in the name were on the Columbia River near its confluence with the Deschutes. Lewis and Clark discovered the Deschutes on October 22, 1805, on their travels down the Columbia, but in their journals they used the Indian name Towornehiooks. However, they called the same stream "Clarks River" on their return. Farther south, Klamath Indians referred to the Deschutes as Kolamkeni Koke, which when translated means "a stream where the kolam [a wild root used for food] grew."[42]

The Deschutes courses mainly through lands under the jurisdiction of the Deschutes National Forest Service. However, in Bend and for about a dozen scattered miles upstream, its banks are in private hands. (The lodge of A. M. Drake, early-day founder of Bend, overlooked the Deschutes which, at that time, was a swift-flowing stream. The power dam had not yet formed Bend's placid Mirror Pond.) Upstream, the Sunriver resort community and other recreational subdivisions and long-established ranches border the Deschutes. Downstream from Bend, the Deschutes and its main tributaries, the Metolius and the Crooked rivers, join forces to power turbines that generate electricity for the energy-hungry Pacific Northwest.

Source of the Deschutes

Sources of rivers are exciting places. How many explorers have traced rivers upstream into the unknown to determine their origin! In normal years, the Deschutes flows out of Little Lava Lake in the High Country just east of the Cascade crest. However, in times of heavy water run-off, following above-average snow falls, there is a flow of water from Big Lava Lake into Little Lava Lake. It is believed by many that water from Elk Lake flows underground through lava beds to Hosmer Lake, then underground again to Big Lava Lake.

Little Lava Lake, nestled in a lodgepole forest, lies near the southwest base of Bachelor Butte, which prominently looms over the lake. Broken Top and South Sister are clearly visible to the north. Water pours out of the southwest part of Little Lava Lake, slowly at first, but within 40 yards a slight gradient gives impetus to the water to send the Deschutes on its way as a fully fledged stream. The river immediately swings to the south into a broad meadow where it promptly slows. Beyond the meadow, it cuts and roars through a lava flow, then spills into a second meadow and forms its own small lake.

A short distance to the south, the Deschutes comes out of its forest hiding place and exposes itself as a fast-flowing mountain stream to motorists traveling the Cascade Lakes Highway at Deschutes Bridge Guard Station. But what a stream! The ice-cold waters sparkle in the sunlight. Stones at the bottom of the river are clearly visible. Tall prairie-like grasses that flank the Deschutes are sprinkled with lupines, Indian paint brush, and daisies. Here, the stream attracts anglers who cast for trout, photographers seeking that prize-winning shot, or picnickers looking for an attractive spot for lunch.

Crane Prairie Reservoir

The next phase of the Deschutes River in its flow to the south is at Crane Prairie Reservoir. Here, the Deschutes, Snow Creek, the Cultus River, Cultus Creek, and Quinn River empty into the seven-square-mile, irregular-shaped reservoir. Most of these tributaries are short streams that originate in the eastern slopes of the nearby Cascades. Crane Prairie today is a popular camping and fishing area. Because the prairie was the home for cranes who fished the Deschutes for their food supply, the prairie and then the reservoir assumed the name of the bird. However, in 1923, a *Bulletin* editorial called for the reservoir to be named West Lake, in honor of Ex-governor of Oregon, Oswald West, who was partly responsible for creation of the reservoir. Also, the lake would be in the extreme west of Deschutes County, while East Lake in Newberry Crater is in the opposite corner of the county.

A rock-filled dam was constructed in 1922 to provide storage for water to irrigate the dry lands of Central Oregon located far to the north. Waters, backing up behind the dam, flooded most of the prairie and part of the adjacent forestland, killing many trees. Attempts were later made to recover merchantable timber, mostly lodgepole pine, from the reservoir site. To do this, the reservoir was drained and, in at least two instances, strange phenomena resulted. In August, 1923, the sudden draining of the waters stranded trout in the snags of trees. The Bend paper reported that the fishing was good, providing people used either a ladder or a shotgun. In March, 1924, receding waters left ice chunks 6 to 8 feet thick and 40 to 50 feet in diameter hanging from trees. The sudden fall of the ice chunks to the ground discharged a thunderous crash that resembled "seige guns."

Failure by the North Unit Canal Company to remove sufficient trees and debris from the Crane Prairie Reservoir site prompted former Oregon Governor West, early in 1929, to threaten to "dynamite the dam." For a while the dam was put under guard but by May of that year the matter was peacefully resolved. A new dam, 285 feet long, was built by the Bureau of Reclamation in 1939 and 1940 because of leakage through the earlier dam. Irrigation districts served by Crane Prairie waters include the Arnold and Central Oregon districts near Bend and the district of Lone Pine near Redmond.

Before it was inundated, Crane Prairie was described as a natural meadow sliced by the meandering of the deep-blue Deschutes River and the tributaries mentioned above. The Deschutes was stated to be a fisherman's paradise, abundant with trout. The meadow was the site of a camp for R. L. Williamson, Lt. Phil Sheridan and Dr. J. S. Newberry who, in the summer of 1855, were seeking a railroad route through the Cascades.

The landscape at Crane Prairie today shows the results of flooding the meadow land. Tall, bare stumps and limbs like grey ghosts rise from the lake. These snags provide nesting places for osprey, large birds that feed on fish in the shallow waters of the reservoir. With luck, visitors to the Crane Prairie Osprey Management Area may spot osprey "fishing" in the reservoir. The birds fly 50 to 100 feet above the water. After sighting a fish, the osprey dives with half-closed wings, enters the water with a splash and grasps the fish in its strong talons.

The osprey arrive in early April. Females lay two to four eggs which take 28 to 35 days to incubate, and the young remain in the nests 8 to 10 weeks. In October, the osprey leave Crane Prairie, heading south for Central and South America. Crane Prairie is the home of the largest nesting colony of American osprey in the Pacific Northwest. In August, 1970, the Crane Prairie Osprey Management area, covering 10,600 acres, was dedicated with ceremonies at Quinn River campground. The osprey area is also home to blue herons, cormorants, kingfishers and many other bird species. In the surrounding forests there are herds of deer and elk. A small resort at Crane Prairie provides boat rentals, gas and oil, and features a general store with groceries and tackle.

Wickiup Reservoir

The Deschutes River, now checked by the Crane Prairie Reservoir Dam, continues its southward course through lodgepole pine and ponderosa pine, then tumbles into Wickiup Reservoir, which, when full, is the largest body of water in the Deschutes National Forest. Preliminary work on Wickiup Dam reservoir site was started in the summer of 1938 by Civilian Conservation Corps boys, many of whom soon found the upper Deschutes area to be too much a wilderness and returned to their more tamed homelands in the South and Midwest. During World War II, some of the clearing work done at the Wickiup site was performed by Mennonites who were conscientious objectors. An educational program including a background history of the Mennonite church, Bible instruction, music, and first aid were offered outside working hours.

Long before the white men considered the Wickiup area for a reservoir, Indians had used the site as a campground for their fall hunting and fishing expeditions. Left behind by the Indians were wickiup huts that sheltered the Indians. Ranchers who grazed their livestock in the basin applied the name "wickiup" to the area. Originally, the site was spelled

Wikiup but, in 1939, the Oregon Geographical Board officially changed the spelling to Wickiup. In September, 1934, while excavations for a test pit for the proposed reservoir site were taking place, stone-age relics were discovered buried under volcanic debris and above or in coarse gravels believed to have been deposited by glacial wash.

Dr. L. S. Cressman, former curator of anthropology at the University of Oregon, in studying the archaeological site, noted that the hunting ground of the Deschutes tribesmen of prehistoric days was buried by pumice from Mt. Mazama (Crater Lake) which erupted about 6600 years ago. Later, volcanic eruptions occurred in not-so-distant craters, as evidenced by the coarse nature of the wickiup pumice. Three stone knives, roughly shaped from obsidian, indicated to Cressman that Indians had lived in the area in Pleistocene times. Some of the Indian poles were still standing when the 90-foot-high, earthen-filled dam was completed in 1949.

Water stored at Wickiup Dam was destined to be used by the North Unit Irrigation District in Jefferson County, about 100 miles from the storage site. Initially, considerable water leaked from the reservoir. Drainage of the reservoir in the summer of 1948 revealed the presence of three large fissures along a fault that extended toward Davis Mountain, a large timber-covered volcano to the south. The fissures, which were allowing 150 cubic feet of water per second to escape, were finally sealed by Bureau of Reclamation engineers. One may wonder, though, how vulnerable the Wickiup Reservoir would be, should an earthquake occur along the fault zone.

Flowing from the west into Wickiup Reservoir, and thus a tributary of the Deschutes River, is Davis Creek, which drains 4 miles underground from Davis Lake beneath a large lava flow before surfacing. Davis Creek is joined by water gushing from large springs in the lava. Because the water level of a full Wickiup Reservoir is higher than Davis Creek, only when the reservoir is drained does the creek flow into the reservoir. When the reservoir is full, water backs up to the lava flow, submerging the springs.

Today, the cool waters of Wickiup Reservoir are used extensively by anglers and infrequently by swimmers. The

Crane Prairie Reservoir. A rock-filled dam built on the Deschutes River in 1922 flooded the Crane Prairie Meadow and nearby forests. Today, Crane Prairie is a popular fishing reservoir. Snow-capped mountains in background (left to right) are South Sister, Broken Top, and Mt. Bachelor. *(Oregon Dept. of Transportation)*

Davis Lake, shrunken by a dry summer, still provides recreation for fishermen and duck hunters. The lake, named after a Prineville stockman, "Button" Davis—who kept cattle in the area late in the nineteenth century—is a large lake during years of normal precipitation. Water flows underground from Davis Lake into Wickiup Reservoir beneath extensive lava flows (background).

surrounding landscape remains unchanged, while the receding water level of the irregular-shaped reservoir exposes more and more mud flats as the summer demands for irrigation water—far to the north—drain the temporarily trapped waters of the Deschutes River.

Pringle Falls

An example of the Deschutes in its wildest moods is seen at Pringle Falls. Indeed, a recreational subdivision almost hidden by lodgepole and ponderosa pine, on a high bluff adjacent to Pringle Falls, is aptly named "Wild River." Here, the Deschutes plunges over exposed and broken basaltic barriers, and white and blue turbulent water roars and cascades down to a grassy meadow where the river, now tamed, subsides into riffles and eddies and gently makes a slow, curving sweep around the meadow. All this occurs within a distance of 400 yards.

Pringle Falls was named for Octavius M. Pringle, who came to Central Oregon in 1873 and established a ranch at Powell Butte. Pringle took the first "stone and timber" claim on the Deschutes in 1902, near the location of the falls. At one time the falls were known as the Fish Trap. In July and August of each year, Dolly Varden fish, seeking their spawning grounds at Davis and Odell lakes, were trapped by Indians at the falls as the fish swam through the narrow channels between lava rocks.

In 1915, work was underway on a power dam at Pringle Flats. That same year, the Deschutes was bridged at the falls. Directors of the Pringle Falls Electric Power Co., in August 1916, authorized installation of the first unit of the power plant to develop 2200 horsepower, sufficient to supply power for irrigation in La Pine as well as light for Pringle Falls and nearby ranches. By 1916, a townsite, advertised as the "most beautiful in Central Oregon" was platted. Today, scattered pieces of lumber and metal are found on the east bank of the Deschutes at Pringle Falls. Except for a narrow footbridge crossing the Deschutes, Pringle Falls is now devoid of cultural features. Large pine trees flank the Deschutes where water smashes into exposed lava rock, sending the turbulent water into a mad frenzy to escape downstream. Yet, on the edge of the stream, quiet eddies, even pools of stagnant water, fringe the "wild river."

La Pine State Recreation Area

Below Pringle Falls, the Deschutes slowly meanders this way and that, cutting through the easily eroded alluvium where the river deposited bedded sediments followings its damming by lava flows from Newberry Volcano. While Newberry flows pushed the Deschutes westward, basaltic lava flows and ash-flow tuffs from the Cascades were pushing the river eastward. Aerial photographs of the Deschutes and Little Deschutes reveal countless features of meandering streams. Meander scars, ox-bow lakes, and in places, swampy ground indicate that the streams have been cut down to base level for a long time.

Floating the Deschutes is an experience many canoests enjoy.[43] The 8 miles from Pringle Falls to La Pine State Park can be made with one short portage around the Tetherow Log Jam (2½ miles below Pringle Falls). From La Pine State Park, the Deschutes can be floated without portage to Sunriver, 16 miles downstream. The river flows about 2 miles per hour and passes through forests and meadows, where wildlife on the banks and in the water may be expected at any turn in the river, along with peace and solitude along inaccessible stretches.

La Pine State Park was planned in 1964 when the Oregon State Parks System purchased 1500 acres of land from the Bureau of Land Management. Included in the purchase was a quiet stretch of the Deschutes where the river is noted for its fine boating and fishing. La Pine State Park today provides separate areas for overnight camping and day use along the river banks.

Fall River

Fall River is a small, 8-mile-long tributary of the Deschutes that joins the main stream a short distance downstream from La Pine State Park. Its source is a series of streams where crystal-clear, cold water literally bubbles out of the ground or pours from flower-decked grassy banks. The instant stream, 30 yards wide, is placid in its upper reaches as it heads through a forest of jack pines, cutting northeast into Lake La Pine sediments adjacent to High Cascade lava. Downstream 4 miles, the river cascades 100 feet in a series of small falls—falls that give the stream its name. Here is the Fall River Trout Hatchery, operated by the State of Oregon Fish and Wildlife Department. Neat, attractive white buildings are laid out in a park-like landscape.

The potential for a fish hatchery at Fall River was noted in 1917. A newspaper reported that the stream was "the proper temperature for brooding fish, and has a level gravel bottom."[44] A fish hatchery was built in 1926, but in 1929 it was destroyed by fire. It was rebuilt in 1930 on the same facilities. Today, the Fall River Trout Hatchery, which employs three people year-round, raises 1,300,000 Brook trout, 65,000 legal-size rainbow trout, and 400,000 fingerling rainbow trout, some of which are used in airplane planting in lakes in the High Country.

A short distance upstream from the trout hatchery, the Fall River Resort operated for several years after World War II. It consisted of a lodge, with meals provided, and a small number of cottages which were rented to fly fishermen who tested their skills in Fall River. The resort was sold in 1965 and was promptly closed. Only happy memories for those who experienced the comradeship of the guests and the hospitality of the owners, Mr. and Mrs. Ranyard.

One of the few places to cross the Deschutes by highway is at General Patch Bridge, a wooden structure that gracefully spans the river. General Patch bridge was built by U.S. Army Engineers who were stationed at Camp Abbot (present site of Sunriver), and named after Lieutenant General Alexander M. Patch who commanded engineers in their military training maneuvers in Central Oregon in the fall of 1943. It is a popular place for fishermen, campers and boating enthusiasts. Lodgepole pine and red-barked ponderosa pine crowd the terraces overlooking the Deschutes—at this spot a green sluggish-flowing stream about 40 yards wide.

Just north of General Patch Bridge, Stage Stop Meadows —a 160-acre residential development—borders the leisurely flowing river. Homesites are nestled amidst the pine forest but residents have common access to one mile of the Deschutes. Underground utilities and building restrictions help preserve the livability of the upper Deschutes country. Tennis courts and bike pathways provide recreation for the energetic. In Deschutes County, only 22 per cent of the land is in private hands, so few people have homesites bordering the scenic river.

Little Deschutes River

Just south of Sunriver, the Little Deschutes River, locally known as Little River, joins the Deschutes or the Big River. Headwaters of the Little Deschutes is on Cappy Mountain (elevation 7392 ft) in Klamath County, 10 miles north of Mount Thielsen. It then flows east and north, meandering through alluvial deposits extending north to Sunriver. For virtually all of its 50-mile journey, the Little Deschutes is a small, tranquil stream, bordered by many grassy meadows or slicing through dense thickets of jackpine. Captain Fremont, describing the Little Deschutes on December 7, 1843, wrote:

> . . . To-day we had good traveling ground, the trail leading sometimes over rather sandy soils in the pine forest, and sometimes over meadow-land along the stream. The great beauty of the country in summer constantly suggested itself to our imaginations; and even now we found it beautiful, as we rode along these meadows, from half a mile to two miles wide. The rich soil and excellent water, surrounded by noble forests, make a picture that would delight the eye of a farmer.[45]

Many of these meadows along the Little Deschutes were homesteaded in the nineteenth century and some of the original homesteads are still holdouts against land devel-

The Deschutes River at Pringle Falls. Here, the river cascades through lava rock. The area on the left was the site of the Pringle Falls townsite. *(Oregon Dept. of Transportation)*

The Vandevert Ranch, known as the "old homestead," is picturesquely located near the Little Deschutes River, a few miles south of Sunriver. The initial two-room cabin was built in the winter of 1892. Additions were made in 1895 and again in 1909. The cabin was used for many years before the late Claude Vandevert constructed a more "modern" cabin just a few yards away. The original Vandevert cabin, at one time, served as a stage stop on the route between Bend and Silver Lake.

opers and subdividers. One of the best known of these homesteads is the Vandevert Ranch. A few years ago the author interviewed the Vandeverts. It was not difficult to turn the clock back to 1900. Cattle grazed the open meadow as deer contently joined them. The Old Homestead still carried momentos and memories. Outside, the Little Deschutes, bridged by an old wooden structure, rippled along, quietly secluded by tall grasses and willows.

Eight miles upstream, an old wooden barn and miscellaneous buildings mark the site of Rosland. According to Lewis A. McArthur, the Rosland post office was established in April, 1897, but in 1910 a new townsite 2 miles to the south was platted by the La Pine Townsite Company.[46]

Near the confluence of the Little Deschutes and the Big Deschutes is the site of Harper, a small community that at one time boasted a hotel and school. *The Bulletin* of May 29, 1912 reported that the Harper Hotel was "under construction and nearly completed. The 25 feet by 50 feet building will have 9 rooms, a barn, and a small store." McArthur, while on a trip to Paulina Lake, in 1916, visited Harper and noted that "Harper bursts into publicity before you get there with an inviting sign announcing 'Livery Stable, Hay and Table Board' or words to that effect."[47] Today, Harper Bridge, just south of Sunriver, is about the only legacy of the old town, which was named after an early homesteader.

Just south of Harper Bridge is the Allen Ranch, another small meadow that was homesteaded long ago. On July 31, 1912, *The Bulletin*, reporting weekly progress from outlying parts of Central Oregon, noted that at the C. B. Allen Ranch, "Wheat, oats are maturing well and in the garden beets, carrots, gooseberries, currants and turnips are doing splendidly." Curiously enough, today much of the upper Deschutes is considered too vulnerable to summer frosts for successful agriculture.

Spring River

Spring River is one of the shortest rivers in Oregon, gushing from an underground source only one mile from its junction with the Deschutes River. Geologists believe that both Fall River and Spring River emerge from lava tunnels in the basalt on the west side of the Deschutes drainage. In 1908, the City of Bend thought of securing title to 40 acres of land at the head of Spring River for $800 and constructing a 20-mile pipeline to Bend to "assure (the city) with the finest, purest water in the state of Oregon."[48] The ballot measure was voted down 37-21 on December 7, 1908. In 1912, a small power dam was constructed across Spring River, its purpose being to pump water for irrigation.

After World War II, a small resort was in operation at the head of Spring River. It featured ten cabins, a combined store and restaurant, and catered to fishermen and hunters. Owners Ross and Ruth Cooper provided rental boats, conducted float trips down Spring River to the Deschutes River, and served as guides for fishermen seeking Rainbow trout. Family-style meals were served at the resort. In the 1960's, after it had been sold to California-based Spring River Land Corporation, the resort closed. Cabins were sold for $200 and removed. Today, there is no sign of a resort at Spring River. The State of Oregon was offered the opportunity to purchase the unique spot, but declined. The area around the head of Spring River is private and fenced.

Sunriver

> Our course this morning lay through a fine prairie, from half a mile to two miles in width, and bordering with pine timber. The river wound through the middle of an open space, concealed from view by a line of willows, and the trail followed its general course. The soil was mostly of a pumice stone character, but there was an abundance of fine grass.[49]

This description was made by Henry Larcom Abbot while conducting the Pacific Railroad Survey on September 2, 1855. The "river" referred to was the Deschutes and the "fine prairie" is where Sunriver, a resort-type community, is now located, some 18 miles south of Bend. Sunriver has been described as a "vision that came to life," and has been recognized nationally as a place where the word ecology has had meaning. It is a planned community where the concept of "design with nature" has largely been achieved.

Volcanic activity along the flanks of Newberry Volcano occurred up to about 6000 years ago. Lava Butte, located on a fault that trends northwest from Newberry, erupted creating the cinder cone. Lava broke through the southern side of Lava Butte and spread westward, blocking the ancestral channel of the Deschutes River. An extensive lake formed behind the blocked river and sedimentation brought down from the Cascades and Newberry Volcano was deposited in the lake basin. In time, the Deschutes River cut a new path around the lava flow where Benham Falls is now located. The lake basin, drained of its waters, became the basis for Sunriver meadow. The Deschutes River is now a quiet stream that meanders along the western edge of that meadow.

Indians camped here long before white men explored the Upper Deschutes Basin. An ancient Indian trail coursed along the eastern bank of the Deschutes north to the Columbia River and south to the territory of the Klamath and Modoc Indians. On the High Desert lands around Fort Rock, southeast of Sunriver, archaeologists have unearthed many evidences of Indian occupancy dating back over 13,000 years ago. Obsidian artifacts have been discovered on Sunriver meadow and it is generally believed that Indians lived along the shores of the lake impounded by the Lava Butte flow and, indeed, until modern times.

Although the main north-south highway through Central Oregon does not pass through Sunriver, early-day travelers, moving up and down the upper Deschutes Basin, used trails that passed through the site of Sunriver. The first settlement of the Sunriver area came in the 1870's when cattlemen such as John Y. Todd and Joel Allen, enticed by the lush grasses, brought cattle into the area. Trapping took place near the Big Meadows (as the Sunriver meadow was called) and upstream. In a three-year period the Simer brothers gathered $3000 worth of pelts from fur-bearing animals that lived along the Deschutes. The furs were taken to The Dalles, only to be destroyed in a warehouse fire.

Even in those early years, the recreational assets of the Sunriver area were recognized by ranchers who, along with

The imposing entrance to Camp Abbot frames Mt. Bachelor. Camp Abbot operated from 1943 until 1944. During that period, 90,000 men trained at the military reservation. Maneuvers were conducted throughout many parts of Central Oregon. *(Sunriver)*

The Great Hall, the only legacy from the Camp Abbot era, is used for conventions, weddings, dances, films, and special lunches and dinners. The former Officers' Club was purchased by the Bend Elks for $1,701, and for a while was known as Elkhorn Lodge.

other residents of Central Oregon, caught arm-stretching fish in the Deschutes and hunted deer that grazed the meadows. In 1904, Fred A. Shonquest purchased 200 acres of the Pelton place—"one of the finest hay ranches on the river"—at Big Meadows for $2,300. He had visions of putting a steam launch on the Deschutes River for hunting and fishing excursions.[50]

In October, 1942, came the announcement that an army camp was to be constructed on the nearby Atkinson place. Soon hundreds of construction men were working overtime to build barracks, mess halls, firing ranges and roadways. Cinders for the roads came from a cinder cone located near US 97 near the Sunriver turn-off. Today the demand for red and irridescent cinders continues, and only a skeleton of a volcano remains.

The huge military facilities, built at a cost of $4 million, assumed the name Camp Abbot, after the West Point graduate who, as stated above, passed through the area in 1855. Camp Abbot was activated March 6, 1943 and by June the camp was described as having taken on the "atmosphere of an old, established army post as hundreds of new trainees may be seen daily, marching and countermarching amidst swirls of dust from the camp streets. . . .The program of training is so arranged that trainees move from one facility to another—rifle ranges, hand grenade course, anti-aircraft course, chemical warfare, mine fields, bayonet drill, bridge building and other specialized subjects."[51]

On September 2 of that year, the exact date that Abbot and his soldiers had camped on that meadow 88 years before, the camp was dedicated. On that day, residents of Central Oregon viewed the Corps of Engineers in various phases of training, toured buildings, watched the battalion pass in review, and listened to speeches by high-ranking army officials. *The Bulletin* described the inspiring background scene, the same one that greets visitors to Sunriver today: "The setting, always beautiful, was never more majestic than on dedication day. Visitors toured the grounds in brilliant sunshine which outlined the startling spires of Broken Top's jagged rim, the white tip of South Sister and snow-streaked Bachelor reaching above a forest of pine that sweeps down to the parade ground meadows."[52]

Camp Abbot existed as an active army camp only until 1944, but in its brief existence, 90,000 men in 9 phases took advantage of the diverse landscape types in Central Oregon. Led by General Alexander M. Patch, maneuvers were held on 10,000 square miles of deserts, forests and mountains. As part of their maneuvers, engineers from Camp Abbot completed bridges over Fall Creek, Soda Creek (both near to Sparks Lake) and the General Patch Bridge over the Deschutes River (described above).

In November, 1945, the Camp Abbot property was put up for sale, the property being advertised "As is, where is— buildings and improvements."[53] The various bids for the $5 million improvements totaled $79,000. In April, 1947, the Camp Abbot site was declared surplus and was offered for sale. Under the regulations of the surplus property act, the state and local governments were to have first priority, but the lands were purchased by the Hudspeth Land and Livestock Company. For several years, cattle again grazed the meadows that had witnessed an interesting history. This time, weeds grew through shattered foundations of the former Army camp, the silence broken only by the purr from a small sawmill located in the area.

Late in 1962, details for a planned community to be built on the Hudspeth lands were revealed. The development, originally to have been named Castellaras, after a planned community in the Riviera of South France, was projected to accommodate 16,000 people. The Deschutes River was to have been diverted into several of its ancient channels that are still seen on the meadowland, especially from the air. In 1965, a master plan for developing the former Camp Abbot site was prepared by architects Skidmore, Owings and Merrill. By now, the project, renamed "Sunriver, was the kind of development of which Oregon could be proud. Planning was to retain the natural beauty of the setting and to enhance Central Oregon's wealth of natural recreational resources. By 1968, construction on the project was well underway.

By the early 1970's, Sunriver had earned a national reputation for largely achieving the goal established by John Gray, the developer of Sunriver and of Salishan, located on the Oregon Coast. Today, the planned recreational and resort community encompasses 3300 acres. Several features, natural and man-made, make Sunriver a distinctive and popular part of Central Oregon. The huge sunburst entrance sign greets all visitors. Back door to Sunriver is the Deschutes River, which winds through forests and past the meadows that have been the scene of historical changes. Because the Deschutes at Sunriver is slow moving it is ideal for boating. Except for a 4,500-foot paved and lighted airstrip, riding stables, cycle pathways and part of the 18-hole golf course, the meadow area has been left as common property. Cattle still graze the meadowlands, which open for vistas of the Cascade peaks to the west and angular-shaped Paulina Peak to the east. Lava Butte is a distinctive landmark a few miles north of Sunriver.

Timbered lands, mainly lodgepole pine but mixed with ponderosa pine on better drained lands, surround the meadow. The lodgepole grows in dense stands, providing excellent screening for homes. All houses at Sunriver must pass an architectural review committee to ensure their harmony with the forest setting. Even so, Sunriver is not made exclusively for the wealthy. Many modest-sized cabins and factory-built modular units mingle with spacious custom-built houses.

Most of the land at Sunriver is level, but gently rolling terrain in places enables planners to diversify developments and isolate one neighborhood from another, thus allowing for a greater sense of privacy. Each neighborhood, using the cluster concept, is separated by acres of common land; and each cluster neighborhood has its own identity with names such as Overlook Park, Meadow Village, Forest Park, and Mountain Village, that reflect the geography of the area.

A distinctive system of red-surfaced, all-weather roads curve around trees and rocks or simply curve for no other reason than to slow down traffic. A few principal roads carry through traffic, but many of the residential areas are located on a complex series of cul-de-sacs and secondary roads where privacy and quietness are better ensured. Bicycle use at Sunriver is strongly encouraged. Some 26 miles of bike paths, completely separated from the roadways, connect residential neighborhoods with various recreational facilities and with the Lodge, Great Hall, and the Sunriver Shopping Mall.

Perhaps the town center for Sunriver, if there is such a thing, would be the Great Hall—Lodge complex. The Great Hall is the only legacy from the Camp Abbot era— but what a legacy! The imposing structure could be described as an oversized rectangular-shaped log house. Built as a training accomplishment of the Army Engineers, it has well withstood many cold, snowy winters of the Central Oregon High Country.

Some of the huge timbers forming its main structural support came from the fir forests of Western Oregon. Lava rock, 10 tons of it, was used for constructing two great fireplaces. The trunk of a tall ponderosa pine supports a spiral staircase leading to balcony canopies which overlook the main hall. This main hall has witnessed an endless variety of social events, including formal dances, film shows, meetings, church services, dinners, weddings, etc.

In contrasting architectural style is the Sunriver Lodge, an imposing structure completed in 1969. This tri-level, 38,000-square-foot building is located on the eastern edge of the meadow on the site that housed the Big Meadows School in 1894, where a dozen or so pupils attended one of the first schools in all of Central Oregon. Sunriver Lodge facilities include several dining areas, a cocktail lounge, conference and banquet rooms, sauna baths, a pro-golf shop, administrative offices and registration lobby. Although the lodge itself does not have accommodations, condominium and guest lodges are located nearby. The condominiums consist of several different units with architectural styling and building materials similar to those used for the lodge. The units are staggered, giving them a greater feeling of isolation and an equal view of the mountains. To further enhance the aesthetics at Sunriver, parking is divided into small areas, each separated by trees, rocks, and natural landscaping, and in some instances, wooden fences.

The name "Sunriver" and "Recreation" are virtually synonymous. Recreational opportunities include two full-size golf courses, 18 tennis courts, swimming, horseback riding, polo, bicycling, canoeing, and fishing. Sunriver boasts a nature center staffed year-round by a resident

Sunriver Lodge is a tri-level building located on the edge of the meadow. Facilities include dining areas, a cocktail lounge, conference rooms, saunas, pro-golf shop, administration offices and the registration desk for visitors using the lodges and condominiums. The wooden bridge crosses Sun River, a small spring-fed stream. *(Oregon Dept. of Transportation)*

Winter landscape at Sunriver. Condominiums overlook a fairway where cross-country skiing, not golf, is the likely attraction. *(Oregon Dept. of Transportation)*

naturalist, David Danley. Danley arranges nature talks, hikes and displays, as well as field trips that take residents and Sunriver visitors to the High Desert and to the Cascades. He also advises Sunriver on the ecological impacts of developments on the property.

The Sunriver shopping center—the Country Mall—opened in 1974, a cluster of small shops linked by a covered boardwalk using wood from an old irrigation flume that once carried Bend's water supply. Red corrugated metal roofing and heavy rough-sawn timber beams used in the mall construction were designed to keep the history of Central Oregon alive. Landscaping features widespread use of local lava rock, native ground-cover plants and bark chips. The mall includes a delicatessen, an antique store, a boutique, post office and a bakery where the pleasant aroma of baking entices even the most tight-fisted shopper. Extensions to the mall in 1979 and 1985 provided additional stores and professional offices.

Sunriver, literally a new town, provides a modern sewage treatment plant, its own fire and police protection, and road maintenance. All utilities are underground. The community has its own citizen participation in the decision-making processes; utlimately, the residents of Sunriver, not the management, will "operate the town." Future growth will probably see light industries in its industrial park and additional services. The year-round population exceeds 1000; in summer this increases to over 4000 at times, some of whom are people attending the many conventions Sunriver hosts. Others are renting condominiums, but many are owners of second homes.

Seasonal changes in the High Country create different landscapes and moods. While brilliant, warm sunshine at Sunriver seems to bring out the entire resident and visitor population to use the recreational facilities, the winter scene —with snow covering the pines and the meadow—almost seems like another world. On those precious, clear winter days that follow a four-inch or more snowfall, the crisp air and bright blue skies are conducive to cross-country skiing. Trails head across the snow-covered golf course and meadows and wind through the pine forests. A pleasant aroma from wood-burning fireplaces pervades the air and while it may tempt some skiers to retreat back to a blazing log fire, the invigorating air is an equally strong incentive to exercise. The Sunriver experience, where man and nature generally operate in harmony, is almost unique in this modern world where, too often, technology dominates and nature takes a back seat.

Benham Falls

Five miles downstream from Sunriver, the Deschutes swirls, roars and tumbles past piles of black, jagged rock that burst forth from Lava Butte some 6000 years ago. Benham Falls, like other "falls" along the upper river, is a series of untamed rapids. The area was named after J. R. Benham, who filed on land just above the falls in 1885. The U.S. Government, however, rejected Benham's claim at this place and Benham subsequently homesteaded land located halfway between Bend and Redmond until 1938.

Captain Fremont, while traveling along the stream in December, 1843, described the rugged beauty of the upper Deschutes: "In all our journeys we had never traveled through a country where the rivers were so abundant in falls, and the name of this stream is singularly characteristic. At every place where we came in the neighborhood of the river, is heard the roaring of falls."[54] Today, Benham Falls has largely retained the untamed setting that must have confronted Fremont, Benham, and others who saw the area before the turn of the last century.

Early in the twentieth century, the Deschutes River was tapped for irrigating the juniper country near Bend. The stream was also eyed for its power potential, which has now been realized downstream at Pelton and Round Butte dams. As early as 1903, *The Bulletin* noted that at Benham Falls, 13 miles south of Bend, the river drops 300 feet in a half mile, making it an ideal spot for the "utilization of the grandest water power on the Pacific Coast."[55]

Israel C. Russell, a geologist who surveyed the lands of Central Oregon in 1905, in his report, "Geology and Water Resources of Central Oregon," outlined detailed plans for the development of water power at 18 different sites along the Deschutes River, including Benham Falls. That was just the start of the Benham Falls Dam Project controversy. Basically, the issue that delayed and ultimately squashed the project centered around the geology of the Benham Falls area. Geological studies indicated that the Lava River Cave, called Dillman Cave in earlier years, and located 4 miles southeast of Benham Falls, might drain water from the proposed storage reservoir. During the 1920's and 1930's, considerable geological testing of the Benham Falls site was undertaken. In 1940, a geological report showed that badly fractured rock lay under the proposed dam site. Undaunted, further geological studies were made in the late 1940's, and in 1949, it was announced that the Benham Falls Project would consist of a dam and reservoir with an estimated 70,000 acre-foot capacity.

In 1950, a new geological study revealed that a feasible site for a dam in the area would be 5 miles upstream from Benham Falls on what was the site of the Camp Abbot Army Camp. Preliminary plans for the dam to be built were announced in 1955. The dam, to cost $4¼ million, would consist of a 4000-foot dike holding 78,000 acre-feet of water. The intended reservoir would flood a cemetery (with 3 graves), a landing strip, 3 summer homes, a schoolhouse and the Camp Abbot site. The U.S. Bureau of Reclamation project delayed sales of lots in the Deschutes River Recreation Homesite subdivision in 1961. The dam never materialized, as did not yet another proposal, to build a 9-mile concrete canal from Benham Falls to Bend to by-pass Lava Island where precious water is lost in lava fissures.

The Benham Falls Project, which was first investigated in 1911 and which had cost the Bureau of Reclamation a half million dollars, did not die easily. In June, 1965, a conference in Bend once again raised the issue of a Benham Falls dam. Although plans for the Sunriver development were beginning, many at the conference felt that irrigation waters, which could be stored in the Deschutes River, would be more valuable than the recreational use in the Camp Abbot area. As the Sunriver community developed, the Benham Falls Project finally died.

For many years, Benham Falls was the site of the Shevlin-Hixon Company picnic. Actually, the first of many annual picnics, in July 1920, was at Dillon Falls, a few miles downstream. The Benham Falls site, located next to the Deschutes River where the stream swings north around a large rhyolitic dome, was described as being "well secluded in a pretty grove of pine, the ground carpeted with moss, grasses and pine needles." *The Bulletin*, July 26, 1920, reported that 1840 men, women and children attended the picnic, consuming 100 gallons of ice cream, tons of watermelons and kegs of lemonade. The watermelon-eating contest was described as a "revelation to mothers who wondered where their boys had learned such manners."

Shevlin-Hixon Company picnics were subsequently held on Labor Day. The company provided transportation from Bend and from the logging camp, using logging rail flat cars, equipping them with long benches. Buntings decorated the picnic specials and an air of festivity prevailed, with the company band providing entertainment. The train ride from Bend afforded scenic views of the Deschutes River, the Cascade Mountains, and the pine forests. Free lunches were served to single men and families were provided with ice cream, coffee, watermelon and lemonade. Sports were conducted throughout the day, and the final event—the big dance—was held in late afternoon. Then the picnickers boarded the flat cars and made the trip back to Bend and the camp as dusk descended on the High Country. As many as 24 flat cars and uncounted autos brought 3000 people to the Shevlin-Hixon picnic in 1923. In 1926, 4,500 people attended. The last company picnic at Benham Falls was held in 1930.

This picnic area today is a quiet spot. The railroad bridge that spanned the Deschutes and carried timber to Bend and picnickers to the Labor Day festivities is broken, charred from fire and unusable. However, a footbridge built by the National Guard provides access to Benham Falls from the old Shevlin picnic area. There are probably few who come to visit Benham Falls who "hear" the whistle of the logging train or the shouts of laughter and gaiety echoing from the grove of tall pines next to the Deschutes River. But the white waters of the river still cascade over jagged lava, escaping all of man's attempts to tame Benham Falls.

Ryan Meadow and Dillon Falls

Downstrem from Benham Falls, the Deschutes continues to rush and tumble past the western flanks of the 6000 acres of lava which gushed from the breached flank of Lava Butte. In places such as Ryan Ranch Meadow the river is released from its constricted flow and leisurely meanders through delightful meadows.

In early days, the small meadows along the upper Deschutes were used by stockmen who grazed their cattle in the lush pastures. The river was also the focal point for wildlife. Ducks swarmed on the Deschutes and, indeed, still do. Deer and bear abounded in the adjacent forests. Today, visitors to one of the upper Deschutes meadows, site of the former John Ryan ranch (The Tules), can reminisce about the past. Here, bleached remains of the Ryan corral and fences are situated amid the tule grasses. The nearby Deschutes lazily drifts by.

Just a short distance downstream, near Dillon Falls, groves of tall, mature ponderosa pines have seemingly miraculously survived the lumberman's axe. In 1919, The Shevlin-Hixon Company, which was railroad logging the area, announced plans to save the pines at The Tules and at Dillon Falls. The Bend newspaper on reporting the story stated that "all the timber will be spared so that to one standing at the falls it will appear as though there were an unbroken stretch of forest around him."[56]

Dillon Falls is an especially scenic spot easily reached from forest service road 1808, a red-cindered road that links the Cascade Lakes Highway (just west of the Inn of the Seventh Mountain) with the Sunriver area. Dillon Falls was named after Leander Dillon, a pioneer settler who homesteaded land near the falls between 1886 and 1891. However, Dillon did not get his land surveyed and his claim was refused. In 1906, Dillon became involved in a law case when a Miss Carrie Olson, who established a residence in a cabin near Dillon Falls, filed a homestead claim and water rights to use Dillon Falls as a power site, only to find her

Start of the Labor Day picnic for Shevlin-Hixon workers and their families. Benches were set on flatcars for people to ride the decorated "picnic special" to Benham Falls. *(Brooks-Scanlon)*

In the mid-1950's, a huge stockade that was initially used by United Artists for the filming of "The Indian Fighters" was constructed near Benham Falls. The stockade, dubbed "Fort Laramie," was on a promontory overlooking a bend in the Deschutes River. The crew of 150 from Hollywood was supplemented by local extras and 100 Warm Springs Indians. "Fort Laramie" became the setting for several westerns before vandalism and fire danger prompted the U.S. Forest Service to destroy it in 1963. *(USFS)*

claim challenged by the Northern Pacific Railroad. Dillon Falls today is under the jurisdiction of the U.S. Forest Service. Groves of tall pines, thoughtfully left by the Shevlin-Hixon Company when it logged the area, provide shade and add beauty for campers who use the small and primitive campground.

The sluggish appearance of the Deschutes just upstream from Dillon Falls is deceptive, and the two nearly red warning signs "Falls" mean just that. The Deschutes, restricted by mounds of lava, roars and cascades through a 40-foot-deep canyon, and like Benham Falls, is a series of rapids. Water is violently hurled against rocks, throwing spray high into the air. On warm summer days, the wind-blown mist provides a cooling effect. In winter, the errant mist, which has fallen on rocks and shrubs, is frozen solid, making a winter wonderland. Near the upper reaches of the falls, water emerges in profusion from the base of the lava flow and discharges into the Deschutes. Rimrocks on the west bank of the river support both pine and manzanita. Trails parallel the Deschutes and lead to spectacular viewpoints, but visitors should exercise caution as overlooks are not fenced. Leander Dillon saw the falls area for its potential power, the site for a sawmill, and upstream, an excellent place for storage of logs. Visitors to the area today, note the untamed and wild beauty of the area. A dollar amount cannot replace the aesthetic dimension of Dillon Falls.

Lava Island Falls

Downstream from Dillon Falls, the Deschutes once again plays a Jekyll-and-Hyde character. Near Aspen Camp it flows through a valley entrenched between barren lava fields on the east and pine-forested terraces on the west. The valley, in places, is wide and moist enough to grow tall reeds and white-trunked aspens. In the fall, when seen from the old Shevlin-Hixon railroad grade on the terrace above the west bank of the Deschutes, the scene is pastoral and photogenic, with a kaleidoscope of colors. At their best, the aspen leaves glow a fluorescent orange. Marshy lands next to the river reflect the passing of the seasons and bushes and reeds have become tan colored. The Deschutes is a sparkling blue while the black lava beds on one side of the river are in marked contrast to the bright green of the ponderosa pine on the other. Numerous aspens lining the stream add a special character to the landscape, especially in fall when the warm, friendly glow of their golden leaves seems to provide a fluorescent color in dramatic contrast to the blue waters of the Deschutes River, the dark green needles of the ponderosa pine, and the spectacular flows of black lava.

At Lava Island, the river angrily charges against the mounds of jagged lava that dare impede its flow northward. The volcanic rock at Lava Island is riddled with cracks and fissures which absorb and discharge tremendous quantities of water underground. On September 2, 1961, for some unexplained reason, the recording chart of the Lava Island gauge recorded a loss of 15,660,000 cubic feet of water, enough water to cover 36½ acres to a depth of 10 feet. The loss occurred at 3:15 p.m. on September 2, and lasted until 6:15 a.m., September 3, before the flow returned to the river channel. It was thought that the top of a lava tunnel in the area had suddenly collapsed, providing a bypass of the recording gauge. All this occurred about the same time a series of earth tremors were recorded in the Pacific Northwest.

In early days, the Bend Livery Stable completed a 10x60-foot ice house near Lava Island on the west bank of the Deschutes. A small dam was built to back up water over the tules. After the water froze in the winter, the ice was gathered and packed in sawdust brought in from the Pilot Butte Company sawmill in Bend.

Just upstream from Bend, the Deschutes flows past the "back door" of the Inn of the Seventh Mountain. The Inn, situated on a high bluff overlooking the river, faces the Cascade Lakes Highway and is described in the chapter that covers that part of the High Country. The Deschutes is a fast-flowing stream, incised in a deep canyon between Lava Island and the Brooks-Scanlon Mill. Along the east bank of the river, a few homes cling to the top of the rimrocks, but for the most part, the canyon is still in its natural wild beauty.

Downstream from this canyon, the Deschutes makes a curvaceous sweep. In this area, years ago, pioneers forded the river, and settlers considered the site a suitable place to establish homesteads. Lumbermen visioned giant mills adjacent to the river and real estate agents laid out a town—no, a city—the City of Bend—on the Deschutes.

5.
Cascade Lakes Highway

The neighborhood of Bend is one of the nation's playgrounds. In big game shooting, fly fishing, canoeing, and mountain climbing, there is sport to tax the strength of the most robust; and the invalid who cannot find life and vigor in the pines, the altitude and the sunshine, cannot find it anywhere. As roads are built out from Bend to the lakes, streams and waterfalls and mountain fastness, there will be no more famous playground. . . .[57]

These words written over half a century ago summarize the characteristics of some of the High Country now opened up by the Cascade Lakes Highway. Although the lands west of Bend for many years were either inaccessible or reached only by those brave enough to combat thick dust or mud or deep snow, the natural beauty tucked away in the Cascades was well known to Central Oregonians. Many of the early tourists, however, were those traveling by horseback. In this section we will follow the story of the construction of the Cascade Lakes Highway and review some of the developments that have changed the landscape. We will also journey around that highway, noting some of the geological and scenic attractions.

Building of the Highway

The Cascade Lakes Highway is a loop that starts and finishes in Bend. It takes in the highway west of Bend past

Bachelor Butte and Sparks Lake, south past Elk Lake and Crane Prairie Reservoir, then east to U.S. 97 north of La Pine, and finally on to Bend. Many old-timers still refer to "Century Drive" when talking about the same loop. Because the loop route was approximately 100 miles long, the late Judge H. C. Ellis of Bend suggested that it be named Century Drive. And so it was for more than three decades. There still may be old signposts around that point to "Century Drive."

In the early twentieth century, few people were thinking in terms of a 100-mile road. Most of the attention was focused on getting from Bend to the Sparks Lake area. In the summer of 1907, plans were announced for a log-cabin-style hotel to be built in the "Forest Reserve" at Soda Springs, where the springs rushed down the hillside 2 miles north of Sparks Lake.[58] The site was described as an "ideal location where one can go and live the simple life for a few weeks." Recreation in the area included fishing in the numerous streams and lakes and hunting ducks, geese or deer which abounded near Soda Springs. In 1909, the Forest Service granted a permit to open a wagon road from Bend to the springs.

Although the resort at Soda Springs was never built, for many years *The Bulletin* featured news articles on the beauty of the area. In 1910, for example, the area was described as a "sportsman's paradise and perhaps the most beautiful to be found on the eastern slopes of the Cascades."[59] In 1913, Soda Springs was called "a most remarkable natural water resort and . . . a great attraction for tourists."[60] By 1912, some work on the Bend—Soda Springs road was underway, but the primary purpose of the road at that time was to aid the Forest Service in fire fighting and in administering the National Forest.

Perhaps the resort did not get constructed because not until 1920 was a wagon road finished to connect Bend to Sparks Lake and Elk Lake. The road naturally brought excitement to Bend recreationists. The local newspaper touted the fact that the new road to the mountains from Bend (25 miles) would shorten travel time to two or three hours. Previously, a trip to Broken Top and back took all day. Before the Cascade Lakes Highway was built, Broken

Top was reached from Bend by taking a dirt road past what is now Shevlin Park, then west into Happy Valley and on to Crater Creek.

The 28-mile road to Sparks Lake, completed on September 23, 1920, cost $10,000; it had taken 6000 pounds of TNT to blast through lava rock. Ironically, the day after the opening, eight inches of snow closed the highway on the southern end near Elk Lake. Eventually, the winding, dusty road was linked to Elk Lake but it was only just prior to World War II that the first few miles of the Cascade Lakes Highway from Bend were graded and paved. Elsewhere cinders were put on a graded portion from Big Springs to Dutchman Flat. Then, in 1941, all road work stopped for nearly a decade. Surfacing of the portion of Cascade Lakes Highway to Dutchman Flat was not completed until 1950, the same year that grading other sections occurred. Finally, in 1956, almost half a century after plans for the Soda Creek resort were announced, the Cascade Lakes Highway was completed.

Along the Cascades Lakes Highway, heading west from Bend, snow-covered mountains loom on the horizon, confronting the motorist at almost every turn but cultural landmarks along the highway are few. Tourism has encouraged some commercial activity—the attractive Entrada Lodge, located a few miles from Bend on the edge of the Deschutes National Forest Service boundary, is a favorite motel for winter skiers, summer visitors, and indeed any traveler who seeks quiet accommodation. The Inn of the Seventh Mountain, with the Deschutes River as a 100-foot step down from the back door of the Inn, faces the highway.

Inn of the Seventh Mountain

The Inn, built in 1970 and expanded in the mid-1970's, provides condominiums for purchase, tourist rental and convention guests. Conventions as large as 500 can be held here. The only other convention facility of that size in the Central Oregon High Country is at Sunriver.

Recreational facilities at the Inn are many and are located amidst lawn areas and tall ponderosa pines. There are

The Inn of the Seventh Mountain, located 7 miles west of Bend, offers accommodations and year-round recreation. Facilities at the Inn include a restaurant, two swimming pools, tennis courts, riding stables, and a rink for roller skating (ice skating in winter). The Inn is only 15 miles from the Mt. Bachelor Ski Area.

Winter scene of the Three Sisters and Broken Top from Dutchman Flat. The area in and around Dutchman Flat is popular with Nordic Skiers. *(Oregon Dept. of Transportation)*

swimming pools, saunas, tennis courts, a small putting green, areas for volleyball and basketball, a play area for tots, an ice-skating rink in the winter and riding stables with rental horses. Forest Service lands surround the Inn and extensive riding trails wind through the pine forests and along the Deschutes River. The restaurant caters to inn visitors as well as Bend residents seeking an evening out. An adjacent lounge offers nightly entertainment, and a gift shop is stocked with a variety of gifts, ski clothing, and everyday needs that visitors may have left at home. In the winter it offers rental skis, both alpine and Nordic.

The setting of the inn is an attractive one. A trail winds down to the Deschutes River, which is incised in a canyon "behind" the resort. The condominiums have natural wood exteriors and shake roofs. Many units have far-reaching views that include Pine Mountain and parts of the High Desert to the east, Newberry Volcano and Lava Butte to the south, and some of the major Cascade peaks to the west. The inn is only 15 miles to Mt. Bachelor Ski Area, and in the summer, within 30 minutes' drive of many of the lakes and trails of the High Country. Its proximity to Bend and its location along the Cascade Lakes Highway make the Inn of the Seventh Mountain a popular resort.

Beyond the inn, the Cascades Lakes Highway climbs steadily, cutting through forests of ponderosa pine, lodgepole pine, fir and then hemlock. At lower levels, where logging has obviously occurred, green manzanita bushes mingle with new-growth trees and stands of reforestation. The highway sweeps around a forested hillside, then, without warning, Mt. Bachelor dramatically looms up ahead, its snow-streaked summit rising over 9000 feet in the sky. Whatever the season, this sudden vista of Mt. Bachelor is inspiring but, for the traveling motorist, it is all too fleeting. Another curve in the road and Tumalo Mountain's smooth, red summit is prominent on the right.

Dutchman Flat and Tumalo Mountain

Wedged between the two mountains is Dutchman Flat, a remarkably flat, desert-like pumice area that provides close-up views of Mt. Bachelor's northern slopes, including the various colored chairlifts that, in winter, carry gravity-minded skiers up the snow-covered runs. The panorama of the Three Sisters and Broken Top is inspiring, summer or winter. According to McArthur, Dutchman Flat was named for a Bend rancher, Dutch John Felderwerd, who used parts of the High Country around Sparks Lake for pasturing sheep and cattle during the summer months.[61] Dutchman Flat is about 6400 feet in elevation, the highest place on the Cascade Lakes Highway and one of the highest on any paved road in Oregon.

Tumalo Mountain, elevation 7775 feet, is a prominent little-glaciated volcano towering over the eastern edge of Dutchman Flat. In winter, its highest slopes, confronting fierce snow-laden winds, are literally plastered white. Remarkable snow sculptures are created wherever buffeted and dwarfed evergreens are coated with snow and ice. Energetic Nordic skiers ski-tour up Tumalo Mountain, and any talk of plans for "developing" the mountain for alpine skiing are met with resistance by these skiers. In summer, Tumalo Mountain is relatively easy to climb. The trailhead, located one mile east of Dutchman Flat, is signposted but affords little room for automobile parking. The trail climbs steadily up a now disused jeep road, then follows a narrow foot trail to the summit. The view from the summit is extensive. Nearby Mt. Bachelor shows its volcanic ridges and lone summer snowfield.

Broken Top and Three Sisters dominate the skyline to the northwest, but between these peaks and Tumalo Mountain, the view (in summer) looks down on green alpine valleys and forested ridges. The southeastern view takes in the hazy blue bulk of Newberry Volcano. The arid flat lands east of Bend lack details, but beyond, observers can spot Smith Rock (near Redmond), Powell Buttes, and Pine Mountain.

Todd Lake

Beyond Dutchman Flat the Cascade Lakes Highway is closed by deep snows all winter and is usually not open for summer travel until late June or early July. The red-surfaced highway cuts through a forest of hardy firs and drops 400 feet in elevation in one mile, providing excellent views of nearby South Sister and Broken Top. The turnoff to Todd Lake is located at the site of a small meadow hemmed in by lava—which flowed from Bachelor Butte— and by a vertical, evil-looking cliff. An excellent close-up view of Mt. Bachelor's northwest flank is obtained from the meadow.

The graded dirt road to the parking area serving Todd Lake is only half a mile. Although this road continues up to the Broken Top country and on to Three Creeks Lake and Sisters, the road is primitive and not recommended for travel by vehicles with low clearance. This road was ready for use in August, 1923—a "scenic road opening up the heart of the Cascades." But in recent years it has become controversial. There are those who feel that the Todd Lake —Sisters Road is the only vehicular access to alpine meadows of the Broken Top country and should be maintained. Many environmentalists, expressing alarm at the abuse of the fragile meadows by irresponsible motorists, seek closure of the Todd Lake Road.

Todd Lake was named after John Y. Todd, a pioneer of Central Oregon who built Sherars Bridge in 1860, the first bridge across the Deschutes River. He lived at the Farewell Bend Ranch for many years and later grazed cattle in the upper Deschutes, moving to Prineville in 1890, then the Willamette Valley early in the twentieth century.

For many years Todd Lake was named Lost Lake because it was difficult to find. In 1921, the Bend Commercial Club petitioned the U.S. Geographical Board to change the name from Lost Lake to Lake Bend, explaining that other lakes in the Cascades were also called "Lost Lake." The Board would not accept the name Lake Bend, feeling that it seemed to advertise the town. Historical names were then solicited. Lake Shevlin was suggested but the final decision, in June, 1922, was Todd Lake.

The lake has long been a favorite picnic spot for Central Oregonians and visitors to the area. For example, in the summer of 1921, it was the scene of the Bend merchants'

Summer view of the same scene. Dutchman Flat is the highest section of the Cascade Lakes Highway, with an elevation of 6,400 feet. *(Oregon Dept. of Transportation)*

Todd Lake, 1930. Although the scene is basically the same today, motorists are now not permitted to drive to the lake. Hillside to the west has been close-cropped by sheep. *(USFS)*

picnic. Over 100 autos brought 500 people to the grassy banks of Todd Lake, where ball games, foot races, tiny-tot races, pie-eating contests and swimming races were staged. Merchants supplied large quantities of ice cream, coffee and watermelons. The Shevlin-Hixon band provided music. Today, the camp sites are only for walk-in campers because much of the lakeshore became overused by vehicles and people. Todd Lake is a favorite of Nordic skiers because of its nearness to the Mt. Bachelor Ski Area and its wintertime charm.

Sparks Lake

The Cascade Lakes Highway beyond the Todd Lake turn-off drops 600 feet to Soda Creek, Sparks Lake, and Fall Creek. Once again, the highway affords spectacular views of the Cascades. South Sister, rising nearly 5000 feet above the Cascade Lakes Highway at Sparks Lake, presents an inspiring and beautiful view. Photographers may wish to travel the cinder road leading around Sparks Lake and include the lake along with the mountain background in their shots.

Sparks Lake lies virtually in the shadow of Bachelor Butte's symmetrical slope. Soda Creek and Fall Creek both drain into the lake, and during the time of spring runoff, the lake expands and spreads over low-lying swampy ground. Toward the end of the summer the lake shrinks again, leaving acres of green meadowland as pasture for cattle.

In 1855, members of the Pacific Railroad Survey party passed through the Sparks Lake area, following an "old Indian Trail up a beautiful little valley with a stream flowing through it" (Fall Creek Trail), then descended to a "series of small lakes" (Green Lakes) "at the base of the snow peaks" (Three Sisters). Sparks Lake, named for "Lige" Sparks, another pioneer Central Oregon stockman, is popular with fishermen and canoeists who like to explore the various inlets around the very shallow lake. Camping is available just off the Cascades Lakes Highway, adjacent to Soda Creek.

South Sister forms a backdrop to picturesque Sparks Lake. This shallow lake shrinks in size by late summer but still offers fine fishing and canoeing. Beyond the lake, the Devils Hill obsidian flow crowds the Cascade Lakes Highway. *(Oregon Dept. of Transportation)*

Left: Sailing boats take to the ruffled waters of Elk Lake. The lake is noted for its excellent sailing conditions—a wide expanse of water, afternoon breezes, and restriction of high-speed power boats. Sailing enthusiasts hold races from the Fourth of July to Labor Day, competing for the Clark Van Fleet Trophy. South Sister is in the background. *(Oregon Dept. of Transportation)*
Right: View looking west across the lake at the Cultus Lake Resort. The lake activities include water skiing, boating, swimming and fishing. Many anglers seek the large Mackinaw fish. The resort has rental cabins, a restaurant, and small store. *(Oregon Dept. of Transportation)*

Devils Garden

The Cascade Lakes Highway skirts the northwestern part of Sparks Lake then passes a small but scenic area (right) known as the Devils Garden. A series of springs surface from the edge of a huge lava flow, creating a small meadow. At one time there was a small campground at Devils Garden but overuse of the fragile environment forced its closure. The meadow has lush grasses interspersed with moss formations, blue lupines, Indian paintbrush and rivulets of meandering water. Huge fire-glazed rocks tower over the meadow and the Cascade Lakes Highway. Some of the boulders from the dacite extrusions that extend north toward South Sister spilled over onto the meadow.

Indians must have passed by the Devils Hill flow, as it is called. Pictographs, painted on the face of a huge dacite boulder, probably depicted an ancient Indian trail. "An Indian legend relates that a Warm Springs brave induced a Klamath maiden to return north with him, and that later, he and a band of his warriors were ambushed at the pass by Klamaths led by a rival lover. Every Warm Springs Indian was killed and the Klamaths inscribed these pictographs as a warning for all Warm Springs people to stay on their side of the pass."[62] Unfortunately, the Indian art, which survived centuries of sun, snow and frost, suffered at the hands of vandals in 1975. In 1971, a chip of dacite from the Devils Garden area was deposited on the moon by Astronaut James R. Irwin, who along with other astronauts visited Central Oregon.

Devils Lake

Beyond Devils Garden, the Cascade Lakes Highway skirts the edges of Devils Lake, a small and shallow lake fed by Hell Creek from the north, Tyee Creek on the west, and a series of springs that discharge from the steep southwest sides of Devils Hill. Despite the frequent use of evil-sounding names in the vicinity, Devils Lake is a popular recreation area. The aqua-colored lake, like a jewel in a green ring, hosts campers, canoeists, fishermen and children who find pleasure splashing in the shallow waters.

A trail from the lake climbs north up Hell Creek to Moraine Lake, a favorite base camp for groups climbing South Sister. Another trail originates west of Devils Lake near Tyee Creek, heading westward to Wickiup Plains and Rock Mesa (see section on "Three Sisters"). Just over 2 miles south of Devils Lake, an unpaved access road (on the east) leads to Quinn Meadows, where the U.S. Forest Service has constructed a corral and equestrian trails.

Elk Lake and Hosmer Lake

Elk Lake, the next stop on the Cascade Lakes Highway, has long been a favorite of campers, picnickers and sailboat enthusiasts. Like so many of the High Country lakes, it is very picturesque. When calm, the lake mirrors the adjacent pine forest and South Sister; when breeze-ruffled, sailboats take over. The lake received its name because of the large number of elk that used to be seen nearby in summer.

As early as 1918, Elk Lake—which is about one and a half miles long and three-quarters of a mile wide—was considered as a possible location for a summer resort. By 1922, a log hotel was under construction, and two years later Elk Lake had its own post office (closed in 1954). For many years, the lake was famous for its fishing, with Eastern Brook trout an important species, and it was also long known as a source for fish eggs. For example, in January, 1919, some 350,000 Eastern brook trout eggs were gathered there, brought to Bend by sled, then dispatched by auto to the Bonneville Hatchery. In recent years, there has once again been a report of good fishing.

Throughout the years, Elk Lake has managed to retain its beauty and charm. The rusting buildings blend well with the forest environment. Cool breezes blowing from the lake make it a pleasant place to camp, boat or visit, and the chilly nighttime temperatures can be tempered by a campfire.

Elk Lake Lodge, 1924. The building is still used although the tent cabins have been replaced by wooden cabins. Elk Lake Resort sells groceries and camping and fishing supplies, serves meals, and has boats and canoes for rent. The recreational value of Elk Lake goes back to before 1920 when a packer from McKenzie Bridge stocked the lake and brought in wealthy recreationists to camp and fish. One of these visitors—interested in a more permanent summer home—got crews to clear a road from La Pine, hauled in lumber, and built the first of the summer cabins, operating under a U.S. Forest Service lease. *(USFS)*

Hosmer Lake, located about a half mile southeast of Elk Lake, was named in memory of Paul Hosmer, long-time Bend resident and, for many years, editor of Brooks-Scanlon *Pine Echoes*. Hosmer Lake was known as Mud Lake because of silt stirred up from the bottom by trash fish. These fish have since been killed and the lake stocked with Atlantic salmon. Grassy meadows fringe the lake which, like Sparks Lake, is shallow and fine for canoeing. *(Oregon Dept. of Transportation)*

Mink Lake Basin

Just south of Elk Lake, a trail leads west from the Cascade Lakes Highway through dense forests to Blow and Doris Lakes (2 miles) and then across the Cascade Divide descending into the Mink Lake Basin (5 miles). Here, a multitude of small lakes occupy pockets in the ground, and during the summer months the area is a breeding ground for countless mosquitoes. While some of the lakes in this part of the High Country are noted for fine fishing, large doses of insect repellent need to be applied to combat the pests.

Lava Lakes

Both "Big" Lava and Little Lava Lakes are reached by Forest Service road 1927, located on the east side of the Cascade Lakes Highway, 4 miles south of Elk Lake. Both lakes are popular with fishermen and campers. However, "Big" Lava Lake boasts a small resort with boat rentals. The Deschutes River flows out of the west end of Little Lava Lake and starts its journey toward the Columbia River—by flowing south!

In the winter of 1923-24, Lava Lake was the scene of a triple murder. Three trappers, seeking fox furs, were found shot, the foxes killed, and their pelts taken. The incident greatly disturbed the people of Deschutes County and reports of the murders quickly spread over the Northwest. After a succession of false leads, a suspect, wanted on other charges, was apprehended in Montana in March, 1933. The case was never proved; the suspect had alibis. Thus the Lava Lake murders remain unsolved.

Cultus Lake

South of Lava Lakes, the highway slices through the Deschutes forests, paralleling the river for three miles near Deschutes Bridge. The setting here is most attractive, with lovely meadows and a rippling stream fringed by forests. The highway next crosses spring-fed Cultus River, which discharges into Crane Prairie Reservoir 2 miles away.

Cultus Lake is signposted on the west side of the highway one mile south of the Cultus River, and a paved road (No. 2025) leads to this popular lake.

This lake, which is 3 miles long and averages a little over one half mile wide, is used extensively by water skiers, campers and, near the shallow east end, swimmers and picnickers who make use of the small sandy beach. A trail parallels the north shore, connecting with other trails that lead south to Little Cultus Lake and north to Winopee Lake and Mink Lake Basin. Depending on the depths, Cultus Lake assumes different shades of blue which strongly contrast with the miles of deep-green forests sloping away from the shore. Cultus Mountain (6759 feet) is prominent to the south, rising over 2000 feet higher than the lake.

Old-timers believe that Indians camped at both Cultus Lake and Little Cultus Lake to the south. "Cultus," used quite commonly in the Pacific Northwest, is a Chinook Indian word meaning "bad or worthless."

According to Steve Steidl, Bend, the name may be associated with a group of 19 Indian graves Steidl saw on top of Cultus Mountain in 1906. The graves are no longer visible— a forest-service fire lookout was unknowingly constructed over the graves. What tragedy overtook the Indians has never been revealed. The burials atop Cultus Mountain remain a mystery.[63]

One of the main cultural features of the lake is the resort constructed in 1956. Located on the east side of the lake, it has cabins for rent, a restaurant, general store catering to recreationists, and boat rentals. A deck and small lawn area in front of the restaurant overlook a small beach. As with the main beach just to the north, cool westerly breezes frequently temper the afternoon heat. However, by evening, the dry air of the High Country leads to rapid radiational cooling and nights that may require wood fires for the cabin occupants, and campfires for the campers.

Twin Lakes

On returning to the Cascade Lakes Highway, you turn south, travel past the Osprey Management Area at Crane

Prairie Reservoir (3 miles) (see chapter on Deschutes River) and proceed to the Davis Lake junction. The highway that continues south leads past Davis Lake and connects with Highway 58. This road, some of which is now paved, is part of a highway once planned to link Crater Lake with Bend. In 1938, $50,000 was allocated for the highway to "extend along the lofty ridge of the Oregon Cascades," connecting such places as Diamond Lake, Windigo Pass, Willamette Pass, Waldo Lake, Cultus Lake, Elk Lake and Bend. The present highway has achieved part of that proposal. At this point it heads east, skirts Brown Mountain and crosses the Deschutes River, where it becomes a small but charged-up stream. The unpaved road to the north (left), before crossing the Deschutes River, leads to the Crane Prairie Dam and Reservoir. A half mile east of the Deschutes River, the turnoff to the south is to Twin Lakes and Wickiup Reservoir.

Twin Lakes—North Twin and South Twin—are of volcanic origin. These circular lakes, both about a half mile in diameter, were formed when rising magma within the earth's crust came in contact with groundwater. The resulting explosion, similar to that which formed mile-wide Hole-in-the-Ground near Fort Rock, created the depressions which later filled with water. The geological name for the "crater" is maar (meaning "lake").

Twin Lakes have long been noted for their fine fishing. Indeed, in 1940, former President Herbert Hoover journeyed to Twin Lakes just for the fishing. A resort at South Twin has new and rustic cabins, furnished and equipped with electric heat and cooking facilities. The adjacent lodge offers meals, sells groceries and fishing equipment, and rents boats. Set amidst beautiful pine trees, the resort attracts those who seek a quiet retreat, leisurely fishing for rainbow trout from Twin Lakes—or German brown from nearby Wickiup—and those who just want to enjoy the clean, fragrant air of the High Country.

Pringle Falls Experimental Forest

East of the turn-off to Twin Lakes, the Cascade Lakes Highway makes a beeline through groves of tall ponderosa pine, then (after 4½ miles) diverges. Motorists may either head for U.S. 97 past the source of Fall River and General Patch bridge or continue east to U.S. 97 past Pringle Falls and Rosland, the former site of La Pine.

Just south of Pringle Falls is a large tract of land set aside for research. The Pringle Falls Experimental Forest, started in 1931, is an 11,000-acre area operated by the U.S. Forest Service Silviculture Laboratory in Bend. It is a giant outdoor laboratory where the environmental factors that control timber stands—soil moisture, temperatures, nutrients and diseases—are studied. Research at the station includes seeking the best methods of harvesting, thinning, and pruning trees—estimating the potential to produce lumber. Researchers also investigate the use and effect of fire, and the interactions among fire, insects and diseases in manipulating plant communities. The station is used extensively by forestry students from within the United States and, at times, by foreign students.

The Cascade Lakes Highway loop, starting and finishing at Bend can be driven in but a few hours. However, to visit and really enjoy the many recreational areas may actually involve several separate visits. Leisurely days could be spent at any number of the places mentioned. Only then can the landscapes be fully appreciated.

6.
Newberry Volcano

A conspicuous feature of the Central Oregon High Country is the large shield-shaped volcano centered 20 miles south of Bend and about 35 miles east of the crest of the Cascades. Newberry Volcano is similar to Mauna Loa or Kiluea in the Hawaiian Islands, and Mount Etna, Sicily, in that it is a broad, rather gently sloping shield of lava; it has a deep caldera and its flanks are dotted with dozens of cinder cones.

In its own way, Newberry is a giant. Across the base it is about 25 miles in diameter. Indeed, motorists using U.S. 97 south from Bend are steadily climbing the lower sides of Newberry's swollen shield as they ascend the grade near Lava Butte. Although its highest point, Paulina Peak, is a rather modest 7,985 feet above sea level, much of the Newberry Volcano rises 3000 feet above the surrounding High Lava plains. The caldera, locally referred to as Newberry Crater, is about five miles east-west and four miles north-south.

Newberry is so large that it creates its own weather and climate. Air masses moving eastward across Newberry's bulk are forced to rise. In doing so, the air cools and its ability to hold moisture is decreased. As a result of this meteorological occurrence, Newberry receives up to 25 inches of precipitation, about twice that of nearby Bend. As most of this falls in the winter from Pacific-born storms, snow depths on Newberry are considerable and long lasting. Throughout much of the winter, the crater, its two lakes

(East and Paulina) and two lakeside resorts are accessible only by snowmobile or cross-country skiing. Early fall snows often dust Paulina Peak and the crest of the crater rim, signaling the end to summer recreational use of Newberry Crater. Winter snows show up well on the sides of Newberry wherever vegetation is sparse, such as on lava flows or steeper slopes.

During the summer months, periodic influxes of warm, moist air from California invade Central Oregon. These unstable air masses are also influenced by Newberry to the extent that dark thunderheads tower over the volcano, discharging jagged lightning flashes, detonating thunder that reverberates between the crater walls, and cooling the air with a refreshing rain. Persistent clouds that cling to Newberry's higher peaks and rims seem to add an element of mystery and moodiness to that already provided by the volcanism. During a summer day, Newberry Crater may experience snow, sun, hail and wind that, within minutes, whips up swells two to three feet high.

The drying winds on the lee side of the volcano sweep over the High Desert country, leaving it sunny, arid and windswept. So dramatic is this meteorological phenomenon that the division between forests that cling to Newberry's slopes and the far-reaching desert is almost a straight line lying perpendicular to the westerly winds.

Newberry was named by Israel C. Russell, a geologist who extensively explored and studied Central Oregon early in the twentieth century. Russell, the first geologist to describe this volcano, named it after Professor John S. Newberry, a scientist who passed through the Deschutes Country in 1855 with the Williamson Pacific Railroad Survey party.[64] An 1881 map of Oregon, compiled by the Corps of Engineers, showed Paulina Lake, Paulina Mountain to the north, but no East Lake or Paulina Peak. Early in the twentieth century, though, both lakes appeared on maps while, at the same time, the mountains north and south of the lakes were named "Paulina."

Newberry attracts both professional and amateur geologists. It is readily accessible, its volcanic history is recent, and many of the volcanic landscapes can easily be studied in a small geographical area. During the summer, Newberry

Crater is a focal point for anglers, campers and sightseers, and snowmobilers find the deep winter snows ideal for their sport.

Newberry's chief development took place in the Pleistocene epoch but volcanic activity continued on and off until only a few centuries ago. According to Howel Williams, its foundation is probably Columbia River Lavas, perhaps as much as a mile thick.[65] Its volcanic shield was built up by flows of basalt low in viscosity and highly fluid. Later, huge outflows of molten lava leaked out from the slopes of Newberry, draining the central feeding pipes, thereby removing support of the bulky summit. The top of Newberry collapsed through concentric faulting about 6000 years ago, resulting in the creation of a single caldera.

Following sinking of the floor of the volcano, the walls of the caldera began to collapse (Halemaumau in Hawaii did likewise in the 1920's), thereby widening the caldera. Evidence of faulting in and near the east, north, and south sides has been noted by geologists. Lines of cinder cones north of Newberry further testify to the presence of fissures beyond the north rim. At first, one "crater" lake occupied the caldera but subsequent activity built a "dam" across the center of the ancestral lake. An outflow of basaltic lava into the bottom of the lake started the dam construction. Later eruptions built up two volcanic tuff rings (similar in occurrence to well-known Fort Rock) which, although their bases were underwater, grew and eventually emerged above the lake's surface. One tuff ring (Little Crater) rises 200 feet above Paulina Lake although a large part of its mass is submerged. Pumice Cone, a younger volcanic feature, towers 750 feet above Paulina Lake and measures about one mile across at its base. At the summit of Pumice Cone is a steep-walled crater, 250 feet deep. A third pumice cone, located south of the road that links Paulina and East Lakes, is partially covered by the Big Obsidian Flow.

Large quantities of light pumice erupted from these cones and escaped over the rim of Newberry, showering the outer slopes of the volcano, especially on the eastern flanks. Basaltic cinder cones such as Pumice Butte (really a cone of red cinders) and the Dome (located southeast of East Lake) and the vast deposits of pumice found on parts of the High

Desert south of Pine Mountain are examples seen today that reflect the tremendous quantity of pumice exploded from Mt. Newberry. Trees killed and burnt by the hot pumice have been dated by the radio carbon method, establishing the Pumice Cone eruption at about 2,000 years ago.

While eruptions were occurring in the caldera, extensive lava flows poured out of fissures on the slopes of Newberry. Cinder cones developed on many of these fissures. Meanwhile, within the caldera some of the eruptions taking place were explosive. Fountaining of scoria occurred on the east and the north wall of the caldera above East Lake. Younger yet were the obsidian flows within the caldera. One of these, the Big Obsidian Flow, is among the largest in the United States. The source or vent of the Big Obsidian Flow is close to the south wall of the caldera. From this vent the sticky lava crept northward down a slope for more than a mile. At the bottom of the slope, the obsidian flow was diverted by the existing pumice cone mentioned above. Obsidian piled up to bury the south rim of the cone and cascade obsidian into the inner slopes of the cone's crater. The jagged snout of the Big Obsidian Flow towers 100 feet high.

Mount Newberry has not erupted for several centuries, but to say that the volcano is inactive would be premature. Interest in Newberry Volcano for its geothermal potential periodically makes the news media. Many environmentalists shudder at the thought of a geothermal plant located anywhere in the caldera or on the slopes of Newberry. In 1981, a temperature gradient hole, located east of the obsidian flow, was sunk, by lease agreement, to 3000 feet. Other exploratory holes had been drilled on the flanks of Newberry. By 1987, an environmental assessment report had not been completed. Other geothermal explorations in the High Country have been conducted in the Melvin Butte area near Sisters.

The geology of Newberry is but one aspect of the Newberry story. The cultural geography of the volcano is much less apparent to visitors. Indeed, apart from the two lakeside resorts, Paulina and East, eleven summer homes, and the U.S. Forest Service campgrounds, there is little other evidence of man's activities. However, Indians are known to have taken obsidian from the Newberry Caldera. In 1930, *The Bulletin* reported on the attempts to locate a lost spring on the northern outer slopes of the volcano (North Paulina Peak). The spring, an underground flow of water, apparently was known to early-day Indians. In a letter to *The Bulletin*, F. V. (Jack) Horton—who had been stationed in Bend as a forest service grazing examiner—stated that he had made the acquaintance of a Warm Springs Indian who said that Indians had established a campground on the slopes, using water from a hole in the lava. This hole was covered with a slab of rock when the Indians left it. Investigations of old stream beds on the north slopes of the Paulinas had been conducted in 1917, but no water source was discovered.

Camping sites of aborigines—old teepee poles and masses of chipped obsidian flints—have been discovered in different places around the outside slopes of Newberry. Indian trails converged on Newberry's slopes and led down to East Lake. Indians traveled long distances—from the Columbia River on the north and Klamath Marsh on the south—to obtain obsidian from Newberry's caldera. About 1915 the discovery of a mass of skeletons in the crater's lava beds indicated that the Indians using the caldera were not always friendly.[66]

The first white men of record to visit Newberry Crater were members of Peter Skene Ogden's fur-hunting party who, in the fall of 1826, explored the then unmapped territories of Central Oregon. Ogden had traveled up the Deschutes Valley, the Crooked River and the Harney Basin before discovering Newberry Crater. His visit here was noted 150 years later when, in September, 1977, the Deschutes County Historical Society commemorated the event by erecting a plaque adjacent to the Peter Skene Ogden Trail near the Big Obsidian Flow.

It was not until around the turn of the present century that a "road" connecting The Dalles—California Highway (now U.S. 97) with Newberry Caldera was completed. A Paulina Prairie rancher, Ralph Colwell, blazed a wagon track up to Paulina Lake and constructed a dam at the lake's outlet to store water for irrigation. Both the wagon road and the dam were in existence by July, 1911, when Harold E. Smith, forest ranger on the old Pine Mountain District of the Deschutes National Forest, visited the area.

The first auto trip to Newberry Crater was made by a party of Bend men in June, 1914. For half a century the road from U.S. 97 was little more than a rutted one. Then, in 1954, the road—18 miles in length—was paved, providing easier access to the crater for thousands of visitors. The only other road into Newberry Crater is a little-used cinder one that enters the crater by the "back door." This road, which connects with the "China Hat Country" and the High Desert, crosses the eastern rim of the volcano and plunges down to East Lake near the lakeshore resort.

The "front door" to Newberry Crater is via the road sign posted from U.S. 97, about 25 miles south of Bend, or 5 miles north of La Pine. The highway climbs steadily through country which was logged over many years ago. Second-growth ponderosa pine now hides most logging scars. As the highway ascends the slopes of the volcano, the grade steepens, twists and turns through dense thickets of lodgepole pine, then suddenly levels out adjacent to Paulina Falls. A short distance east of the falls, the highway enters Newberry Crater. Paulina Lake is directly ahead but visitors have the choice of continuing on the paved road to East Lake, taking the cinder road on the right to the summit of Paulina Peak—which towers over the crater—or visiting nearby Paulina Lake Lodge. Near the lodge, a dock extends into Paulina Lake, which is quite shallow at this spot. The lake level has been raised artificially by the completion of a dam near the outlet to Paulina Creek. Throughout summer, boats cluster at favorite fishing spots, often near the northern shore of the lake.

Although fishermen now recognize East and Paulina lakes for their great fishing potential, both were barren of fish until a Central Oregon sportsman packed in trout in 1912. The lakes were originally stocked with fish by the Oregon Game Commission in 1914, but the first year that fishing was permitted was in 1915. By 1939, over 1000 anglers used Paulina Lake alone. These lakes are now the favorite fishing spots for over 63,000 anglers each season. Best fishing is usually early in the season or late in the fall.

The Paulina Lake Resort features a general store, tackle shop, and cabins. The lodge serves complete meals—breakfast, lunch and dinner with a Saturday night "Prime rib night." The store is stocked with a wide variety of groceries, beverages and sundry items. Fishermen can get everything from license to boat rental, tackle, and free advice as to where the Kokanee salmon or rainbow trout are biting. The resort is open nearly all year, catering to snowmobilers in winter.

Paulina (shown here) and East Lake are noted for their excellent fishing. Newberry Crater has five major campgrounds, and rental boats are available at the resorts at each lake. Paulina Lake is about 200 feet deep and fed by water percolating from East Lake and by springs, some of which on the northeast shore have temperatures of almost 110° F. *(Oregon Dept. of Transportation)*

In the warm days of summer, the trout move to deeper waters. Catches of 9- to 14-inch rainbow trout are quite common. Brook trout to 16 inches and weighing to 5 pounds are taken. German brown trout over 10 pounds have been landed, but arm-stretching records go to the angler who hauled in a 37-inch German brown that tipped the scales at 35½ pounds. Fishing methods include trolling with a spinner and bait, and bait angler with eggs and worms.

During the winter season—a long one at mile-high Newberry Crater—the landscape is dominated by snow and ice. Both Paulina and East lakes are usually frozen solid except for a small area near the East Lake hot springs. However, Paulina Lake is not frozen over as long as East Lake is, possibly due to its greater volume of water and its exposure to westerly winds. In 1953, Paulina Lake remained ice free even in late January.

The presence of hot springs at East Lake is well known, but less known is the presence of hot springs with water temperatures of 96-113° F—discovered at Paulina Lake in 1911. *The Bulletin* stated that the hot springs water contained numerous mineral substances with medicinal benefits and predicted that a health resort would be located there.[67] While such a resort failed to materialize at Paulina Lake, hot alkaline springs, charged with sulphur and soda and having a temperature of 120° F, became the site for a resort located on the southeastern shoreline of East Lake.

The highest part of Newberry Volcano is Paulina Peak, elevation 7985 feet. North Paulina Peak, located north of the caldera, is actually only 300 feet lower but is much less conspicuous. Certainly, Chief Paulina, the notorious Snake Indian who terrorized the region during the years 1866-68, has been well remembered by Central Oregonians. From U.S. 97 north of La Pine, Paulina Peak dominates the eastern skyline. The peak is accessible by motor vehicle after the winter snows have melted, usually by early July. The unpaved but graded road to the peak starts just south of Paulina Lake Lodge and is signposted. Morning is the best time to visit most viewpoints in Central Oregon and Paulina Peak is no exception. The cindered road slices through evergreen forests, skirts the bulging western flanks of Newberry and affords far-reaching vistas across miles of forests to the glacial Cascade peaks. Toward the summit, the road swings around the south slope of the volcano, then climbs, twists and turns through alpine vegetation before abruptly ending at the confined summit parking area. Beyond, the ground literally drops away nearly 1600 feet, down boulder-strewn slopes to a deep-blue Paulina Lake.

The entire Newberry Crater is then visible in one sweep. Deep blues of Paulina and East lakes contrast with green forests and glistening white-pumice deposits, all contained within the caldera. The Big Obsidian Flow is distinctive, with concentric circles marking the flow of the highly viscous lava. The only structure on the summit of the peak is a formidable pumice-block structure once used as a radar early-warning station.

No road circles the rim of Newberry Crater as is the case with Crater Lake. Not that such a rim road has never been dreamed of. In 1929, foresters from the Deschutes National Forest Service planned a rim road which would extend from Paulina Peak along the southern rim, providing scenic views and fire protection for the adjacent forest lands. The road was never constructed but a trail for hikers and horseback riders was completed in 1976. This trail, about twenty-six miles in length, circles the caldera.

Unlike Crater Lake, Newberry Volcano does not have national park status. However, in 1920, then again in 1940, geologists suggested that Newberry be made a national park or national monument, but no action has been taken.

Lava Butte

Traveling along Highway 97 some 10 miles south of Bend, first-time visitors to Central Oregon may be surprised to be confronted by a "volcano" rising 500 feet above a jumble of black and jagged lava adjacent to the highway. This steep-sided cinder cone, capped by a small fire lookout tower and observation building, is actually but one of dozens in the area. However, none is so conspicuous, so perfectly shaped, or so accessible from the main highway as is Lava Butte.

East Lake Resort in 1921. The resort, started in 1915 by Fred Shintaffer, consisted of an eight-room hotel (left), a bathhouse (mineral baths 25 cents), kitchen, dining room (center), bunkhouse, and rental cottage (right). The resort was completed in 1919 and taken over by the stockholders of the East Lake Resort Company. Hot water from the natural hot spring was pumped from the ground by gas engine. The resort was destroyed by fire on November 5, 1923. *(USFS)*

Dedication of the Newberry Volcano trail system, in 1976, was held at the Paulina Peak summit. Trails at Newberry circle both the volcano rim and Paulina Lake, and switchback up to Paulina Peak. The idea of creating a Newberry Volcano National Park was suggested first in 1920 and again in 1940, when Dr. R. L. Nichols from Tufts College proposed including the Lava Cast Forest, Lava Butte, and the Lava River Caves as parts of the park. Timber interests argued against the proposal. *(Don Peters)*

The spiral road that winds around and up the butte lures many tourists from the main highway to drive up to the vista house at the summit. The narrow red-paved road that climbs Lava Butte demands full attention. Passengers who are the least bit apprehensive of heights have the choice of some back-seat driving or just nervously peering over the guard rail at the receding lava flow and forest below. The distant horizon constantly changes as the motorist spirals the cinder cone.

Ample parking is available at the summit, except on holidays and during July and August. Immediately, a variety of interests command the attention of all those who leave their vehicle. Beyond a wooden railing bordering the parking area, the side of the cinder cone virtually disappears beneath the feet of the viewer. Between a scattering of tall ponderosa pines, visitors look over a vast, forbidding lava field that extends to the west and north of Lava Butte. Beyond, a forested countryside merges with the base of the Cascades.

Early morning in May or June is perhaps the best time to view the Cascades from Lava Butte. The air is generally cooler and clearer than in late summer, and usually considerable snow covers not only the higher peaks but also some of the lesser known volcanoes along the Cascade Crest. Identification of the major peaks is a popular game. "Is that Three Fingered Jack or Mt. Washington?" "Broken Top sure looks closer to the Three Sisters than it does from Pilot Butte." "Way off, in the distance, is that Mt. Hood?" "No, there is Hood. That peak beyond. It can't be Rainier?" (Mt. Adams, 130 miles away is visible on clearer days.)

To the southwest, Cowhorn Peak and Diamond Peak are less conspicuous than the Three Sisters or Mt. Jefferson. However, Mt. Thielsen is easy to identify by its slender finger-like spire. Mt. Scott, which overlooks Crater Lake, rises above the distant Cascade horizon to the southwest, but Mt. Shasta in northern California is not visible from Lava Butte. The southern skyline is dominated by bulky Newberry Volcano. To the north, the City of Bend is barely visible, marked only by the roads that seem to scar Awbrey Heights and, perhaps, by smoke drifting from the lumber mill.

By now, the visitors' attention may well be diverted from the spectacular view to what is close at hand. The U.S. Forest Service Observation Building and fire lookout rises above the red north wall of the volcanic crater of Lava Butte. And, literally at their feet, tourists often find that they are approached for handouts from a half dozen or more furry friends. Cute, playful golden-mantle squirrels and striped chipmunks never seem to tire of begging for tidbits, and a steady stream of visitors never seems to tire of responding.

The precipitous western inside wall of the crater is comprised of deep red cinders, pocketed by small caves here and there. These caves provide convenient hideaways, storage places, and refuges for the squirrels. Overhead, perched on branches of lightning-scarred ponderosa pine, a chorus of protests over preferential treatment comes from raucous blue jays and Clark's nutcrackers. Actually, the wildlife at Lava Butte is much more varied than most visitors realize. During the summer of 1950, the fire lookout at the summit was manned by a graduate student of zoology. During his sojourn, the student noted 23 species of birds and 6 species of mammals, including a visit by a bobcat.

Most visitors to Lava Butte make the walk from the parking lot to the observation building. The pathway is short but fairly steep and at a 5000-foot elevation. Lowlanders and indeed those who are "out of shape" may find the exertion and thinner air temporarily exhausting. The 360-degree panorama from the top is breathtaking and rewards those who make it with glimpses of the edge of the High Desert country to the east—and a chance to study the geological and botanical displays in the observation building.

Prior to 1975, this wooden cabin was manned by a forest ranger who helped interpret the geology and geography of the Lava Lands and other parts of Central Oregon. Forest Service interpretive personnel are now housed in the more extensive Lava Lands Visitor Center located near the road entrance to Lava Butte.

The summit lookout is literally glass enclosed. To help identify key horizon landform features, a mural is painted above the windows on three sides of the building. By standing back from the display cases, visitors can line up one or more familiar peaks, then use the mural to name those not identified. The 72-foot mural was painted by Mrs. A. L. Schatz of Bend in 1963. Ed Parker and Phil Shoemaker of the U.S. Forest Service provided photographs and scaled sketches respectively. The vertical scale of the mural was exaggerated three times the horizontal scale to highlight the distant skyline. Mrs. Schatz, working from pictures enlarged from 35 mm slides, spent about four hours a day for three months painting the impressive mural.

The fire lookout office, located over the observation building, is open to the public when fire conditions allow. A naturalist is on duty and will demonstrate fire equipment and techniques. During thunderstorms, the lookout literally jumps as lightning can, and does, strike Lava Butte. The number of scarred and dead trees around the crater top testifies to the fact that high points are prone to lightning strikes. Several years ago the author spent two summers working for the forest service at the visitors' center at Lava Butte and can clearly recall that it was a hair-raising experience during severe thunderstorms. Employees in the lookout, perched on stools supported by glass castors, are alternately dazzled by brilliant lightning flashes and deafened by the crash of thunder.

The history of Lava Butte—geologically and culturally—has been eventful. Lava Butte came into existence about 6150 years ago, but its youthful-looking appearance caused early-day geologists to grossly underestimate its age. Perhaps the first description of Lava Butte was made in August, 1858, when A. S. McClure, prospecting the Deschutes Valley, noted in his diary the "huge mass of basaltic rock, or cinders rather, covering acres in extent and forming something like a semicircle around a butte about five hundred feet high. The butte is covered on the north side by pine and other species of timber and upon examination it was found to be the crater of a volcano. . . ."[68]

Israel C. Russell was probably the first geologist to study Lava Butte. In 1905, he described it as a conspicuous lapilli cone with a deep crater in its summit, from the south base of which a stream of basaltic lava was poured out and flowed toward the northwest at a recent date.[69] Noting the lack of vegetation, he estimated its age as "at least a hundred years and probably more than a hundred and fifty years...."[70]

In 1934, W. O. Crosby, a geologist involved with the geological study for the planned site of a dam and reservoir at Benham Falls, stated that "5000 years would not be unreasonable for the date of the Lava Butte flow, based on the time needed to cut a 50-foot gorge through massive rhyolite, especially with clear water unarmed with sand and gravel."[71] In 1957, the geologist, Howel Williams, estimated the age of Lava Butte to be less than 1000 years.[72] Certainly the rugged black lava, spread over 6000 acres at the base of Lava Butte, gives little indication that volcanic activity occurred over 6000 years ago. However, the cold, relatively dry climate of Central Oregon is not conducive to the rapid weathering that occurs in a hot, humid climate such as Hawaii.

Lava Butte was born and formed, along with scores of others, on the Northwest Rift Zone, a line of faults and fractures northwest of Newberry Volcano. Initially, lava bombs and cinders were shot into the air to build up the cindery flanks. Prevailing southwesterly winds carried the light cinders and built up the northeast side of the cone higher than the southwest. Some of the lighter cinders (lapilli) were carried as a plume northeast of Lava Butte to deposit a layer of ash several inches thick as far as a mile away.

It was this plume that prompted geologists to search for clues to the true age of Lava Butte. In August, 1976, attempts were made to find traces of carbonized wood that might have been preserved in the ash deposit. About fifty holes were hand dug in the volcanic ash before a suitable piece of carbonized wood was located. This wood was sent to Menlo Park, California, for carbon isotope study, which dates material by the extent of decay. The age of Lava Butte?—6160 years.[73] This date coincides quite closely with the date of other eruptions along the Northwest Rift Zone, including the Lava Cast Forest, described below.

Following the eruption of cinders and building up of the cinder cone, the final phase of Lava Butte vulcanism occurred when streams of lava, in a relatively viscous form, burst out of the central vent, broke through the thinner south wall of the cone without destroying the cone, and spread westward. The lava flow, as high as 50 feet high, no doubt flowed quite rapidly, but the surface, exposed to the air, cooled and formed a surface crust which was carried along by the molten under-material. The surface material became broken and pushed up into irregular heaps, forming the "aa" type of rough-faced lava.

Of particular interest to visitors is the lava "delta," the spot where the high-density lava escaped from the base of the cone. Lava flows built up a lava gutter—nearly vertical walls of black, rough-looking lava where the molten lava chilled on the sides. Then pulsating discharges spread out toward the west of Lava Butte, filling the ancient channel of the Deschutes River. The time span for the whole eruption of Lava Butte may have been as short as 1 to 10 years, by analogy with the activity of comparable modern volcanoes.[74]

A short paved trail, starting from the Lava Lands Visitor Center adjacent to Highway 97, twists and turns through parts of this lava field. A self-guided tour allows visitors to interpret several geological features located near the lava gutter. Beyond the jagged lavas, the Cascade skyline contrasts markedly with the black foreground. Here and there, twisted limbs litter the lavas, adding further desolation to the somber landscape.

The first road up Lava Butte was opened in December, 1932. The enterprising Skyliners immediately eyed the road and sought to use it as a ski runway. In February, 1933, the Skyliners, working with blueprints used for the construction of the ski jump at the 1932 Winter Olympics at Lake Placid, New York, planned a similar ski jump on the north side of Lava Butte. This jump was to replace the McKenzie Highway jump that was deemed too small for competition. Although Lava Butte was used for winter sports from time to time and receives much more snow than Bend, snow depths throughout the winter proved insufficient to warrant developing a ski resort there.

In the spring of 1946, a new road at Lava Butte was completed. The maximum grade of this road was 10 percent compared to 19 percent for the old one, and the new alignment added an extra half circle to the spiraling highway. The road, which measures 1.155 miles from the base to the summit, was paved in July, 1950.

Aerial panorama of Lava Butte showing the top part of the spiral road, the crater, the fire lookout and observation building on the summit. Lava flowed from the southern base of the cinder cone 6,000 years ago, spreading over 6,000 acres. More recent "volcanism" occurred in September, 1914. Portlanders, visiting Central Oregon to view real estate, made a stop at the base of Lava Butte. At a prearranged signal, members of the Bend Ad Club detonated, at the top of the butte, hundreds of pounds of black powder along with fireworks. According to eye witnesses, "The entire top of Lava Butte seemed to tremble. Lava boulders were hurled high into the air and aerial bombs rattled like volleys of thunder, and streams of writhing fire ran through the lava fields." *(USFS)*

While Lava Butte is perhaps better known for its geological story and interpretive center, the summit of the cinder cone has long been important as a vantage point for a fire lookout. The lookout shown here was in use in the 1950's. Not the wire anchoring the building to the summit. *(USFS)*

Lava Butte affords a full 360-degree panorama and is a natural site for forest-fire detection. The first lookout at the butte was established in 1924. It was reconstructed in 1962 with the lower part housing the visitor information center. While most of the Deschutes National Forest Service fire lookouts have been abandoned in favor of spotter planes, Lava Butte continues to be manned during the fire season, usually from May to October, depending on local weather conditions.

Lava Butte attracts thousands of visitors each year. In 1986, an estimated 90,000 people took time to visit the Lava Lands Visitor Center adjacent to Highway 97. This compares with 7,846 in 1948 and 25,321 visitors at the Butte in 1951. No visit is complete without a drive to the summit for the spectacular view and examination of the 150-foot crater. The quarter-mile walk on a cindered pathway around the crater rim provides an additional scenic and educational experience. The trail "starts" at the summit observation building and "ends" at the paved parking lot. Some tourists walk the trail in reverse but it is perhaps more logical to get an overview of the geology from a higher vantage point before starting on the trail. The forest service has placed small signs at intervals to explain features that are of geological and botanical interest. The walk provides a different perspective to the crater and a chance to peek down at the source of lava flow to the south.

Lava Cast Forest

In 1926, a forest service lumberman, Walter J. Perry, while scaling timber in a Shevlin-Hixon Company timber sales area, came across remnants of a forest buried by one of the many lava flows that scar the forested lower northern flanks of Newberry Volcano. Although molded casts had been known to exist on the north slopes of the Paulinas for several years, they were believed to be "blow holes" formed by gases escaping the ancient lavas. Perry noted that in the casts were impressions of tree bark, limb holes and even lightning scars. One cast was of a giant tree whose interior held lava stalagmites and stalactites. Another cast, about 40

The Lava Lands Visitor Center at the entrance to Lava Butte, dedicated in September, 1975, houses a variety of exhibits including a diorama which depicts the geological story of the Lava Lands. Two self-guiding tours originate behind the visitor center. One, described as a "Trail of the Molten Lands," is a half-mile paved trail winding across the lava flow. Markers signify points of special geological interest. A shorter tour, "Trail of the Whispering Pines," focuses on the ecology of the grove of ponderosa and lodgepole pine trees, along with associated shrubs that have evolved following logging in the area in 1918. *(Oregon Dept. of Transportation)*

The Lava Cas' Forest was created when molten rock spread from a fissure on the north slope of Newberry Volcano. The lava engulfed acres of ponderosa pine, felling or surrounding the trees. The lava cooled on contact with the bark, forming stone casts. Some of the casts are standing upright, up to 15 feet tall in places. Others are horizontal, as shown here. *(Oregon Dept. of Transportation)*

feet long, held the stony impression of a lightning scar on the tree around which the cast was formed.

Lava Cast Forest was created long before the coming of white men to the Central Oregon country. A sea of molten rock, breaking loose from a fissure on the north side of the Paulina Mountains, spread over thousands of acres of ponderosa pine forest, felling and igniting trees as the fiery rock continued on its course. Contact with the trees chilled the lava outward from the bark, forming the impressions or casts, before the trees were burned away.

Since Perry's discovery, further studies of the casts have been made. Among other finds was an instance where one lava flow engulfed a previous flow. Protruding lava from the first flow appears through the fresher lava. The time lapse between the two flows was so great that a forest of pine had managed to grow on the first flow, only to succumb later to a fiery death. One puzzling question has been why the lava did not completely consume the tree before a cast solidified. In explanation—the lava had traveled nearly a half mile before reaching the forest and in places only three feet deep was becoming sluggish in its flow. A living tree with all but its outer bark saturated with moisture and oxygen excluded, even with the most extreme heat would maintain its form for some time. While in most cases the inner surfaces of the casts are smooth, in a few instances, possibly of dead trees rich in pitch, the temperatures of the casts were sufficiently raised again to create clinkers on the wall. Clinkers seem to occur especially in the root ends of casts where the pitch would have been richest.

That same year, 1926, discoveries of more lava-cast forests were made by Bert C. Boylen, organizer of the Deschutes Geology Club, whose organization requested that the U.S. Forest Service set aside the Lava Cast Forest as "an area possessing objects and monuments of special scientific interest." At that time, part of this forest was on Shevlin-Hixon land, and an exchange of lands was suggested. In a *Bulletin* article, June, 1936, Emil Nordeen, long-time Bend Nordic skier and amateur geologist, stated that less than 10 percent of the lava-cast forest had been explored. Nordeen called for surveying, mapping and recording the geology of the area, along with seeking precautions to protect the lava casts against vandalism. The most accessible area of the forest is 10 miles east of U.S. 97 from the Sunriver Junction, 15 miles south of Bend. A cindered road climbs 1000 feet between the highway and the forest, but the grade is gradual. The U.S. Forest Service has provided parking facilities, and in June, 1973, opened a self-guided, paved trail through some of the area. Although the trail takes in only part of the total area of lava casts, visitors can see a wide variety of casts adjacent to the nearly mile-long trail.

Lava Caves

Lava tubes, or lava caves as they are more commonly called, are to be found in several different parts of the volcanic lands of Central Oregon. However, the lower outer slopes of Newberry Volcano have some of the best examples of lava caves to be found anywhere in the continental United States. Some of the caves are named, mapped and frequently visited. Others are little known, unnamed and not mapped. It is likely that many caves are still hidden amid the rugged lava flows on Newberry Volcano.

Lava caves are formed when a stream of molten lava moves downslope from its source, is chilled underneath, on the sides and on top, while the interior of the flow remains hot and fluid. Pressure of the liquid mass may lead to a break at some point at the lower end of the flow, resulting in a breakthrough. The fluid lava then drains the interior core, leaving a lava tube.

The best known of the lava tubes is Lava River Caves, a state park, located some 12 miles from Bend, just south of Lava Butte and adjacent to U.S. 97. Cimarron-barked ponderosa pine tower over the parking lots, picnic area and the cave entrance. Visitors experience the beauty of these trees, their fragrance, their bright green foliage and the ever-present stirring of their upper needles by an invisible wind. Sunlight filtering between the needles strikes and brightens the tan pine needles that cover the light pumice soils. The picnicker's lunch is often interrupted by impatient, noisy blue jays aloft and by scurrying but quiet chipmunks and golden mantle squirrels at their feet—all seeking handouts. (No water is available at the Lava River Caves State Park, so plan to provide your own drinks.)

Visitors may notice the crumbling remains of an early road, the old route of The Dalles—California Highway, just east of the cave entrance. In 1925 the Shevlin-Hixon Company was logging their lands adjacent to this road. Rather than despoil the beauty of the area along the highway around the Lava River Caves, they left untouched the grove of mature pines referred to above and deeded the timbered area to the state of Oregon.

The geological story of the cave is told on signs located near the cave entrance. In early days, artifacts were found near here, pointing to the fact that Indians probably hunted in the vicinity. Pioneer settlers in the upper Deschutes Valley may well have used the cave to store venison in the cool 40° F ice box. At one time, the cave was named Dillman Cave after James Dillman, an early rancher. In 1927, when the cave was designated a state park, it became officially known as the Lava River Caves State Park.

Access to the cave is where a part of the tunnel roof collapsed, possibly following earthquake vibrations. Although the cave extends in two directions from this point, entrance to the eastern part of the tunnel is blocked. The part open for exploration extends almost one mile within volcanic terrain. From the cavernous mouth, the trail descends over volcanic rock bridged by stairs. From the entrance, stairs lead upward to the main tunnel, which at this point compares in size with highway tunnels. The ceiling is 50 feet high and the walls at least that far apart, and long shadows cast by lanterns or flashlights create a Halloween effect.

Farther into the cave the tunnel slopes down about the same degree as the ground above it. Evidence of the lava draining the tunnel shows in the rounded shelves at varying levels on the sides. The walls are coated with a glaze and here and there small volcanic stalactites are suspended from the ceiling. The walk through the cave, which averages 20 to 30 feet wide and 15 to 20 feet high, includes a lava surface and a walkway of sand.

Interior of the Lava River Cave. Visitors may rent lanterns or use their own in touring the cave. The cave extends west one mile from its entrance. While temperatures may be 90° F outside in July, visitors to the cave should prepare to defend against a chilly 40° F. *(Oregon Dept. of Transportation)*

Lavacicle Cave, previously known as the Plot Cave, was discovered by forest service crews following control of the large Aspen Flat forest fire in 1959. The cave was so named because of the many "lavacicles" suspended from the cave roof and protruding from the floor. These lava stalagmites—1 to 3 feet high—and stalactites were formed when lava drained and left hot rock dripping from the ceiling. In places, large pieces of the ceiling fell into a still hot lava, creating swells and waves which, in turn, were frozen in motion. Lavacicle Cave is open for visitation only under guided supervision of the Deschutes National Forest Service, located in Bend.

The sand in the Lava River Cave is considerable. Its origin is unknown but theories as to how it came there include its being filtered through cracks in the roof or deposited by water after Lava Butte backed up the Deschutes River 6000 years ago. One of the features of the cave is a "sand garden" where water has dripped on the sand and constructed delicate formations. Toward the end of the cave the sand becomes more abundant and moister, finally reaching the roof closing the tunnel.

Attempts to go beyond this sand unsuccessfully took place in 1919 and 1920 when geologist W. O. Crosby was investigating the feasibility of a dam on the Deschutes River at Benham Falls (see section on Deschutes River). Early in 1936 further excavations of the sand choking the cave were made in the hope of breaking through to another long stretch of the cave. It was thought that the tunnel might extend to the ancestral gorge of the Deschutes River. After considerable effort, state park crews cut through 310 feet of sand before work was halted. Sand tested was identical to that at the Benham Falls Reservoir site, and was found to include strata of clay intermingled with the sand.

The cave was dedicated a state park in July, 1927, when the Lions Club (Bend) staged formal and informal ceremonies underground. In 1978, approximately 60,000 people visited this park. Its nearness to the Lava Lands Center helps visitors gain a better understanding of the many volcanic features in the Central Oregon High Country. Indeed, operation of the caves is now being transferred to the U.S. Forest Service.

A red-cindered surface road, U.S. Forest Service road 1821, sometimes graded, sometimes washboarded, heads southeast from U.S. 97 about 5 miles south of Bend and, within a dozen miles, leads to several lava caves on the lower slopes of Newberry Volcano. A U.S. Forest Service map shows the names and locations of several of these caves.

Aptly named Skeleton Cave, adjacent to Forest Service road 1854, one mile off road 1821, was the site of some interesting discoveries over half a century ago. In March, 1926, explorers of the cave came across 42 teeth of carnivorous creatures, deeply encrusted with silica. Some of the teeth were identified by Dr. J. W. Gidley, Smithsonian

Institution, Washington, D.C., as being from a giant bear, probably one known as *Arctotherium*. Other teeth were from an extinct species of horse which ranged over ancient Oregon; still others were from an Arctic fox, *Alopex*. Later that year, the skull of an animal was discovered, which was subsequently identified by University of California paleontologists as a pleistocene-age wolf of the same species found in the Rancho La Brea pits of Southern California.

Further discoveries were made in Skeleton Cave in 1940 by Mrs. J. O. Lammi of Bend, when the mineralized teeth of an extinct horse, *Equus niobrarensis*, were found 2000 feet back in the spacious cave. This find was significant because the horse was known to have ranged from Texas to Arizona but never before was believed to have been in Oregon. All the useful finds in Skeleton Cave were of teeth, protected by enamel; all skeletal bones had turned to dust in the dry cave. Why so many animal remains in Skeleton Cave? One theory is that the animals became trapped after falling into the sunken entrance of the cave while moving across the lava plains. Another theory is that seismic activity caused bone fragments to work gradually through lava fissures into the cave.

Charcoal Cave, an extension of Arnold Ice Cave (described below), is a vast underground chamber whose floor is covered two feet thick with the debris of burned wood. Here, traces of Indian habitation—obsidian fragments, arrowheads and bison horns—were found in September, 1930. One of the perplexing aspects of the find is why so much burned wood, estimated to be equivalent to 100 cords, was found in the cave. Chiseled on a rock near the entrance to Charcoal Cave is the name A. W. Holt, a member of an 1884 surveying party.

Some of the caves in the volcanic High Country are virtual ice boxes, storing naturally formed ice—even in the hot summer months. Circulation of air in winter and available moisture dripping from the ceiling help form the ice. During the summer, poor air circulation, good insulation from the thick basaltic roof and, in many instances, a north-facing entrance keep the ice from melting.

Some ice caves on the slopes of Newberry Volcano provided ice for early-day residents of Central Oregon. Homesteaders in Fort Rock Valley obtained it from East Ice Cave. Arnold Ice Cave, near U.S. Forest Service road 1821, provided it for Bend residents in the hot summer of 1910, when ice sold for as much as $40 a ton. The Deschutes *Pioneer Gazette* had the following to say about Bend and Arnold Ice Cave:

> In all America, Bend is believed to have been the only town that obtained its ice from a cavern. Over a period of several years, it is recalled, ice was hauled here from the Arnold cave, some 12 miles to the south. The ice was cut in the cave, from the dark-surfaced cavern glacier, removed with block and tackle up a steep incline and hauled into Bend on horse-drawn wagons. One year, old timers say, a local saloon keeper obtained a monopoly on the Arnold ice supply and enjoyed a fine business through the hot summer in selling ice-chilled beverages.[75]

Origin of the name "Arnold" for the ice cave came about long ago. At one time, a road extended east from the old Sisemore place (south of Bend). A sign pointed to Arnold's (the homestead of William Arnold) and to the ice cave. Newcomers, not knowing of the homestead, believed the sign led only to the ice cave.[76]

Arnold Ice Cave is virtually blocked by a mass of ice near its entrance. As with Lava River Cave, a grove of trees was left near the cave. In 1927, Brooks-Scanlon, which was logging the area, left 80 acres of virgin forest adjacent to the cave. Other mapped ice caves in the High Country are the Edison Ice Cave, located east of Bachelor Butte, and South Ice Cave, located on Newberry's southern flanks. South Ice Cave was discovered by Walter J. Perry, U.S. Forest Service employee. Under a heap of ice, Perry discovered a mass of bones, including the skull of a small bear with tusks well worn. Near the small skull were skulls of huge bears. The skeletons were only revealed after Perry crawled snail-like through a small opening into an inner cave where ice was three to four feet deep.[77] Another cave, Cleveland Cave, was found by loggers near Edison Ice Cave, as recently as 1958. Quite likely other ice caves await discovery in the High Country.

A few miles east of Bend, lava caves have further proved that Indians once made caves their homes. In 1931, explorers discovered basketry made from reeds, juniper bark, and grass, and a small shoe woven from reeds in Barlow Lava Cave. Traces of fire at different levels indicated that the cave was occupied at different time periods.

The Devils Garden

A few miles southeast of Newberry Volcano, on the edge of the High Desert, is a little-known area of volcanism. The Devils Garden, covering about 45 square miles, is an area of black pahoehoe lavas which originated from fissures in the north and northeast. On the northeast side are some of the best examples of spatter cones, spatter ramparts and lava tubes found anywhere in the continental United States. Two giant spatter cones, known locally as the "blowouts," were formed by lava bubbling up a semi-molten lava. Nearby, a half-mile-long lava tube, Derrick Cave, played host to geologists seeking information preparatory to the lunar landing. This cave, named after one of the early-day ranchers, H. E. Derrick, has a sand-covered floor at the entrance. The cave is huge; visitors are amazed at the height of the roof, over 50 feet. Flat benches on the sides of the cave show quite clearly that molten lava flowed here at different levels.

About 1920, there were reports of sighting a diminutive type of bear in the Devils Garden lava beds. The bear, to be known as a "lava bear," soon became an object of controversy. Speculation ranged from the discovery of a new species to the possibility that the bear was a small type of grizzly or a small black bear living in an inhospitable environment. Throughout the years, several small, brown bears were caught in the Fort Rock region—all anatomically similar to black bears. One bear, caught in a trap in 1922, weighed only 35 pounds. Another weighed but 25 pounds. This latter bear was placed on exhibition and, in Portland, some 8000 people paid to see it. The animal was later sold, without authorization of the trapper, for $7,000 and subsequently found its way to a New York museum.

Four stunted lava bears were captured in Northern Lake County in 1933. (However, one of them grew rapidly when fed by a trapper.) The name "lava bear" was adopted by members of the Bend Commercial Club. In September, 1934, this group suggested that the Bend High School football team be called the "Lava Bears." The name was acceptable because the animal was of the Central Oregon region and was ferocious. Today, all athletic teams of Bend High are known as Lava Bears. Home games are played, naturally, on Bruin Field.

7.
Logging the High Country

One of the several distinctive features of the High Country of Central Oregon is the vast territory covered by forests. Except for the alpine areas, the lava flows, the lakes and the riverine meadows, forests blanket the entire region. The potential of the pine forests was noted as early as 1843 when John C. Fremont explored the area. In his journals, December, 1843, he wrote:

> Today, the country was all pine forest, and beautiful. . . .The timber was uniformly large, some of the pines measuring 22 feet in circumference at the ground, and 12 to 13 feet at six feet above the ground.[78]

Early settlers in the forest lands did little to use the timber. Pioneer stockmen herded cattle and sheep amidst the pines each year, but except for small local mills in and near Bend, there was no way of moving lumber out of the region. In 1877, a sawmill was operating on Willow Creek near Grizzly, north of Prineville. In Bend, the Pilot Butte Development Company mill was constructed in 1901 on the banks of the Deschutes River, and two years later, the Steidl and Reed mill was established just north of where Pioneer Park is located. These and other small operations served local needs in the construction of irrigation flumes, homes, barns, stores and homesteads on the High Desert.

Giant Lumber Mills Come to Bend

The lumber industry was late in coming to Central Oregon. By the time of the Civil War, having exploited the timber in New England, large lumber industries had moved into Minnesota and Wisconsin. In both regions, water played an important part in the timber industry. Melting snows in spring carried logs to the mills, and logs were stored in mill ponds. At first, in New England, waterwheels powered mill machinery but, in the Midwest, steam power was used for energy. By the 1880's, the timber supply in the Midwest was diminishing rapidly and soon giant corporations such as Pope and Talbot, Weyerhauser, and Dant and Russell—with the nearby California market in mind—began to appear in the Pacific Northwest. Development of the timber along the Lower Columbia River and in the Puget Sound area already had taken place.

About this time, foresighted lumbermen from the Midwest, awaiting completion of the railroad to Bend, started assembling large tracts of valuable timber in Central Oregon. In many instances, settlers, taking advantage of the 1878 Timber and Stone Act, secured 160 acres of land at a nominal $2.50 an acre. The act, originally designed to help people obtain stone and timber for building dwellings, was later misused. Settlers (illegally) transferred their claims to speculators who, in turn, sold to timbermen. This practice continued until July, 1903, when almost all the remaining unlocated claims were withdrawn and designated part of the Deschutes National Forest Service.

The federal history of the Deschutes forests actually dates back to September 28, 1893, when President Grover Cleveland withdrew land from public domain and created the Cascade Range Forest Reserve—then an area west of the Deschutes River between Jefferson Creek and Cottonwood Creek. Lands east of the Deschutes River that are now in the Deschutes National Forest (the Fort Rock District) were the ones withdrawn in July, 1903. Other minor withdrawals followed, but by September 17, 1906, the Cascade National Forest was formed on lands west of the Deschutes River and the Fremont National Forest land to the east of the river. On July 1, 1908, the Deschutes National Forest was created. At that time it encompassed the Ochoco National Forest, but the Ochoco lands were only part of the Deschutes National Forest until 1911. Boundaries were periodically adjusted until 1938, when the present Deschutes forest area was established.

In September, 1907, a considerable tract of land south of Bend was thrown open to settlement. What took place in the latter part of September and the early part of October was perhaps representative of the feverish attitude of those seeking timber claims. Prior to the filing date (September 28, 1907), the woods were alive with people cruising the timber. Some were setting up shanties and attaching notices to trees ahead of time, a violation of the regulations. In timber east of the Big Meadows (present site of Sunriver), as many as 17 people camped on the same one-quarter section. The night before the filing date was disagreeable with a cold rain falling. At midnight, people—thoroughly drenched—were hurrying through the woods, trying to run their lines by lantern.

Even before the "great timber rush," investing companies had assembled large acreages of timber through acquisition of state indemnity lands. For example, the A. J. Dwyer Pine Land Company acquired 16,000 acres along the Deschutes River, a few miles upstream from Bend. The Mueller Land and Timber Company bought 16,000 acres in the La Pine area. Brooks-Roberts Company secured 16,000 acres southeast of Bend. All of these purchases were completed before 1896.

After the timber rush, investment companies became involved in the forests of the upper Deschutes region. S. S. Johnson, of Minneapolis, bought the holdings of the A. J. Dwyer Pine Land Company, then in the hands of a trustee in bankruptcy (in later years the Johnson interests added additional tracts of land until the ownership totaled 60,000 acres). R. E. Gilchrist, of Alpena, Michigan, purchased 60,000 acres mostly in Lake and Klamath counties. In 1906, the buying of land intensified with involvements that included, among others, the Shevlin interests, the Scanlon-Gipson Lumber Company, and the Alworth-Washburn Company.

Frank P. Hixon, of La Crosse, Wisconsin, joined T. H. Shevlin in 1907 in purchasing other large areas of timber land. In November, 1911, Hixon and Shevlin formed the Fremont Land Company, which was successful in grouping large tracts of land necessary to carry out logging. Trades were made and consolidated holdings of the Fremont Land Company, the Brooks-Scanlon Lumber Company, Bend Timber Company, and the Alworth-Washburn Company became larger. The Shevlin-Hixon Company was formed, May 5, 1915, and in June, 1916, acquired the holdings of the Mueller Land and Timber Company and title to large tracts of land on both sides of the Deschutes River as far south as Klamath County.

Meanwhile, in October, 1911, the railroad reached Bend and this fact—along with the securing of large holdings of land—opened the way for timber to be extracted from the High Country. On May 10, 1915, the eagerly awaited announcement was made that the Shevlin-Hixon Company would build in Bend on the west side of the Deschutes River on 140 acres of land donated by the Bend Company. Estimates at that time indicated that the mill, a (planned) box factory and logging operations would provide employment for 500 men, "who will receive an average wage of $3.00 per day."[79] The monthly payroll was figured at $39,000.

It was then estimated that, with cutting 80 million feet of timber a year, enough lumber was available to supply the mill for over 25 years. Bend rejoiced at the mill news. On the afternoon of May 10, 1915, all businesses closed. A procession of 45 automobiles, headed by the Bend band, paraded the business streets, finally stopping at the lawn of the Bend Company office. Here, speeches were made and the band played. *The Bulletin* staff had worked all night to issue an eight-page extra edition, many of the copies being mailed out of town. As expected, real estate business became very active and many pending deals were closed at once.

Work on the rail spur across the Deschutes River began immediately. Laborers earned $1.40 a day and teams were paid $5 a day. A trestle (still standing), 880 feet long and built of fir timbers, and a dam across the river were constructed in less than two months. On August 18, 1915, Dr.

Left: This was typical of the pine forests near Bend when representatives of large lumber companies surveyed the High Country for the potential timber. This photo, taken in 1909, shows the mature pines in a park-like landscape with an absence of undergrowth. *(Oregon Historical Society)* Right: Early-day faller using a large saw that was attached to a slender piece of rubber (called a "rubberman"), cutting down a large pine. Todays fallers would be alarmed at the lack of safety—no hard hat and no face guard. *(Brooks-Scanlon)*

High wheels used in early-day logging of the High Country. Logs were bunched and secured by a chain to a long, heavy tongue. A team of horses, moving the high wheels forward, lifted the front end of the logs off the ground. The light vegetation of the area enabled the logs to be dragged to the landing. *(USFS)*

A two-ended Clyde skidder used by Brooks-Scanlon in the 1920's to move logs from the forest to the landing. This machine was fueled by wood. *(Brooks-Scanlon)*

Track-laying by Brooks-Scanlon crew through the pine forests of Central Oregon about 1930. The grade was prepared the year before to let the surface settle. The crew set down hand-hewn ties, then steel was placed in position and the track spiked. After the logging was completed in the area, the track and ties were removed and reused elsewhere. Note that none of the crew wore protective hats. *(Leo Bishop)*

D. F. Brooks announced that Brooks-Scanlon, Inc., would also build a large mill along the Deschutes River, opposite the Shevlin-Hixon site. Mill operations at the Shevlin-Hixon plant started, March 23, 1916. On a typical Central Oregon, cold March day with snow on ground, Shevlin-Hixon cut its first logs—the start of logging operations which were to last 34 years.

The Bulletin, in a timely edition, proudly reported every conceivable fact about the Shevlin-Hixon plant—height of the smoke stacks (197 feet), capacity of the mill (150,000 feet of lumber for each of 2 ten-hour shifts), number of boilers (11), etc. An article also acclaimed the builder of the plant, J. P. Dion of Dion and Horskotte, who had just completed his 28th mill, with the Shevlin-Hixon plant the largest. And so it was, the Shevlin-Hixon sawmill started on schedule without the slightest difficulty.

Brooks-Scanlon began operations, April 22, 1916, with employment of 250 men in the mill and an additional 150 men in the forests. At that time, the company and "allied interests" controlled 32,000 acres of timber lying south and east of Bend, enough to supply the mill for 20 years, running one shift a day.

Logging and Living in the High Country

Logging in the High Country included some operations that were unique to the area. For example, the level terrain and an absence of undergrowth on much of the Deschutes plateau was conducive to "high-wheel logging." These high wheels became part of the regular scene of early-day logging in the Central Oregon forests. Today, high wheels are to be found in wayside logging museums like the Collier State Park, located on Highway 97 north of Klamath Falls, to which, in January, 1956, the Brooks-Scanlon Company donated logging equipment from the abandoned town of Shevlin. Included in the donation were three logging cars, a bunkhouse car and a cookhouse car.

During the era of railroad logging, crews and their families lived in camps that periodically followed the logging operations. Each camp provided small cabins for married workers and their families and bunkhouses for single men. The single men ate their meals in a dining car and were served by two or three "hashers." Family cabins consisted of two small rooms, each room serving a dual role. One room contained a kitchen and an eating area, while the other alternately served as a bedroom and a living room. Furniture in this room included chairs, a dresser, and a bed which, by day, folded against a wall and was screened by a curtain. A wood stove kept the cold out of the uninsulated cabins. Large families had two cabins put together. A connecting doorway gave access to two extra bedrooms. In 1935, rent at the Brooks-Scanlon camp was $5 a month, plus $1 a month for water.

Water was hauled from Bend by rail tank cars as most of the timbered country away from the lakes and streams is devoid of water. The tank cars were connected to stand pipes from which camp residents carried water in buckets to their cabins. Severe winter cold frequently froze the water in the stand pipe. Each camp had hot shower baths and electricity provided by a generator.

A lesson in economy and ingenuity for creating low-cost school building was provided by Brooks-Scanlon at their Lava Butte camp. A logging engine switched a boxcar into the camp. Workers cut out a door at each end, then built steps and a platform for easy access. A partition part way across the boxcar created two "rooms," one for storing books and lunch boxes, the other for hanging coats; the main part contained the students' desks, the teacher's desk and a heating stove. Teachers were expected to do the cleaning, light the stove, carry in firewood (unless she could get a student to help), as well as teach 12 to 15 students in grades one through eight. Students not only received instruction from the teacher but older ones were expected to help the younger ones. In 1927, the Bend School District included two Brooks-Scanlon and two Shevlin-Hixon camp schools.

The schoolhouse was the hub of camp activities. It was used for social purposes including holiday programs staged by the children and for dances. Brooks-Scanlon provided free weekly motion picture shows, using a hand-operated projector. These attracted not only camp residents but visitors to the camp. Except for the time needed for changing reels, the shows were described as being comparable to those in the best-equipped theaters in the "big city," with newsreels, comedies and a main feature. Brooks-Scanlon camps also provided a library car with Deschutes County providing the books. Interest was quite high; in 1928, for example, the circulation was 1465 books, with the men favoring westerns and northern stories, while the women favored books on home life. Church services were not organized at the Brooks-Scanlon camp but a Sunday school was held for children. The mobile town of Shevlin had a small church and conducted marriages. This church building was moved to Camp Sherman, northwest of Sisters, in 1956, where it was renovated by residents of the community.

Each camp had a commissary boxcar with basic needs for the residents—canned goods and vegetables, fruit, kerosene for table lamps, tobacco, work gloves, etc. On pay days, men bought commissary books. As supplies were needed, purchases were made with scripts from the books. During late summer, fruit was brought from the Willamette Valley, Hood River Valley, or from the Cove orchard (located in the Crooked River canyon now flooded by Round Butte Dam) and used for bottling and canning for the winter months. Trucks with food came from Erickson's grocery store in Bend—or, at times, logging trains, returning from Bend, brought stocks of eggs, cottage cheese, milk, butter, etc., back to the camp. Ice for the camps came from the various ice caves located on the flanks of Newberry Volcano.

Moving days at the logging camps were exciting times. First, dishes, vases and other breakables were placed in galvanized wash tubs, copper wash boilers or boxes. Dressers were placed on their backs and beds secured against the walls. Porch floors and roofs, which were hinged, were folded against the front doors. Cabins were built on skids so that the "cats" could pull them to the rail spurs. Cables were then hooked to the skids, and the cabins were lifted and placed on railroad flat cars. Moving was done quickly and efficiently. For example, in November, 1921, Brooks-Scanlon camp #1 moved to a new location 3 miles distant in two hours without so much as breaking a dish.

Logging camp in the pine forests. During the period of railroad logging, loggers and their families lived in the woods. Camps had bunkhouses for single men and separate cabins for families. Shevlin, a mobile town, had up to 700 people and included a post office, barber shop, gas station, community hall, store, and school, all set up near the railroad tracks. *(Brooks-Scanlon)*

Brooks-Scanlon logging-camp cabins on the move. Through the years, the camps of Brooks-Scanlon and Shevlin-Hixon moved several times. This move, in 1946, was from the Bull Springs area west of Bend to the junction of the McKenzie and Santiam Highways on the edge of Sisters. The cabins are used as permanent residences at that location today. *(Brooks-Scanlon)*

The town of Shevlin, population 600 to 700, had its own post office, barber shop, gas station, community hall, gift shop, grocery stores, school, Sunday school, bath house and pool halls, all of which were on wheels. These buildings were on spur tracks at one end of the camp, while the family cabins were at a separate part of the camp along the "residential" streets. Moving all of the cabins and commercial buildings and engineering sheds took longer than the smaller Brooks-Scanlon camps. Even so, when Shevlin moved from the Finley Butte camp, 3 miles east of La Pine, to Summit Stage Station on the Fremont Highway, in 1942, all 400 buildings were moved in 4 days. Altogether, Shevlin (while owned by Shevlin-Hixon) moved at least 16 times.

After the Shevlin-Hixon interests were sold to Brooks-Scanlon, Shevlin moved for the last time (a situation which pleased map makers and the U.S. Postal authorities). In 1950, Shevlin came to rest at a place appropriately named The Timbers, about 5 miles north of Gilchrist. Brooks-Scanlon modernized the cabins and installed indoor plumbing and electrical wiring. Shevlin had started in 1916 near the brickyard west of Bend and journeyed south. Today, travelers on Highway 97 can still see some of the Shevlin cabins at the Jack Pine Motel south of La Pine.

Railroad logging in the High Country lasted for many years, but by the 1940's trucks were beginning to replace the trains. In 1946, Brooks-Scanlon moved its logging camp from a site near Bull Springs, 6 miles west of Bend, to a location on the western city limits of Sisters. The small, maroon cabins are still picturesquely nestled amidst the tall pines. In December, 1956, the last trainload of logs was moved from the Pole Creek country, south of Sisters, to Bend. The steel rails between Sisters and Bend were then torn up and sold to a representative of the government of India. Some 80,000 tons of steel were moved by 250 railroad cars from Bend to Portland docks. The Indian government used the steel for supporting power lines, as termites were having some good meals on the wooden poles. In many instances, logging trucks used the abandoned railroad grades, but not without some problems. Pressure from the fast-moving trucks occasionally unearthed tire-piercing rail-

Locomotive hauling loaded flatcars into Bend for milling. Rail lines crisscrossed the pine forests of the High Country. In 1923, Brooks-Scanlon had 40 miles of tracks, operated 5 oil-burning locomotives, 135 logging cars, and a steam track-laying machine. The discerning eye can still detect old railroad grades throughout the forests. *(Brooks-Scanlon)*

Rail trestle across Tumalo Creek near Shevlin Park, west of Bend. This trestle enabled Brooks-Scanlon to log in the Sisters Country and move the timber to Bend by rail. The trestle was removed following the end of railroad logging in the area. *(Brooks-Scanlon)*

road spikes. To locate the spikes, large magnets were moved slowly over the grades.

Economic Impact of the Lumber Mills

When the railroads reached Bend in 1911, the city had a population of approximately 1000. Imagine, then, the impact on the city when the Shevlin-Hixon and Brooks-Scanlon mills opened for business in 1916. Shevlin-Hixon, in addition to its logging and mill operations, also ran a sash-and-door and a box factory.

The Shevlin-Hixon plant occupied a 200-acre tract of land, the buildings themselves covering 11 acres. In 1923, in a 16-hour day (a double shift), the mill had a daily output of 600,000 feet of lumber. The plant's annual capacity was 150,000,000 feet. Employment by Shevlin-Hixon totaled 1200, including 400 at the logging camp, and the annual payroll in 1923 totaled $1,750,000. Shevlin-Hixon, in cooperation with Brooks-Scanlon, maintained a hospital in Bend and all necessary medical and surgical treatment was given workers for a nominal monthly charge. Logs were brought to the Shevlin-Hixon mill by rail. For many years, logs were floated down the Upper Deschutes to just above Benham Falls. They were then taken by a steam-operated loader directly to empty cars that were backed onto a bridge crossing the stream. The mile-long mill pond in Bend stored logs until they were conveyed into the mill.

In 1923, Brooks-Scanlon, which undertook a major expansion that year, was producing 175,000,000 feet of lumber. Employment that year including 700 working at the mill and an additional 300 in the woods. Brooks-Scanlon was then shipping 6,500 carloads of lumber a year from the plant. Between 1916 and 1933, Mill A manufactured approximately one billion feet of lumber. At the height of operations in Bend, considering shift changes and lunch breaks, whistles from the two mills echoed across Bend 13 times a day.

The enormous appetite for timber by two companies as hungry as Brooks-Scanlon and Shevlin-Hixon had a tremendous impact on the landscapes of the High Country south of Bend. Travellers along the Dalles-California Highway (now

What is possibly the final resting home for Brooks-Scanlon logging camp cabins is the cluster of such cabins near Sisters. Here, fittingly within the pine forest, some are still used as residences.

The Shevlin-Hixon Company, located on the west banks of the Deschutes River in Bend, occupied 200 acres of land. In 1923, the mill was producing 600,000 board feet of lumber daily. That year, the payroll for the 1200 employees was $1,750,000. The office building (lower right) was later moved across the Deschutes River and for many years was used as the administration office of the Bend School District. *(Brooks-Scanlon)*

U.S. 97), arriving in Bend, frequently voiced loud complaints on the massacre of the forests. Photographs from Lava Butte taken in 1933 reveal how extensive the logging had been. As the forests were cut, large sections of land were turned over to the Deschutes National Forest. Thus, the story of logging in the High Country involves the formation of part of a National Forest as it exists today.

As early as the 1920's, fear was expressed that Bend was placing too much dependence on the lumber industry and that the forests could not keep on supplying timber for two giant mills. That fear materialized when, on November 21, 1950, the Shevlin-Hixon Company, with only three years' standing timber supply left, announced that their operations were about to stop. At that time, Shevlin-Hixon employed 850, including 225 in the woods at the town of Shevlin, then located near Chemult. News of the mill closure stunned Bend.

In December, 1950, Brooks-Scanlon purchased all of the Shevlin-Hixon holdings, including the town of Shevlin, the logging railroad, sidings, telephone lines, water rights and mill property. In the snow-covered Chemult country, 65 miles south of Bend—without ceremony—Vern Callihan and Edward J. Aasen, cut the last tree for Shevlin-Hixon at 3:30 p.m., December 9, 1950. On December 19, a 52-car train moved the last load of logs into Bend. The final mill operations took place on December 23, 1950, when J. N. Mahoney, who was at the controls when the first log was sawed, March 23, 1916, cut the last log for Shevlin-Hixon. At 12:45 p.m., on an unusually balmy 60° F. day, a whistle echoed across Bend, signaling the end of the operations of the Shevlin-Hixon Company.

Late in January, 1951, the last railroad car left the Shevlin-Hixon plant. Fittingly, two Scandinavians, Emil Nordeen and Nels Skjersaa, loaded the car. In 31 years of loading, these two "work-horses" had stacked nearly one billion board feet of lumber. Few of the Shevlin-Hixon buildings are standing today. In March, 1956, the two burners, the larger one weighing 920 tons, were toppled by dynamite.

Today, logging objectives in the woods are basically the same as 50 years ago. The trees are cut, bucked, assembled

Logging near McKay Butte, west of Newberry Volcano, in the early 1930's. Note the skidder trails on the hillsides. *(USFS)*

Photo taken in 1972, from the same point as the 1930's photo, showing the restorative ability of nature in recovering from the scalping of the land. *(Don Peters)*

in bunches, loaded, then transported. However, the technology involved in carrying out these procedures has changed so dramatically since early days that old-time woodsmen may well express surprise at the changes made. Instead of notching the tree 3 or 4 feet above the base with an axe, then felling with crosscut saw, fallers now notch and cut the tree close to the base, using a power chain saw. The butt of the tree is then marked (to identify the faller) and the branches are trimmed. The faller next measures off lengths to fit the log truck and the tree is bucked. (cut to lengths). A good faller, working in mature ponderosa pine and favorable terrain, would cut 40,000 board feet of timber a day.

Scalers follow the fallers, measuring the volume of wood cut. Every minute or so, the woods reverberate as another pine thumps to the forest floor. There is no sound of "timber!"—just the penetrating drones of the chain saws, a warning call "Hoe!" followed by a distinct creak as the tree momentarily resists gravity, then a crash as the upper branches smash through anything in their way. Heavy machinery is used to assemble the logs. Instead of the high wheels and horses and gopher men, "cats" and "skidders" quickly drag, push and lift the logs, stacking them in piles along the roadway. Instead of the giant steam-operated McGiffert loaders affixed to a rail, smaller mobile hydraulic and front-end loaders are used to move logs on to maneuverable trucks. For many years the latter have replaced the nostalgic rail engine and their line of flat cars. The hydraulic loader, deftly manipulated by a skilled operator, snatches up a 32-foot log as if it were a toothpick, rapidly whirls it over the bed of the truck and gently sets it in place.

The trucks are loaded with large diameter logs in about 10 minutes, or with smaller logs in about 18 minutes. Drivers check the weight and the distribution of weight on each of 3 axles by reading electronic scales. As soon as the logs are secured, the driver gives a short warning toot on the horn and starts moving the 76,000-pound load to Bend.

No sooner does one truck pull away when another backs into place. The loader's claws immediately pounce on the piggy-back trailer, snatch it up, set it on the ground and resume loading. Every two truck loads hold enough timber

Loading of log trucks by a mobile diesel-operated loader. Trucks, when loaded, haul up to 76,000 pounds of timber. Two such loads would produce enough lumber to build an average-size house. (Brooks-Scanlon)

The High Country has had its share of forest fires. Many visitors and newcomers to the area often do not recognize the explosive fire danger of the forests during the summer. Each season, valuable timber is lost to such fires. In addition, such fires ruin watersheds, cause aesthetic losses and destroy wildlife habitats. The Bridge Creek fire west of Bend (above) in July, 1979, is an example of such losses.

Logging the High Country

to provide lumber for an average-sized house. From the Sisters area, about 40 miles from Bend (depending on exact location of logging), each truck makes 4 trips to the mill every day. Two-way radios in the cabs of log trucks and company pickups give personnel instant communication as to the location of men and equipment.

But logging involves more than the work of fallers, scalers, cat operators, loaders and truckers. On U.S. Forest Service lands, bids are made, sales are awarded, roads are built, and areas where trees are to be cut are identified. Slash has to be disposed of by piling and burning; and on logged-over areas, the land is prepared for reforestation. Because natural revegetation is preferred, the forest is usually replanted with trees similar to those cut in the area. Otherwise, small seedlings from the U.S. Forest Service nursery near Bend are brought in for planting. Thus conservation is assured, with young forests replacing the old.

8.
Communities Along Highway 97

Highway 97

La Pine, Gilchrist and Crescent are three communities that straddle U.S. 97, the main north-south route through Central Oregon. In the southern part of Deschutes County and extending well into Klamath County, this highway is a straight road slicing through miles of lodgepole pine and, in places, ponderosa pine. It parallels, in part, an old Indian trail and travels by explorers Fremont, Wyeth and Abbot. Fremont, in 1843, journeyed along the west side of the Deschutes River. Abbot, in 1855, followed a well-established Indian trail. Meanwhile, in 1853, the Elliot cut-off party, seeking a route to the upper Willamette Valley, rested at Bend after hardships across the High Desert, then struck south, crossing the Little Deschutes near Crescent.

In 1864, the first wagon train, traveling what was later to become The Dalles—California Highway, carried supplies from Fort Dalles (on the Columbia River) to the Klamath Indian Reservation. The wagon train, led by Captain O. C. Applegate, was guarded by soldiers and Warm Springs scouts against possible attack by Chief Paulina and his marauding Snake Warriors. The wagon train camped in Bend adjacent to the Deschutes River (where Pioneer Park is now located) then continued south, a crew of axemen chopping a wagon path through "jackpines." For a major part of the journey an old Indian trail was followed. It took one month for the wagon train to make the trek from Bend to the Klamath Agency.

A north-south roadway had become established in 1910, passing east of Lava Butte, through Harper (south of the site of Sunriver), La Pine and Crescent. Seven years later, the road was made part of the Oregon Highway system, but travel conditions through the pine forests of south central Oregon were poor for many years. In summer, thick powdery pumice soil, once disturbed, sent clouds of choking dust into the air. In winter, the highway was buried by deep snows for long periods. Indeed, winter travel was sometimes by sleigh-drawn horses rather than wheels. Once the snows melted, the roads were even more impassable because of mud.

Thus, for many years, travel on The Dalles—California Highway, as it was later called, was often difficult. For example, in 1920, the first stage of the "season" arrived in Bend on March 12, after taking 24 hours for the trip from Klamath Falls via Crescent. In 1922, the first road trip of the year—by the stage between Klamath Falls and Bend—was not made until May and it took five days to complete the journey. Not only was travel south of Bend an adventure but, for a brief time, it was costly. On March 12, 1925, part of what was then called The Dalles—California Highway was declared a toll road. The tax was imposed to help pay for keeping the highway open all year so that auto stages could meet operating expenses.

Three toll gates were planned—one south of La Pine, one south of Crescent, and one at Beaver Marsh (south of Chemult). The legality of the road tax centered around an 1862 law whereby, in "Eastern" Oregon, which was largely unsettled at that time, the only means by which roads could be built and maintained was through revenue from road taxes. For example, road taxes were levied on the McKenzie Wagon Road at Cache Creek toll station and at Sherar's Bridge across the Deschutes River. Toll charges established on The Dalles—California Highway included 12½ cents for each sheep and hog, 50 cents for horses, mules, donkeys and milk cattle. A four-wheeled vehicle was charged $5, a two-wheeled vehicle $2. No toll was charged for footmen or for persons going to or from a funeral, election or church.

Those "going around the gate" and not paying were liable for three times the toll charge. Klamath County residents were excused from the toll unless they happened to cross into Deschutes County.

Bend and Crescent residents protested the tolls, feeling it would harm tourist business to and from Crater Lake. A meeting on March 23, 1925, resolved the issue—State of Oregon crews were put to work clearing the highway.

In the late 1930's, a completely new road between Bend and La Pine was built. Near Lava Butte the highway was moved east so it would not be inundated by water from the long-proposed Benham Falls Reservoir. In places such as the Lava River Caves State Park the old highway is still to be seen. Today, Highway 97 is the major artery linking Northern California with the Columbia River and eastern Washington State. Traffic counts just south of Bend and toward Sunriver reflect the increasing use of the highway. For example, in 1985, average daily traffic count just south of the Sunriver turnoff was 5000, compared to 1,950 in 1960. At the Bend city limits, 0.01 miles south of Cleveland Avenue, the average daily traffic count in 1985 was 20,700; in 1960 it was only 4,950. These figures compare with a count of 716 vehicles per day recorded at the south city limits on a busy August day in 1926.

La Pine

Thirty miles south of Bend, Highway 97 passes through La Pine, a small but bustling community. Observant travelers may note the variety of commercial activities and express surprise at the number. After all, whatever direction from which you enter La Pine, you see mostly miles of lodgepole pine and—except for Wickiup Junction, 2 miles north of La Pine—little in the way of development. Furthermore, immediately west of La Pine, an extensive but uninhabited meadow further isolates the community. The question is who supports the 130 plus businesses, many of them new? The answer is the 9000 or more people who live in the La Pine area, plus hundreds more who reside in the La Pine

Aerial view of La Pine. Although the commercial area clings to Highway 97, most residents of La Pine are secluded among the miles of pine forests or along the Little Deschutes River (background). *(The Bulletin)*

The Gilchrist Timber Company mill started operations in Gilchrist in 1938. The community, one of the last company towns left in Oregon, employs 240, owns about 86,000 acres of land, and manufactures lumber from various species of pine. The company-owned lands are capable of producing about 25 percent of the mill's needs; the bulk comes from various forest-service lands including the Deschutes, Fremont and Winema. Modernization of the plant took place in 1969 and increased annual production from 40 to 50 million board feet.

service area—Crescent, Gilchrist, Fort Rock, Silver Lake and Christmas Valley.

In many respects La Pine is a unique community. If all the built-up area roundabout were incorporated it would be the third largest city in Central Oregon, after Bend and Redmond. Although most of its growth has occurred since the 1960's, the townsite dates back to 1910. From a climatic point of view, La Pine ranks as one of the coldest reporting stations in Oregon for a large part of the year and has the distinction (?) of being one of the coldest stations in the United States during the summer months, with frosts likely any night. Ironically, one of the earliest advertised economic activities in La Pine was agriculture!

La Pine is located in the extreme southern part of Deschutes County and that, in itself, has created political problems. Many of the community residents live in subdivisions not only remote from the county seat, Bend, but several miles from the La Pine business district—separated by geography and occasionally by a poorly maintained road system. Historically, as we have seen, accessibility to the southern part of Central Oregon has often been difficult.

The townsite of La Pine was platted in February, 1910. However, the forerunner of La Pine was the settlement of Rosland, 2 miles north. The first post office in the area was established in 1897 by B. J. Pengra, 3 miles north of Rosland on the old Bend-Silver Lake stage road. In 1907, when the area was part of the old Cascade National Forest, Rosland was the location of a ranger station. In 1910, the various businesses at Rosland, including the post office, were moved to La Pine. The birth of La Pine meant the death of Rosland.

In those early years, La Pine was projected to be the principal city of southern Deschutes County. Playing a major role in the development of La Pine were Alfred Aya, James Gleason and Bill Riley. According to McArthur, Aya named the community La Pine because of the miles of pine trees in the area.[80] For many years the spelling Lapine (one word) was used but in 1951, on orders from Washington D.C., the post office changed the spelling to La Pine. The post office received many requests from stamp collectors for cancellation of stamps issued for the final day of Lapine and for the first day of La Pine.

In 1912, La Pine was heavily advertised along with other burgeoning communities in Central Oregon including homestead settlements in the High Desert. The town was described as the trading, milling and shipping point of the Upper Deschutes Valley. In a July, 1912, expanded issue on the economic development of Central Oregon, *The Bulletin* made special references to the agricultural potential of the La Pine area. This is surprising as, today, those who know the area well would be the first to admit that agriculture is a poor risk because of an unfavorable climate. Even so, in 1912, newspaper reports focused on the importance of dairying (the introduction of purebred Holstein and Guernsey stock), beef cattle, poultry raising and the growing of oats, wheat and barley, using dry-farming methods. Land was described as level and free from rocks, with rich, deep volcanic ash soils.

A Carey Act project, later known as the Morson Project, was expected to bring water to 28,000 acres of land in the La Pine area by 1914. However, a word of caution crept in as *The Bulletin* warned prospective settlers that the "territory is new and requires in addition to courage and hard work, at least a small surplus of ready cash to keep things going until there is an income from the land."[81] Besides the agricultural potential of the La Pine area, other resources mentioned included water power from nearby Pringle Falls, the clear, sparkling water from shallow wells for domestic purposes, the huge timber reserves, and the nearby recreational opportunities, including fishing at Crescent, Odell and Davis lakes. The newly discovered hot springs at East Lake were reputed to have given bathers some "remarkable cures from rheumatism."[82]

La Pine was heavily advertised all over the continent and inquiries were received from such diverse places as Maine, Canada, Alaska, Mexico, and the Caribbean. Land was listed at $36 an acre and lots in La Pine were offered by the La Pine Townsite Company for as little as $50. The first blow to affect La Pine was a reversal of the plans James J. Hill had to extend the railroad south of Bend. After the construction of several miles of main canals, money for the irrigation project was lacking, and by 1912, progress on the irrigation scheme ceased, at least temporarily.

In 1919, the Morson Project was resumed by Frank W. Tomes, who was prepared to spend $30,000 to complete it. Tomes's plans included digging 17 miles of canals, constructing head gates and repairing the previously dug canal banks. It was anticipated that 10,000 acres of land would be irrigated by 1920. By that time, La Pine had a bank, livery stable, hotel (Riley Hotel), dairy, mercantile store, meat market, grocery and even its own newspaper, the La Pine *Inter-Mountain*. In 1922, this paper had a circulation of 627, although the community had a population of 40. The newspaper was widely distributed with copies sent by auto stage to Silver Lake, Fort Rock, Crescent and Fort Klamath. However, the irrigation project was never completed and even if it had been, the short growing season would have precluded all but the hardiest root vegetables.

In the following years several of the businesses in La Pine burned down and the long-promised railroad had not yet materialized. The nearby outdoor recreational opportunities, especially hunting and fishing, were excellent but these assets were not capitalized on until after World War II. Thus, for many years, La Pine remained a small rural community.

In 1951, small (1¼ acre) parcels of land were offered (by Burdette and Pearl Lechner for $100) as sites for summer cabins. A multitude of land developments followed, some of them preceding land-use controls. For example, one tract of land adjacent to the Little Deschutes River west of La Pine was, in fact, too close to the stream. In spring, high water inundated some of the lots that had been purchased during the dry part of the year! Beginning in the 1960's, septic-tank permits were required before home construction could begin. Only then did some property owners discover that because of soil conditions their land could not be built upon.

By 1963, approximately 900 people lived in the La Pine area. This number doubled by 1971 and by 1987, some 2750 families, over 9000 people, lived in the area, making it the second largest community in Deschutes County. Midstate Electric Cooperative reported 7000 meters in use in the Sunriver-La Pine area, about 55 percent of them at full-time residences. Although perhaps 50 percent of the residents of La Pine are retirees, many younger families, seeking the kind of living offered in a rural setting and access to year-round recreation and clean air, have moved into the area. So, although early dreams of homesteaders were shattered, new "homesteaders" have come to "file their claims" in this part of the Central Oregon high country.

Gilchrist

Of all the communities in Central Oregon, Gilchrist best typifies what could be characterized as a "logging town." Indeed, since the Kinzua plant in Wheeler County ceased operations in 1978, Gilchrist is one of the last company logging towns left in Oregon. It is situated on U.S. 97 about 45 miles south of Bend and 15 miles south of La Pine. Motorists using that highway, having traveled many miles of straight road through a long uninterrupted avenue of pine trees, cannot help noticing the small but neatly arranged houses and the cluster of commercial buildings—all painted the same shade of brown. Gilchrist, along with its twin community, Crescent, provides needed services to travelers moving north or south through Central Oregon.

It was in January, 1937, that plans were announced for a sawmill to be built just north of Crescent. However, land to supply the mill was acquired in the early 1900's. Prior to moving to Central Oregon, the Gilchrists had operated in Laurel, Mississippi and, before that, in Michigan and Wisconsin. The construction of the town and the sawmill began in the spring of 1938. The sawmill started operating and the shopping center was completed by the following year. The original Gilchrist post office was located in the company cookhouse!

The townsite at Gilchrist was laid out in a magnificent forest setting. The commercial section, fronting U.S. 97 yet nicely set back from the highway, consists of several different architectural-styles buildings which offer a surprising array of services. The restaurant sports a modern Norwegian style with a prominent clock tower. Another building uses an Alpine Chalet motif. Included in the cluster of commercial businesses are a spacious supermarket, barber shop, beauty parlor, movie house, bowling alley and post office, all leased from the Gilchrist Company but under private management.

Gilchrist Company workers' houses, 140 of them, are nestled under mature ponderosa pine on gently sloping land east of the commercial section. Small Cape-Cod type cottages are clustered along the lower section of the paved roads. New England salt-box houses of the supervisory personnel dominate the residential section on higher terrain. All the houses have the uniform "Gilchrist" brown paint which blends well with the forest setting. Maintenance of the houses is provided by the company, which has its own plumber, electrician and carpenters. Any additions to the houses have to receive company approval. Many of the residents have put in small lawns and some have fenced their property. Rent at the company-owned houses is modest.

When the Gilchrist Company moved from Laurel, Mississippi, half of the company employees were Southerners. By the end of World War II, there were few original transfers left. However, the company president, Frank R. Gilchrist, and the vice president, Charles Shotts, have been with the company since its move to Gilchrist.

Crescent

Crescent adjoins Gilchrist and one may suppose that together they form Central Oregon's only "twin communities." However, they are not identical twins. While Gilchrist is a company town with the layout and buildings conforming to company standards, Crescent reflects individual choice. Gilchrist dates back to 1937, but Crescent is much older. Both communities, however, are adjacent to the Little Deschutes River, a stream that adds an aesthetic dimension.

The Pacific Railroad Survey party noted the attractiveness of the Crescent area and selected it as a campsite on August 25, 1855. Abbot noted in his diary:

> The dense clouds of dust raised by our animals from
> the ashy soil were suffocating. After riding about 18.7
> miles from camp, we suddenly emerged from the
> dense forest, and found ourselves in the beautiful
> grassy bottom of the Des Chutes river. It was here a
> fine stream about thirty feet in width, and fordable
> although the current was rapid and the bed stony. We
> immediately encamped. . . . The supply of grass to-
> night was abundant, and of fine quality; the water
> was cold, and the position in every respect excellent
> for a camp. Large numbers of delicious trout, marked
> with red longitudinal stripes, were caught with great
> ease in the river.[83]

Crescent was originally to have been on the junction where rails extending south from Bend met those crossing the Cascades from the Willamette Valley. The community was initially to have been named Odell after the nearby lake bearing that name. Since Odell was already in existence near Hood River, promoters then selected the name of another lake, Crescent, only 15 miles distant.

In 1912, *The Bulletin* noted the assets of Crescent: the excellent wagon roads, the expected railroad through Crescent, the vast timber resources, including the use of the "jack pine" for railroad ties and the grazing lands for sheep and cattle. The paper also noted that two years before (1910) the townsite had been simply a ranch with a house, a small school building, a barn and a few outbuildings. In 1912, there were four stores, including a drug store; also a hotel, livery barn, blacksmith shop, saloon pool hall, a U.S. forester's office, and several residences. The school district had raised $3,000 toward a new school building.[84]

Thomas Murphy, in a journey from Crater Lake to Bend in 1916, briefly described Crescent and the landscapes along the north-south highway in the area:

> Nearly the whole distance it [the road] runs through
> forests, chiefly the worthless lodgepole or jackpine,
> which grows almost as thickly as they can stand. We
> ran through those uninteresting trees for more than
> fifty miles without a single village or even a ranch
> house to break the monotony. It was as wild and lone-

ly a country as we had so far traversed and yet in a little shack by the road we passed a station of the Bell Telephone Company—a reminder of the wonderful ramifications of the wires of this great organization.

Crescent, about seventy miles from Fort Klamath, the only village on the road, has a dozen scattering houses, a store or two, the omnipresent sheet-iron garage, and a big wooden hotel. For some distance about the town the jack pines were being cleared and preparations made to till the land, though little had actually been done as yet in the way of producing crops.[85]

Today, in Crescent, a scattering of roadside businesses serves local needs and those of travelers on U.S. 97. The Crescent District ranger office and forest service houses, with their standardized shape, size and color, contrast with the random nature of the rest of the community. Old buildings mingle with new ones. Glistening mobile homes are located close to older frame buildings. To combat the long, cold winters with snow depths representative of the high country, woodpiles are common in the residential sections, and as it is with La Pine and Gilchrist, curls of smoke from chimneys prove the popularity and need for wood stoves.

Gilchrist and Crescent, set amid the forests of south Central Oregon, are quite isolated. In recent years, La Pine has been able to supply certain services, including legal, dental, and medical, that otherwise were obtainable only in Bend, 50 miles away, or Klamath Falls, 98 miles distant. Heavy snows and an almost non-existent frost-free season sometimes makes life arduous for the residents of these three communities. However, it is the same somewhat harsh weather conditions that seem to foster community spirit often lacking in larger settlements.

9.

The Sisters Country

The Sisters Country is distinctive and one of the most attractive parts of Central Oregon. It includes Black Butte, a prominent volcano that dominates the skyline northwest of Sisters; the Metolius River Country north of Black Butte; and Black Butte Ranch, a well-planned community "designed with nature in mind." The town of Sisters is the focal point for this region that encompasses forests, lakes, meadows, and a unique spring-fed river—all with an alpine backdrop.

Sisters

In 1905, Sisters was described as a "little town situated in the midst of the most delightful pine forests to be found anywhere. It is only a short distance from the foothills of the three snow-capped peaks known as the Three Sisters, from which the town takes its name. The stately pines shade the village from the burning summer sun and protect it from the cold blasts of mid winter."[86] In that year, the town, which had been platted July 10, 1901, by the Smith brothers, Alex and Robert, had two general stores, a hotel, blacksmith shop, saloon, real estate office, livery barn and a splendid schoolhouse, costing $1300.[87] Four miles west of town, a sawmill with a capacity of 5000 feet of lumber a day was operating, using water of 20 horsepower taken from Pole Creek.

The geographical setting remains as it was early in the twentieth century but, as elsewhere, the impacts of man on the land and technological changes in communication have, over the years, modified the natural landscapes in and near Sisters. The town is situated on the main highway from Central Oregon to the Willamette Valley. First, the McKenzie Highway, then the Santiam Highway, both funneled traffic to and from Central Oregon through Sisters. In the early twentieth century, a stage from Prineville reached Sisters every afternoon on its way to Eugene. Traffic and movements of herds of sheep and cattle into the high Cascades passed through Sisters because it was on the direct route between Tetherow Crossing on the Deschutes River, north of Redmond, and the junction of the two mountain passes.[88]

The story of Sisters actually began in 1865, the year when Captain Charles La Follette and a contingent of Company A 1st Oregon volunteers crossed the Cascades from Polk County with the intention of subduing Indian uprisings in Eastern Oregon. The troops never did take part in any military action but, rather than recrossing the Cascades, spent the winter of 1865-66 at Camp Polk. Camp Polk was located on Squaw Creek, about 3 miles northeast of Sisters. This creek, known as Why-chus by earlier-day Indians, is the only stream that flows through Sisters from the High Country to the west.

As an establishment, Camp Polk was a wasted effort, but it survived to start a sort of community for later settlers and it gave a geographical name to the area. A post office and store were established at Camp Polk by settler Samuel M. W. Hindman in 1875, five years after the homesteader and his family settled there. For a while, Camp Polk post office was made a stop-off point on the newly contracted mail route which ran over the McKenzie Pass from Eugene to Prineville. At the time of Hindman's settlement, the area between the Deschutes River and the Cascades was basically unoccupied, only four families living in the region in 1880. Eight years later, Camp Polk post office was moved into Sisters, by then a small but growing town.

The site of Camp Polk, sign-posted from Sisters and identified by a rather crude weather-worn sign, still attracts history buffs. Rustic ranch buildings and a weathered rail fence now mark the site of the camp. Gentle hills, studded with pine trees on the west, slope down to the broad meadow where soldiers once paraded. The last of the eight cabins that formed the camp buildings was torn down in the 1940's. On an arid knoll overlooking the parade ground, where a trimmed pine tree stood as a flag pole, is a graveyard with markers of early pioneers and of recent deaths. Beyond the graveyard the landscape is more open and is typical of the juniper lands farther east.

While history characterizes the site of Camp Polk, nearby Sisters has developed into one of the most interesting communities in Central Oregon. The sheep-traffic over the Santiam Wagon Road was responsible for Sisters' initial growth after 1880, when herds of sheep (from Antelope and Shaniko on the grasslands of north Central Oregon) were driven into the high pasture lands of the Cascades. Sisters, the only settlement between Prineville and the mountains, picked up considerable trade, supplying stockmen as well as other travelers passing through.

In 1908, the Forest Service closed some of the High Country pastures to sheep grazing, but by this time cattle raising had become an important industry, centering around the vast holdings of the Black Butte Land and Livestock Company. Sawmills operated on Squaw Creek in 1890 and on Pole Creek two years later.

Not until 1914 was a lumber mill established in Sisters. For years, lumber continued as the main industry. In addition, the U.S. Forest Service and the Barclay Logging Company were major employers of the Sisters area. The Brooks-Scanlon Company (Bend) acquired considerable land to the west, which had previously been the Jim Hill land granted earlier for a railroad over the Cascades. Although the railroad was never completed, alternate sections were given for construction of a road instead. Land ownership patterns west of Sisters are a checkerboard, with alternate sections belonging to Brooks-Scanlon and the U.S. Forest Service.

The last mill in the Sisters area closed in 1963, resulting in a loss of jobs and an outward migration of Sisters residents. For a number of years, it appeared that the town of Sisters might shrivel to a ghost town, leaving only a skeleton of

View looking west along the main highway in Sisters in the 1940's. The photo indicates that the community served travelers at that time, although at a more leisurely pace than since the mid 1970's. *(Tillie Wilson)*

The decision to adopt 1880-style architecture for commercial buildings in Sisters has helped revitalize the economy of the city. The change has created a "sense of place." Shoppers can leisurely browse in stores which feature antiques, gifts, and hand-crafted goods—some of which are made locally.

service activities to meet needs of the passing motorists. Today, however, after an architectural transfusion, the town of Sisters has been revived.

Curiously enough, the revival came through a unique plan to make the business section "look old." In 1972, a comprehensive plan was initiated, prompted by increased development in the area. By 1974, the planning commission and a small citizen advisory committee had established a formal list of objectives, stressing the importance of tourism and related industries being attracted by the "old west" theme, while attempting to preserve the city environment. The architectural theme, which has now been encouraged for several years by the Sisters Chamber of Commerce, features 1880-style fronts on most of the stores. Brooks Resources, developers of Black Butte Ranch and other smaller subdivisions in the Sisters area, have given some financial assistance, but the project, initiated by the community, has been achieved without federal or other public funding.

New buildings and old have been westernized, and Cascade, the main street of Sisters, looks like a part of the Old West. The result of the changes has been far reaching. Residents of Sisters can take pride in their community; it now has a unique identity. Tourists and shoppers from Central Oregon and elsewhere are drawn to its unusual variety of specialty shops. In some instances, the handicrafts which are sold in the stores are also manufactured right there. Even names of the stores invite leisurely browsing — The Hen's Tooth, Scents and Non-Scents, Cook's Nook, Wildfire Pottery, and The Stitching Post. In addition, Sisters now boasts two dentist offices, a part-time doctor, two veterinary clinics, two law offices, and two banks.

During the summer tourist season, the main street through Sisters is often bumper-to-bumper traffic. The surrounding residential and recreational developments, such as Black Butte Ranch, Indian Ford Ranch and others have no commercial facilities and generate business for Sisters. Then, because of the newly found popularity of Sisters, more people have moved to the community. It grew from a population of 161 in 1970 to 762 by mid-1977. Incorporated in 1946, it has a character that gives it a "sense of place." Ponderosa pines tower over parts of the residential areas, especially south of the main thoroughfare. Here and there, between the pines, are glimpses of the glacier-clad Sisters mountains, which gave the town its name. These peaks assume different identities during the course of a day and throughout the changing seasons. During the winter months the peaks hide behind dark storm clouds that bring the needed snow to the High Country.

Residential areas of Sisters, seemingly unaffected by the western decor of the business district, consist of a mixture of old frame cabins, ranch-style houses, modern condominiums, and glistening mobile homes. Outside town, the pine forests have been cleared on three sides, creating meadow lands that open up wide panoramas of the Cascades. It is the town's pine-forest setting, its location adjacent to vast forest service lands and to the Cascades, and its attractive climate that combine to make the area a favorite place to vacation or to live.

Several ranches border Sisters. One of these, the Patterson Ranch, the Pattersons established a working ranch involving approximately 500 llamas, and 100 (Polish) Arabian horses. Why was this ranch located at Sisters? Dick and Kay Patterson, traveling through Central Oregon in 1968, passed the Bailey Ranch and noted the resemblance of the landscape of the Sisters area to parts of New Zealand, where they had visited.

Other factors prompting the Pattersons to move from Richfield, Ohio, to Sisters included the attractive climate, the excellent water, good porous soils, and prospective business opportunities. The Pattersons fly in Arabians from Poland by charter airliner to supplement their stock. Their llama herd is the largest on the North American continent. Hundreds of tourists are attracted to the rather unexpected sight of llamas and camels grazing the 350-acre meadowlands, virtually in the shadow of the Three Sisters. A deluxe barn—adorned with a clock tower housing a 13,000-square-foot covered arena and show ring—is a prominent landmark on the ranch.

Indian Ford Ranch

Those who enjoy the Sisters country have a choice of several recreational and residential areas within a few miles' distance. Some of these, such as Tollgate and Wagon Trail, are hidden away in the pine forest. Barclay Place is perched on pine and juniper-covered McKinney Butte overlooking Sisters and providing panoramic views of the Cascade Range.

Indian Ford Ranch, 3 miles north of Sisters, has an enviable setting, an interesting history, and planning policies and standards that should be the goals of all developers. Indian Ford is a small and secluded stream that flows northeast out of Black Butte Ranch, slices through thickly forested land past the Indian Ford campground adjacent to the Santiam Highway, then creates its own ecosystem within an elongated, poorly drained area. Indian Ford meanders through the meadow in the Indian Ford Ranch property, loops around the south side of McKinney Butte, then joins Squaw Creek.

Indian Ford Meadow, but one of several meadows near to Sisters, is 3 miles long and about ½ mile wide. Bordering the meadow are quaking aspen and willows, deciduous trees which add color to the evergreen ponderosa pine and blue-green Western Juniper that crowd the meadow. During late spring and early summer the meadow becomes bright green; following fall frosts, the willows and aspens turn a golden yellow.

Indian Ford Ranch lies in the transition zone between ponderosa pine, typical of the High Country, and the Western Juniper that is representative of the arid lands of Central Oregon. The western part of the ranch properties is predominantly pine; the eastern is largely juniper. The latter is quite arid. Here vegetation includes sagebrush, rabbitbrush and bitterbrush; the fragrance and yellow coloring of these species is representative of the High Desert lands. There is also a surprising array of wildflowers—goldstars, red dwarf mimulus, white mountain lilies, golden sunflowers, blue lupines and the bright orange-red Indian paintbrush. The nearby skyline is a breathtaking panorama of snow-capped peaks.

Originally, Indian Ford Ranch was an old homestead, the Willow Ranch, which had been settled in the 1860's. Ancient Indian trails crossed the creek; hence the name Indian Ford. The Pacific Railroad Survey party passed through here on September 23, 1855:

> Today we followed the old trail to the "black butte," where we found a paper on one of the trees, stating that the main party was in camp on Why-chus creek, about seven miles towards the south. We struck through the woods, and soon saw the white tents in an open prairie covered with grass and bordered by fine timber. Near it, the brook Que-y-ee, after spreading out into a meadow, disappeared. This little opening, amid forest-clad mountains and grand snow peaks, furnished a camping place, the wild beauty of which I have seldom seen equaled.[89]

Today, Indian Ford Ranch is a recreational and residential community geared to those who enjoy western living, including riding and a chance to raise your own cattle. Riding trails link the corrals, meadows and adjacent Forest Service lands. Both cattle and horses are maintained on the property for a monthly fee. Of the 1700 acres, 300 of meadowland are dedicated for agricultural and recreational purposes, to be preserved in their natural state. Homesites, each an acre or more, surround the meadow. Some are located in the forest lands, some are on the west side of the pine and juniper ridge overlooking the meadows, while others are east of the ridge and, in some instances, have views across the Central Oregon plateau to the Ochocos.

Black Butte

Black Butte is one of the most easily recognized landmarks in all the High Country. Even seen at a distance, from Pilot Butte in Bend or from the juniper lands near Redmond, its isolated, symmetrical cone stands out clearly and darkly against the taller Cascade skyline. Although it was originally named Pivot Mountain by early pioneers,

The Patterson Arabian Ranch west of Sisters lies in the shadows of the Three Sisters. This ranch, one of several in the Sisters area, helps create a more rural character to the community. Besides raising Arabian horses, the Patterson Ranch has llamas.

The meadow at Indian Ford Ranch has been retained in its natural setting. Homesites, many with spectacular mountain vistas, occupy adjacent pine and juniper lands. *(Wm. Van Allen)*

engineer Lt. Henry L. Abbot used the name Black Butte when reporting on his 1855 explorations for a railroad route in Central Oregon.

Black Butte has long been used as a weather prophet. Pioneers knew when it was safe to cross the Cascades and gardeners knew when spring had come and it was safe to plant vegetables by the amount and location of the snow on Black Butte. Its high peak has also served as a vantage point for forest-fire watch since about 1912, when the summit of the butte was linked by telephone line with a nearby ranger station.[90] A summit fire-lookout tower was completed in 1934. Materials for the 83-foot tower were carried up by pack string or hauled by teams.[91] A trail up Black Butte was constructed in the fall of 1908. The spectacular view from the summit (elevation 6,415 feet) is worth the climb.

Black Butte stands guard over the residents of Black Butte Ranch and the Metolius River-Camp Sherman country. With its broad base, symmetrical shape and huge bulk, it is an impressive sight from either area. Furthermore, Black Butte's aesthetic appeal is heightened in the fall and winter seasons. Fall brings out a colorful display on the lower slopes and on the north slopes when the western larch, whose summer green is masked by the ponderosa pine, show their golden glory before losing their needles to the winds which herald winter. On occasion in fall, a cold front, whose origin was the cool waters of the North Pacific, brings early snows to the upper slopes of Black Butte and, if coinciding with the colorful display by the western larch below, creates a scene which is photogenic, to say the least.

Throughout winter, Black Butte's snow line marks the alternate passage of cold fronts and warm fronts which move through the High Country. The lofty summit is, for the most part, locked up in an arctic-like landscape while the lower forested slopes alternately reflect the icy grips of winter and the surprising mildness associated with lower elevations to the lee of the Cascades. A receding snow line in late spring is watched by old-timers who note the butte's barometer before planting their gardens. Certainly Black Butte has a character of its own and greatly contributes to the landscapes of the Sisters Country.

Black Butte Ranch

Some motorists, traveling the road that slices through the pine forest at the base of Black Butte, about 10 miles west of Sisters, may miss the sign unobtrusively located at the entrance to Black Butte Ranch. The entrance road divides after a short distance. To the left, a stable and paddock cater to horse lovers. Visitors seeking the ranch's restaurant follow the road to the right through a grove of quaking aspen, which display their brilliant yellow in the fall. Not until the motorist almost swings back to the main highway (U.S. 20) does he finally discover his goal. It is almost as if Black Butte Ranch wants to remain secluded. It was April, 1969, when Brooks Resources, Bend, purchased Black Butte Ranch and announced plans for land developments on the property. To many old-timers it seemed incredible that one of the oldest ranches in early Central Oregon would be anything but a place for stock raising. The history of this ranch goes back before the turn of the century. The Black Butte Land and Livestock Company was incorporated on March 14, 1902. The company's holdings at the time included the old Allingham Ranch on the Metolius River and the Dry Hollow Ranch. However, on what is now Black Butte Ranch property, a small cabin was built on Glaze Meadows as early as 1881. Here, Till Glaze ran horses and some cattle during the summer months.

Today, part of the Glaze Meadow is included in the Black Butte Ranch. In 1957, the 577-acre ranch, at the southern base of Black Butte, was purchased for $75,000 by Mr. and Mrs. Howard V. Morgan of Monmouth, from the estate of Stewart S. Lowery. In 1979, $75,000 would not purchase any two of the lots in the community development. Black Butte Ranch now covers 1800 acres, consolidating land secured from Brooks-Scanlon, Inc., another landowner, and the original 600 acres.

Since homesites were first put on the market in 1970, sales have been as planned. Indeed, by 1987 all of the 1250 homesites had been sold. Black Butte Ranch is considered by many to be one of the finest examples of creating a large recreational community and, at the same time, not destroying the natural environment that had first made the area so attractive. Cattle and horses still graze the meadowland and dense forests still surround the open meadows. And ranch headquarters, for many years visible from the Santiam Highway, still stands though its function has changed. First and foremost, Brooks Resources developed a master plan that has applied Ian McHarg's principle of "design with nature." All buildings at the ranch are governed by the master-plan concept, where maximum protection for the natural beauty at Black Butte Ranch is paramount.

The large, open meadow has been preserved by placing it in community ownership. Furthermore, the meadow now supports about 500 cattle and horses, more animals than before Black Butte Ranch became a resort. Wildlife habitat in the meadow has increased. Some of the meadow, previously a swamp, has been drained and used for a polo field. Springs gush forth about 24 million gallons of water a day. Because of planned hydraulic studies and dredging, water flow downstream from the ranch on Indian Ford Creek has been increased. All buildings at Black Butte Ranch must be approved by an architectural review committee which allows flexibility with the design but requires that all materials used be compatible with the natural surroundings. Any transplanting of plant materials has to be approved. "Mow-type lawn" are considered "not congruent with the natural vegetation" and are discouraged, and fences must use natural wood materials.

Where higher density condominiums are clustered, several design features typify the master-plan concept. Enclosed parking areas are in the interior of the project. Chimneys are painted natural color and outside lights are screened from view. Even basketball backboards are painted natural colors.

A single road winds around the meadows but innumerable cul-de-sacs leading from this peripheral road provide privacy and tranquility for homeowners. While this peripheral road, for the most part, leisurely twists and turns through forest groves, here and there are vistas of snow-capped peaks or conical Black Butte that dominates the northern skyline.

Black Butte, a 6,415-foot volcano frosted by a mid-fall snowstorm, stands as a sentinel over golfers driving the lush fairways at the Black Butte Ranch golf course. The ranch, designed to preserve the natural environment, offers property owners a variety of recreational facilities including golf, riding, tennis, swimming, and bicycle pathways.

The Allingham Guard Station in earlier years. Established in 1890, Allingham Ranch served as a post office from 1893 to 1896. The ranch house, used as a forest-service ranger station from about 1906, was removed in the late 1960's. *(Kitty Warner)*

It is fitting that most of the roads bearing the names of flora—lupines, snowbrush, foxtail, hyacinth, etc.—reflect one of the important landscape features on the ranch. Because of its location near the foothills of the Cascades and certain topographical features—lava ridges, swales, glacial deposits and low-lying swampy areas—there is considerable variety of flora at Black Butte Ranch. The ranch buildings are actually integrated into a ponderosa pine forest. Willows grow along streams; white-barked aspen border the meadow, while manzanita, buckbrush, and bitterbrush provide ground cover in wooded areas. It is these forest areas that absorb and seclude the growing weekend and summer population.

Many recreational facilities have been designed for property owners and their guests. Two golf courses, tennis courts, swimming pools, miles of bike paths, stables, and a youth recreation hall are at the ranch, but the golf courses and the lodge restaurant and bar are the only recreational facilities open to the public. The 18-hole golf course, completed in 1972, has to be one of the most inspiring in the West. Each hole seems to face a different mountain view. The Black Butte Ranch Lodge restaurant has a reputation for fine food. Dinner reservations, especially for weekends and all summer months, are a must. Dining is located on two levels, each featuring views across the meadow to the Three Sisters and Mt. Washington.

In sum, no single feature makes Black Butte Ranch as attractive as it is. Careful planning, consideration for the environment which nature generously endowed, and providing a place to relax and sooth nerves that have become taut in the urban world—all contribute to the unique Black Butte Ranch atmosphere.

Metolius River Valley

Metolius Valley is located north of Black Butte, tucked away in a predominantly forested landscape about 5 miles from U.S. 20. The most accessible part of the valley extends from the headwaters of the Metolius River almost due north for 10 miles. Green Ridge, an aptly named uplifted block, rises 2000 feet over the eastern side of the valley. Black Butte, which geologically played an important part in the creation of the landscapes of the Metolius River Valley, towers 3400 feet above the southern end of the valley. The valley floor is about 3 miles across at its widest but as the Metolius rushes north toward its junction with the Deschutes River, it is constricted to nothing more than a narrow defile.

The valley lies just a few miles east of the Cascades and although it is the "sunny side" of the crest, because of its nearness to the mountains, it is in the ponderosa pine belt. In addition, western larch (locally called tamaracks) and firs and, in wet spots, aspen and willow add variety to the natural vegetation. On nearby Green Ridge, there is also incense cedar, white pine and spruce.

The volcanic Cascades discharge large amounts of run-off into underground channels feeding countless springs that provide an almost constant flow of water into the Metolius River and its tributaries. This accounts for the several lush meadows that stay green all summer. The rapid flow of the Metolius and the small creeks flowing into it from the Cascade foothills to the west means that there are few suitable breeding places for mosquitoes, an insect that is often the despoiler of recreational areas which are otherwise blessed by the presence of water. The Metolius is very photogenic. The adjacent green meadows open up views of the nearby Cascade peaks rising over the forested foothills. Because these mountains are so close to the valley, their stature seems accentuated. In particular, Mt. Jefferson's cathedral-like spire and the jagged, eroded remnants of Three Fingered Jack are only 18 and 10 miles respectively from the headwaters of the Metolius River, a clear stream unspoiled and largely unpolluted by man. Like the Deschutes, the Metolius is a river of changing moods. For the most part, its waters rush headlong through pine forests, but in its upper reaches it bides its time through the meadows mentioned above.

The Metolius is famous for its rainbow trout stocked from Wizard Falls Fish Hatchery, 5 miles north of Camp Sherman. Upstream from "Bridge 99" (9 miles north of Camp Sherman), the stream is restricted to fly fishing only. Camping, as well as fishing, attracts many recreationists to the valley. The U.S. Forest Service operates ten campgrounds which border the Metolius north of Camp Sherman. Even some of the campground names are inviting—Pine Rest, Smiling River, River Island, Pioneer Ford, Camp Sherman. Each campground, located under tall ponderosa pines, has the river as a "back door," so each campground has the soothing sound of wind moving through upper branches of the pines and of water tumbling and gurgling in its continuous path toward the ocean.

Several resorts in the Metolius River Valley cater to those who wish to rent housekeeping cottages or just furnished cabins. Most of the resorts have been established for many years and have earned a reputation for providing an informal western atmosphere in rustic but clean units. Many of the clientele return to their favorite resort year after year. Even in summer, nights in the Metolius River Valley are usually cool, and it is not uncommon to find guests relaxing in the evening in front of the flickering lights of a log-burning fire.

Some 90 percent of the land in the valley belongs to the U.S. Forest Service; the acreage devoted to resorts and homesites is minimal. Only one modest-sized subdivision, Metolius Meadows, is located in the valley. Even here, forest service property surrounds the meadows on three sides. Approval of this development came after heated debate as to the environmental impact the subdivision would have on the hydrology of the spring-fed waters of the area. Nature has been benevolent to the valley and has left a legacy that includes one of the most beautiful settings in Oregon, and man has generally left this legacy unspoiled. That is how the residents of the valley, few in number but collectively strong in their opinion, want the valley to stay.

One of the earliest descriptions of the Metolius River area was by Captain John C. Fremont who, in December, 1843, noted that the clear waters of the swift-flowing Metolius River were difficult to ford. He also noted that his Indian guide informed him that it was "salmon waters." In September, 1855, the Pacific Railroad Survey, headed by Lieutenant Henry Larcom Abbot, searching for possible railroad routes in the Cascades and adjacent foothills, mentioned the name Mpto-ly-as. Settlement in the valley dates back to 1881 when early settlers engaged in farming of some type. The first post office in the area was established as early as 1888. At that time, the post office was known as Matoles. At first, the post office was on Lake Creek; then it was moved twice, the second and last move being to the Allingham Ranch where Mrs. Margaret J. Allingham was the postmistress from 1893 to 1896. After that time, the office was discontinued.[92]

The Allinghams lived on the ranch from 1890 till 1900, during which time the ground was cultivated, producing hay for cattle and sheep, which were pastured in the Jefferson Park area during the summer. The meadow adjacent to the house was irrigated by water run by ditch from Lake Creek. At that time, supplies came from Prineville, requiring four days' travel. Later, mail was sent weekly by saddle horse from Prineville to Camp Polk. In 1900, the Allinghams sold the homestead to a Mr. Alley who conveyed the title of the property to the government. The first use of the Allingham house by the government was for the first Sisters Ranger Station, occupied by Ranger Perry A. South about 1906. During a remodeling in 1938, walls of the house were found to have been papered with newspapers, once in 1902 and again in 1908.

In early days, cattlemen used the government range land for summer grazing, when cowboys could be seen guiding their herds through the countryside. Later the grazing permits from the U.S. Forest Service were given to sheepmen; then many bands of sheep would slowly make their way through to the summer pastures in the High Cascades.

Around 1916, the first tract of government land for leasing summer homes was opened up by the forest service. Farmers from Sherman County followed signs from the Sisters highway which read "Camp Sherman"—hence the origin of the name of the community of Camp Sherman. This name became official in 1923 when the post office, operated by Frank Leithauser, used it. The Sherman County residents built cottages beside the Metolius River before harvest time, then returned after their wheat had been threshed and sold. Today, 108 leaseholders in six designated tracts pay a yearly lease of $300-400 for their property. Whenever a lease sells, the improvements are transferred along with the lease, but many of the leasees are second and third generations of the first Sherman County owners.

The development of parts of the Metolius River Valley for resorts and ranches goes back nearly three quarters of a century. In 1908, Dan Heising started a resort, mostly catering to fishermen, on land homesteaded in 1885. Later, the resort became the Circle M Ranch, a guest ranch with horseback riding one of the main features. The Cold Springs Ranch was a dairy farm from 1919 to 1945, when part of the property was sold to the Oregon State Fish Commission for use as a salmon hatchery.

North of the Heising resort, the Henry Corbett Ranch was formed as a family vacation ranch in 1919. A further 7 miles down the Metolius River Valley, the "Old Bailey Place" was settled by Meredith Bailey during the time when the area was known as cattle country. Upstream, the Martin Hansen Resort started operations in 1919. In 1935, the Hansen's Resort was purchased by Mrs. Bertha Perry Ronalds, at which time Hays McMullin renamed the resort, Lake Creek Lodge.

The legacy of man's impact on the lands in the Metolius River Valley is evident today but, in many ways, the natural environment is complemented by the rustic homes and ranch houses built some half century or more ago. These structures, mellowed with age, blend into the natural landscape whether it be meadow or forest. An example of this is to be found in the Metolius Meadows subdivision. In 1973, the Metolius Meadows guest ranch was acquired and developed for use as homesites. This subdivision, which not surprisingly used the name "Metolius Meadows," has retained part of the ranch facilities where only houses compatible with the natural environment are approved for building. The ranch house is situated on a small rise overlooking Lake Creek and the adjacent green meadows. Beyond the meadow, pines cover the Metolius Valley, crowding the symmetrical slopes of Black Butte, which rises 3000 feet over the valley.

All the buildings on the guest ranch were built for Mrs. Bertha Perry Ronalds, an elegant American who had previously lived for 30 years in a house in Paris before returning to the United States. After a round-the-world tour looking for the ideal climate in which to live a rustic life, Mrs. Ronalds chose the Metolius Meadows property as the site for her summer home (San Mateo, California, was her winter home). At one time she had 12 servants, including a lady's maid, chauffeur, main house cook, assistant cook, two houseboys, a maid for the help, and two gardeners. She developed a deep interest in horses, adding to the ranch the finest barns, paddocks and equipment and one wrangler, called a groom by Mrs. Ronalds—much to the bewilderment of the hardbitten westerners. And she built 70 miles of trails through the adjacent pine forests. The riding facilities, a swimming pool and open pastureland are now in common ownership for Metolius Meadows subdivision property owners. The ranch house and subsidiary buildings have become private residences.

Secluded from the main tourist activity around Camp Sherman is the House on the Metolius, in one of the most spectacular settings in the valley. The resort's guest units are among ponderosa pines, where the Metolius cascades through one of many gorges before being tamed in its curvaceous path through open meadowland kept green all summer by waters from over 100 springs. The resort is on a slight rise bordered by split-rail fences, mottled by green lichens. A lawn area overlooks the meadow where horses are usually grazing.

A wall of tall pines abruptly closes off the meadow on three sides. The forest's dark-green carpet spreads over the rolling foothills of the Cascades. Beyond, the skyline is dominated by the serrated volcanic remnants of Three Fingered Jack and by the precipitous slopes of Mt. Jefferson, whose glacier- and snow-clad peak rises over 7,000 feet above the Metolius Valley. The author has found that while the eye assimilates the impressive stature of Mt. Jefferson, the normal camera lens does not do justice to the scene.

On this meadow, in 1916, 73 lots on 80 acres of land were offered for sale. The development, known as Metolo, advertised the properties "in a beautiful valley that looks like green velvet snuggling closely to the foot of Mt. Jefferson, with countless cool and sparkling springs. . . .[with] the fish-laden Metolius River winding to and fro."[93] The lots, designed for "summer estates and fishing and hunting retreats," cost from $75 to $125 each. No development on the meadow ever took place but the House on the Metolius occupies the southeastern fringes.

The House on the Metolius was built by John and Elizabeth Gallois about 1925. Once while staying at the Heising Fishing Resort, they walked across the meadow and up the bluff and were so overwhelmed by the magnificent view that they purchased a few acres from Dan Heising, drew out a rough sketch of a house for Heising to follow, and then returned to San Francisco. They spent their summers at the House on the Metolius for the next 20 years. In 1949, the resort was purchased by a Bend businesswoman, Eleanor Bechen, who for many years served meals to guests. However, since 1972, meals have not been served.

Today, the House on the Metolius caters to adults (no children permitted) who simply wish to relax in the quiet beauty of the resort. Guest cabins have no phones or television. On one of the author's visits with the managers, Mr. and Mrs. Laurence Dyer, several guests were testing their angling skills in the clear Metolius which, at this point, is stocked three times a year. Excited shouts of triumph rang across the lush meadowland as one gentleman snared a fine-looking Dolly Varden. Meanwhile, back on the resort's lawn, other guests relaxed on lawn furniture with idle chatter, embroidery and other peaceful leisure pursuits. Clientele for the resort are mainly Californians who return year after year. In many ways, the atmosphere is like a reunion.

Head of the Metolius River

One of the major tourist attractions in the Camp Sherman area is the Metolius Springs. Here, an instant river, 30 yards wide, is born in front of your eyes. Several names have been given to the head of the Metolius River. Though commonly referred to as "The Head of the Metolius," C. E. Hein stated that it has also been known as "Metolius Springs," "Crystal Springs," and "Crater Springs."[94] This crater is a hollow cone, 30 feet high, at the bottom of which

The view here is across the headwaters of the Metolius River to Mt. Jefferson, which rises 7,500 feet over the valley. The aesthetic qualities of the Metolius Springs are many, and in July, 1971, they were dedicated as a scenic area by the U.S. Forest Service. The land was donated to the U.S. Forest Service by former State Representative Sam and Becky Johnson of Redmond. Johnson's father, the late S. Orie Johnson, had acquired 160 acres of land around the springs in 1924, with the hope of building the terminal of a railroad from Bend to open up his timber operations. Today, the 79-acre site, plus scenic easements, is made accessible to the public by the Forest Service, which has built a paved trail to the viewpoint. *(Oregon Dept. of Transportation)*

The Metolius River is well known for its fly fishing. Nearby campgrounds are nestled beneath tall pines. The river is but 35 miles long before its confluence with the Deschutes River at Lake Billy Chinook. Through its course the river roars through canyons and meanders across meadows.

a current of ice-cold water gurgles its way toward the Deschutes River, the Columbia, and finally, the Pacific Ocean.

The view downstream is one of the most frequently photographed in Central Oregon. Countless cameras have recorded Mount Jefferson's glacial-clad spire rising over a pine forest which, in turn, hems in the lush green meadow. The river twists and turns through this meadow before rushing north parallel to the base of Green Ridge. But film cannot capture the sounds of winds passing through the tops of the cimarron-bark pines or the pine fragrance so prevalent in the High Country. The Metolius Springs is a must for all visitors to the valley.

The geological story behind Metolius Springs is interesting. The total flow from the springs at its source measures 45,000-50,000 gallons of water per minute all year. However, other springs and tributaries from the Cascades add 600,000 gallons of water per minute to the Metolius in its short 35-mile journey to its confluence with the Deschutes. According to Peterson and Groh, a sequence of geological events led to the origin of the springs.[95] First was the actual creation of the valley, which occurred when tension in the earth's crust set off movement along north-trending faults to create the valley and cause the eastern block (Green Ridge) to stand as an escarpment. Rocks in Green Ridge date back to the Pliocene age (about 10-14 million years ago). While once the Metolius River flowed from west to east, its drainage was changed when Green Ridge was elevated. The old drainage system was altered so that the river followed the base of Green Ridge, as it does today.

Volcanism in the High Cascades—first the broad base as a result of shield volcanoes, then higher, more recent peaks caused by violent activity—built up landforms to the west. These events occurred during the last 1½ million years. Following the advance of and retreat of glaciers, glacial debris was transported from the Cascades and deposited on the floor of the Metolius River Valley.

Volcanism along a fault in the valley resulted in the birth of Black Butte around 1,000,000 years ago, and blocking the drainages of the Metolius River. In fact, the valley was virtually split into two parts. North of Black Butte is where the Metolius River now flows; the southern part of the

The first store at Camp Sherman, back in 1920, was simply a stack of staple foods placed on a platform and covered by a tent. The existing store was built in 1920, but its rustic appearance is in keeping with the aesthetics typical of the community. This photo was taken in 1933. *(USFS)*

A 1979 photo of the Camp Sherman store. The basic rustic appearance remains although an addition (not shown here) includes the community's post office. The store has long been the hub of activity in the Camp Sherman area.

valley contains Black Butte Swamp, Glaze Meadow, and the upper reaches of Indian Ford Creek. Geologists believe that Black Butte Swamp and Glaze Meadows were, at one time, shallow lakes that discharged water northward along the base of Green Ridge. In other words, the Metolius River originated to the southwest of where Black Butte now stands. Black Butte covers the ancestral course of the Metolius River. The water that once flowed on the surface as a river now percolates downward through the permeable sands and gravels of the ancient channel beneath the volcano and surfaces again at the lowest point just north of Black Butte, which is Metolius Springs."[96] Water collects in the Black Butte Ranch area (300 feet higher than the Metolius Springs), providing a constant hydraulic head for feeding the springs.

Camp Sherman

The focal point for the bulk of the economic and cultural activities in the Metolius River Valley is at Camp Sherman. Here, situated among mature ponderosa pines by the swiftly flowing Metolius—with Black Butte rising up 3000 feet over the valley to the south—is a picture-book community. The general store (complete with hitching rail in front) serves as the supermarket for tourists and a gathering place for valley residents. The store, seemingly, stocks everything, including free advice on fishing, and it is an official U.S. Post Office.

In April, 1948, Camp Sherman residents, headed by Wayne Korrish, built a community hall on one acre of land donated by Hays McMullin. The community donated time and money and held barbecues to raise funds. One such barbecue, featuring mountain trout and venison, attracted 700, who participated in foot races, swimming, and baseball. Elsewhere in Camp Sherman, a small church serves all denominations. The new two-room grade school caters only to elementary grades; older children are bussed to Bend, 40 miles away. Two small cafes and a laundromat cater to the thousands of tourists and campers who descend on the Metolius Valley during the hectic summer months.

The Wizard Falls Fish Hatchery, located five miles north of Camp Sherman, raises rainbow, Eastern brook, German brown trout, kokanee, and Atlantic salmon. There are numerous fish ponds at the hatchery. Fish are graded and separated periodically to reduce the problem of large fish eating the smaller, to help in feeding, and to determine size for transferring to lakes and streams. Besides the rearing of fish, the full-time staff of five, including the supervisor, conducts research in controlled-growth experiments, selective breeding of Atlantic salmon, evaluation of various diets, designing and testing of hatchery equipment, and research on early spawning strain of eastern brook trout. *(Oregon Dept. of Fish and Wildlife)*

Suttle Lake Resort lodge, about 1932. The lodge, built in the 1920's, served recreationists until August, 1939, when the structure burned. In 1941, a replacement was opened for year-round use, catering to anglers, hunters, alpinists, tourists, and winter-sports enthusiasts. The dining-room picture windows looked out across Suttle Lake and up to the spire of Mt. Washington. Cabins, set among tall evergreens, provided accommodations for guests. The resort was sold and purchased several times during the next twenty years. It was renovated in 1973 and early 1974. However, just prior to reopening on Memorial weekend, 1974, fire again swept through the wooden buildings, which included a coffee shop, store, lobby, and guest rooms, leaving only concrete foundations. *(USFS)*

Other commercial businesses at Camp Sherman include a trailer park and tourist cottages. Many of the guests at the trailer park migrate between Camp Sherman in the summer and the warmer, sunnier climates in Arizona or Southern California the rest of the year.

Wizard Falls Fish Hatchery

Five miles downstream from Camp Sherman, a red-cindered road crosses the green and white waters of the turbulent Metolius River, leading to what must be one of the most attractive settings for a fish hatchery in Oregon. The Wizard Falls Hatchery was constructed in 1947 at a cost of $125,000, and the first fish to be released from the hatchery, 30,000 rainbow trout, were used to stock Mirror Pond in Bend. Dedication and public unveiling of the facilities was in April, 1949. A bronze plaque—prepared by Central Oregon sportsmen as a memorial to George Aitken, who discovered the site—was dedicated "to an ardent sportsman of Sisters, instrumental in the establishment of this hatchery." Some 800 attended the dedication, with Superintendent K. E. Morton as host and music provided by the Bend Municipal band. Major improvements and additions were made in 1972. Sale of Oregon angling licenses support operations of the hatchery; very few federal funds are received.

Visitors are welcome to tour the Wizard Falls Fish Hatchery, located on 35 acres of Deschutes National Forest Service land. Each year the Department of Fish and Wildlife hosts over 20,000 visitors, including educational tours by 2000 school children from various parts of Oregon.

Several springs on government-held land, not the Metolius River, supply water for the hatchery. Because of the relative evenness (49° F—53° F) of the water year round, the site is considered excellent for the development of fish from eggs to young fry. In fact, eggs hatched at the station are from other Oregon hatcheries, such as the Willamette Hatchery near Oakridge, the Roaring River station (Linn County), the Oak Springs Hatchery, and the Deschutes

River near Maupin. The eggs are delivered to Wizard Falls to obtain the rapid initial development and growth.

Most of the fish raised at Wizard Falls are rainbow trout. At different times, the hatchery may be raising German brown, Eastern brook trout, kokanee and Atlantic salmon. It was at Wizard Falls that the first Atlantic salmon were successfully raised, in 1950, from eggs obtained at Gaspé Bay, Quebec, Canada. The only domesticated Atlantic salmon brood stock was developed at Wizard Falls. This stock has since been planted in several Central Oregon lakes, providing a bonus fishing experience for anglers. Most kokanee eggs at the hatchery are obtained at Suttle Lake, where 500,000 to a million are taken each year.

Visitors find that feeding the fish in the stock ponds often creates some exciting moments as the fish literally rush and jump to get their share of the food. The fish are fed a special commercial diet consisting of fish, vegetable, and meat meal. Feedings, which are done manually as well as by automatic feeders, take place at carefully selected time intervals. Approximately 150 to 200 tons of food are consumed annually.

Head of Jack Creek

Just a few miles northwest of Camp Sherman, a dusty, red-cindered forest-service road leads to a small geographical area unique east of the Cascades. Here at the "Head of Jack Creek," a multitude of springs literally bubble out from under mossy banks and join to form Jack Creek, but also to provide year-round moisture that supports a verdant forest. The springs that form Jack Creek, a tributary of the Metolius River, are believed to come from water that has seeped into underground streams which have been covered with porous lava from eruptions in the volcanic Cascades.

A short pine- and bark-covered trail constructed by the U.S. Forest Service takes visitors into an ecosystem more typical of Western Oregon. The trail crosses small streams and pools that are crystal clear. The cold, spring-fed waters inhibit growth of algae and bacteria, small organisms that make warmer waters murky. Most of the quarter-mile trail is soft and springy—even damp and musty in places. Hemlock and spruce needles, twigs and leaves cover the ground, then decay and act like a sponge in holding the water. Because water is all around, a variety of water-loving plants grow here. Some of these have adapted to cool shade or scant light or the abundance of water include the Pacific Yew, ferns, coolwort, twayblade, bead-lily (or queen cup) monkey flower, prince's pine, and thimbleberry.

Part of the soil that supports the plants and trees of the forest is derived from the decay of fallen logs. In places, what appears to be firm ground is actually floating islands of pine needles, duff, and twigs supported by tree roots but underlain with running water. Because tree roots must have air as well as water, many of the trees along the Head of Jack Creek Trail have a shallow root system. While the forest surrounding the creek is predominantly ponderosa pine, the abundance of water at Jack Creek supports larch, Douglas fir, vine maple, thinleaf alder, Engelmann spruce, white fir, mountain hemlock and incense cedar. These trees grow so close together that their branches form an almost closed canopy to shade the forest floor from the bright Central Oregon sunshine. It is in this cool shade that the shrubs mentioned above are able to flourish.

Although the eye can readily discern the subtle differences caused by gradations of shade and sunlight, the author has found that the amateur photographer may find it difficult to portray adequately the beauty at the Head of Jack Creek. Visitors here should seek out the trail head near a picnic area and, if available, pick up and use the small, free booklet provided by the Deschutes National Forest Service. This guide helps interpret the story behind the ecosystems on the trail. Along this quarter-mile trail that winds through the area are ten numbered stops identified by wooden markers. The booklet includes a description of each number as well as sketches of birds, plants, and trees that are to be seen in the area.

Suttle Lake—Blue Lake Area

A few miles southwest of Camp Sherman, at the base of the grade leading up to the Santiam Pass, are two lakes,

Suttle and Blue. Each is a different size with a different geological origin. The area, at and adjacent to the lakes, is one of the most interesting in the Deschutes National Forest. Here ample precipitation enables lush vegetation, more typical of the west side of the Cascades, to mingle with the east-side flora. Suttle Lake, by far the larger of the two lakes, was named for John Settle, a pioneer from the Lebanon area in the Willamette Valley, one of the organizers and directors of the Willamette Valley and Cascade Mountain Military Road Project in 1866. While on a hunting trip, Settle discovered the two lakes.

Suttle Lake, of glacial origin, was formed when glaciers from Mt. Washington cut the valley now occupied by the lake. The glaciers piled up a terminal and a lateral moraine —rounded boulders carried down the mountain by the ice —at the place where an outlet now pours out of the lake. The lake is about one and a half miles long, but a mere third of a mile wide. Highway 20 clings to the 400-foot-high slopes that rise precipitously to the north of Suttle Lake. Motorists traveling that highway get a bird's-eye view of the lake, if they are brave enough to take their eyes off the unfenced highway.

Lake Creek drains out of the east end of Suttle Lake near the Santiam Highway. Before Suttle Lake was developed for its recretional role, early ranchers eyed it for its irrigation waters. The first investigation for using Suttle Lake for irrigation came late in the nineteenth century for settlers living near the Metolius River. In 1906-07, L. D. Wiest of Bend further examined the possibilities of using Suttle Lake water for irrigation. In 1912, the Suttle Lake Improvement Company, with headquarters in Bend, laid plans for irrigating 12,500 acres of fertile land near Cline Buttes. The Suttle Lake Irrigation District filed on water from both Suttle Lake and Blue Lake in 1915, but the intended project, to be completed before 1923, and was never finished.[97] Further plans to tap Suttle Lake and Blue Lake waters surfaced in 1926 when the Squaw Creek Irrigation District revealed plans to place a dam at Suttle Lake and back up water to Blue Lake. In 1929, an 18-mile canal was planned to run from Suttle Lake to the Swamp Ranch (Black Butte Ranch), then to Indian Ford and south to connect with

Squaw Creek Canal to irrigate the Sisters-Plainview-Cloverdale communities.

In 1937, yet another storage plan for Suttle Lake was discussed. The "Plainview Project," designed to provide water for 4000 acres, was to involve building a canal from Suttle Lake to Lake Creek, constructing an earth-filled dam on Lake Creek, just below Suttle Lake. Water would have been raised 34.5 feet at Suttle Lake and 16 feet at Blue Lake. Cost of the project was estimated at $480,485 or $120 per acre. In the period 1912 to 1937, there had been 12 different investigations and surveys of the possible use of water from Suttle Lake water. None of the plans materialized, but just east of Suttle Lake, near Highway 20, a short stretch of canal, overgrown with young trees and bushes, remains in quiet, secluded testimony to the attempts. Although the lakes did not supply irrigation water to the people living in the dry lands east of Sisters, Blue and Suttle Lakes have been put to good use by tourists.

The Sisters country is marked by an absence of lakes at lower elevations. Of course, the nearby Cascades have countless alpine lakes but, except for Big Lake, these are not readily accessible to the motorized tourist. Thus it is no wonder that Suttle Lake is so popular with campers, fishermen, and boating enthusiasts. Four campgrounds are nestled among the trees and adjacent to the lake. Recreational use of Suttle Lake dates back half a century. One of the recreational land-use plans for the area, in 1937, was for the forest service to clear a ski hill near the Suttle Lake Resort, which was then planned for year-round use. However, the plans did not materialize. In 1939, a 5-mile ski trail skirting Suttle Lake and Blue Lake was built as part of Civilian Conservation Corps projects.

A Methodist Youth Camp, with a main lodge and cabins, was constructed at Suttle Lake in 1948. However, as early as 1921, young people from Central Oregon churches met there for an Epworth League Institute. Today, the youth camp, under Forest Service special-use permit, offers fellowship and educational programs to Methodist families and age groups from within the Oregon and Idaho Conference. In addition, the camp is rented to others, including outdoor school programs.

A view of part of Suttle Lake. The lake is well-used by boaters and fishermen. Campsites are located on the southern shore. The volcano in the background is Black Butte. *(Oregon Dept. of Transportation)*

Blue Lake, formed as a result of a violent volcanic explosion about 1500 B.C., is a miniature "Crater Lake." The Blue Lake Resort features rental cottages, boating facilities, a small store, and trailer park. A restaurant is located one mile from the lake. The isolated peak on the skyline is Mt. Washington; Cache Mountain is the forest-covered mountain on the left. *(Oregon Dept. of Transportation)*

Blue Lake, a much smaller lake located half a mile west of Suttle Lake, is dubbed the "Crater Lake of the Central Cascades." Although the 300'-deep lake is of volcanic origin, it was first thought that Blue Lake, like Suttle Lake, was of glacial origin. In 1903, H. D. Langille, of the Geological Survey, stated that Blue Lake might occupy a crater resulting from a volcanic explosion that discharged volcanic debris over adjacent lands. In 1965, Ed Taylor, in releasing the results of studies of volcanism in the Cascades, further mentioned the volcanic origin of Blue Lake.[98] Dr. Taylor reported that Blue Lake was the result of a violent upward explosion which ejected volcanic bombs and blocks in all directions from the crater and sent scoria and ashes 3 miles east and southeast. Carbon-14 dating of charred wood from the limb of a conifer buried by scoria and ash indicated that the Blue Lake explosion took place about 1500 B.C.

The source of most of the water that fills Blue Lake (and subsequently drains into Link Creek then onto Suttle Lake and its outlet at Lake Creek) is from large springs at about the 240-foot level underwater, near the east shore. Also, there are several large caves, both underwater and above water level, in the eastern cliffs. The underwater cliffs on both the north and west shores drop off over 100 feet.[99]

As already stated, Blue Lake is a miniature "Crater Lake." Its clear waters take on different shades of blue, depending on the light. A trail circles the crater rim which exposes red and brown volcanoc cinders. A riding stable and pack station located near the Blue Lake Resort, at the east end of the lake, provides rental horses for one-hour rides around the rim and on other adjacent trails, as well as guided pack trips into the nearby Cascade wilderness country. Blue Lake Resort, "hidden" in the forest next to the lake, features rental cottages, a restaurant, store, trailer park, campground and boating facilities.

Camp Tamarack

Dark Lake and Scout Lake are two small lakes situated about 300 feet higher than Suttle Lake, just a short distance away. Both of these small lakes are picturesque in their own way. Scout Lake has excellent day-use facilities by its shores and a reservation group-area campground nearby. Dark Lake is the site of Camp Tamarack, a private camp for girls. This camp opened in the summer of 1935 when Miss Donna E. Gill of Lebanon and Lucile Murphy of Portland found the "perfect spot" to operate a camp.

Sun sparkles on the quiet waters of Dark Lake, which has a smooth, accessible shoreline. The lake is tucked away in the forest, yet it is only a few miles from Highway 20. Endless recreational opportunities are within an hour's drive. With a lease and the cooperation of the Deschutes National Forest Service, the building of Camp Tamarack came about. A road was extended from the old Scout Lake Road, building materials were trucked over the Cascades from the valley, and the camp got underway in 1935.

Camp Tamarack continues to be known for its lack of regimentation, its superb staffing (1 staff member to 4 girls) and its diversified outdoor program. The girls can participate in horseback riding, tennis, swimming, canoeing, sailing, badminton, table tennis, volleyball, hiking and climbing. In the evening, with a log fire blazing in the huge lava-rock fireplace, time is spent in singing, dramatics and square dancing. The main building at Camp Tamarack is a large one-story pine structure which serves as the focal point for dining and most of the camp activities. Small cabins, some adjacent to Dark Lake and others clinging to the forested hillside, provide sleeping quarters.

Epilogue

Here we have identified and visited the major geographical areas of the High Country, one of several distinctive regions that comprise the varied and fascinating Central Oregon country. Throughout most of historical times, man has done little to shape or change the natural landscape of the High Country. To be sure, trails, camps and the presence of artifacts mark the presence of early-day Indians. Bleached fence posts and weathered boards, scattered on riverine meadows, are silent testimony to the settlements of ranchers and homesteaders. Newer frame buildings and mobile homes largely mask the presence of historical structures within the small communities of the region. Even most of the scars left by extensive logging are now healing.

In recent years, the High Country has played host to an increasing number of visitors. Thousands have come to seek the beauty of alpine meadows or the tranquility of secluded lakes and rippling streams. Others have taken the opportunity to ski, fish, boat, hike, camp or sightsee. Those with vacation homes have sought relaxation from urban pressures. Others, ranging from young families to retirees, have moved to the High Country, hoping for a quiet life amidst the pine forests or along the scenic Little or Big Deschutes.

This greater influx of people—recreationists and residents—has put increasing pressure on the land. Special interest groups (skiers, snowmobilers, hikers, equestrians, timbermen, and others) each lobby for their own needs. Most of the High Country is under the jurisdiction of the U.S. Forest Service. Its role in the management of these lands, now mandated by Federal orders, will help determine future land uses.

Pressures on the relatively modest acreages of privately owned lands are even more intense. However, the quality of planned developments, such as Sunriver, Black Butte Ranch, Indian Ford and others, has demonstrated that man can build and live in harmony with nature. Elsewhere, land-use guidelines and controls—controversial though they may be—help create a more orderly process of development than might have been experienced over a quarter century ago.

Lumber companies, such as Brooks-Scanlon and the Gilchrist Timber Company, implementing a sustained-yield program, ensure that the forests will continue to supply the raw materials for lumber production, one of the major economic activities of the region. Thus the High Country of Central Oregon will continue to play a key role in providing tangible and intangible resources for future generations.

NOTES

1. Henry Larcom Abbot, *Explorations for a Railroad Route from the Sacramento Valley to the Columbia River* (1857), p. 74.
2. *The Bulletin*, July 27, 1906.
3. *Ibid.*, July 14, 1909.
4. Information supplied by Bruce Kirkland, Deschutes National Forest Service, March, 1979.
5. Lewis L. McArthur, *Oregon Geographic Names* (1974), p. 133.
6. John C. Fremont, *Report of the Exploring Expedition to the Rocky Mountains in the Year 1842 and to Oregon and North California in the Years 1843-44* (1845), p. 199.
7. Ella E. Clark, "The Mythology of the Indians in the Pacific Northwest," *Oregon Historical Quarterly*, Vol. 54, No. 3, September, 1953, p. 166.
8. *The Bulletin*, September 12, 1961.
9. ___ Abbot, p. 92.
10. *Ibid*, p. 94.
11. Don A. Hall, *On Top of Oregon* (1975), p. 135.
12. See *On Top of Oregon*, by Don A. Hall. Binford & Mort (1974) for a detailed account of this climb and other historical climbs of Cascade peaks.
13. See *Oregon Historical Quarterly*, Volume IV, for a detailed account of the Minto Trail.
14. ___ McArthur, p. 366.
15. *The Bulletin*, May 3, 1926.
16. Robert W. Sawyer, "Beginnings of the McKenzie Highway, 1862," *Oregon Historical Quarterly*, Vol. 31, No. 3, September, 1931, p. 265.
17. *The Bulletin*, September 8, 1924.
18. *Ibid.*, June 11, 1935.
19. *Ibid.*, September 19, 1927.
20. *Ibid.*, September 22, 1927.
21. ___ McArthur, p. 726.
22. Keith Mountain, "Saga of a Dying Glacier," *Old Oregon*, Vol. 57, No. 3, 1978, p. 24.
23. *The Bulletin*, August 26, 1937.
24. *Ibid.*, December 8, 1915.
25. ___ Abbot, p. 79.
26. Howel Williams, *Volcanoes of the Three Sisters* (1944), p. 46.
27. *The Bulletin*, December 16, 1969.
28. ___ Williams (1944), p. 52.
29. *Ibid.*, January 21, 1922.
30. *Ibid.*, January 13, 1926.
31. *Ibid.*, May 11, 1927.
32. On Labor Day, 1927, the unsuccessful hunt for two climbers lost in a blizzard in the Cascades led to the formation of the Skyliners, in part to help organize search and rescue activities and participate in recreational skiing.
33. *Ibid.*, December 28, 1927.
34. Interview with Edith Kostol, Bend, April, 1979.
35. Representing and active in plans for the U.S.F.S. Mt. Bachelor ski area was Jim Egan. The upper lodge at Mt. Bachelor is named after him and was dedicated January 3, 1959.
36. *The Bulletin*, February 22, 1964.
37. George P. Putnam, *The Smiting of the Rock* (1918), p. 106.
38. Israel Russell, *Geology and Water Resources of Central Oregon* (1905), p. 12.
39. *The Bulletin*, September 4, 1903.
40. *Ibid.*, June 5, 1903.
41. ___ Fremont, p. 13.
42. ___ McArthur, p. 216.
43. The U.S. Forest Service, recognizing this, has compiled a small free leaflet "Floating the Deschutes River in the Deschutes National Forest."
44. *The Bulletin*, October 13, 1917.
45. ___ Fremont, pp 202-203.
46. ___ McArthur, p. 630.
47. *The Bulletin*, January 19, 1916.
48. *Ibid.*, September 18, 1908.
49. ___ Abbot, p. 74.
50. *The Bulletin*, September 23, 1904.
51. *Ibid.*, June 19, 1943.

213

52. *Ibid.*, September 3, 1943.
53. *Ibid.*, November 19, 1945.
54. ____ Fremont, p. 202.
55. *The Bulletin*, April 17, 1903.
56. *Ibid.*, November 18, 1919.
57. W. D. Cheney, *Central Oregon* (1918), p. 84.
58. *The Bulletin*, August 16, 1907.
59. *Ibid.*, July 20, 1910.
60. *Ibid.*, June 11, 1913.
61. ____ McArthur, p. 238.
62. Howard M. Corning (Ed). *Oregon, End of the Trail: American Guide Series* (1951), p. 409.
63. "19 Burials on Top Cultus Mountain not yet Solved," *Deschutes Pioneers' Gazette*, January 15, 1955.
64. ____ Russell, pp. 97-110.
65. Howel Williams, "Newberry Volcano of Central Oregon." *Geological Society America Bulletin*, Vol. 46, No. 2, 1935.
66. *The Bulletin*, January 31, 1930.
67. *Ibid.*, August 2, 1911.
68. A. S. McClure, "Diary of a Mining Expedition 1858 of the McClure Family." (no date).
69. ____ Russell, p. 110.
70. *Ibid.*, p. 111.
71. *The Bulletin*, April 25, 1934.
72. Howel Williams, *Geological Map of the Bend Quadrangle, Oregon, and a Reconnaissance Geologic Map of the Central Portion of the High Cascades Mountains*, 1957.
73. Lawrence A. Chitwood, Robert A. Jensen, Edward A. Groh, "The Age of Lava Butte, *The Ore Bin*, Vol. 39, No. 10, October, 1976, p. 162.
74. Conversation with Dr. Bruce O. Nolf; Professor of Geology, Central Oregon Community College, Bend, Oregon, April, 1978.
75. *Deschutes Pioneers' Gazette*, January 26, 1951.
76. *The Bulletin*, April 18, 1927.
77. *Ibid.*, August 27, 1927.
78. ____ Fremont, p. 202.
79. *The Bulletin*, May 12, 1915.
80. ____ McArthur, p. 428.
81. *The Bulletin*, July 3, 1912.
82. *Ibid.*
83. ____ Abbot, p. 73.
84. *The Bulletin*, July 3, 1912.
85. Thomas D. Murphy, *Oregon the Picturesque* (1917), p. 112.
86. *An Illustrated History of Central Oregon* (1905), p. 733.
87. *Ibid.*, p. 733.
88. *Ibid.*, p. 733.
89. ____ Abbot, p. 90.
90. *The Bulletin*, July 10, 1912.
91. *Ibid.*, August 24, 1934.
92. ____ McArthur, p. 472.
93. *The Bulletin*, July 29, 1916.
94. *Ibid.*, June 16, 1971.
95. Norman V. Peterson and Edward A. Groh, "Geology and Origin of the Metolius Springs, Jefferson County, Oregon." *The Ore Bin*, Vol. 34, No. 3, March, 1972.
96. *Ibid.*, p. 47.
97. *The Bulletin*, November 22, 1926.
98. Edward M. Taylor, "Recent Volcanism Between Three Fingered Jack and North Sister, Oregon Cascade Range," *The Ore Bin*, Vol. 27, No. 7, July, 1965.
99. Interview with Ken Lovegren, Blue Lake Resort, September, 1978.

BIBLIOGRAPHY

Abbot, Henry L. *Explorations for a Railroad Route from the Sacramento Valley to the Columbia River*. Washington: Beverley Tucker, 1857.

Ames, Francis. *Fishing the Oregon Country*. Caldwell, Idaho: The Caxton Printers, Ltd., 1969.

Baker, Gail C. *Historical Write-Up of the Deschutes National Forest*. Bend: Deschutes National Forest Service, 1950.

Binns, Archie. *Peter Skene Ogden: Fur Trader*. Portland, Oregon: Binfords and Mort, 1967.

Brogan, Phil F. *East of the Cascades*. Portland: Binfords and Mort. Publishers, 1964.

Brogan, Phil F. *Visitor Information Service Book for the Deschutes National Forest*. Bend, Oregon: U.S. Forest Service, 1969.

Bulletin (Bend), 1903-1979.

Bullard, Fred M. *Volcanoes in History, in Theory, in Eruption*. Austin: University of Texas Press, 1962.

Cheney, W. D. *Central Oregon*. Portland: The Ivy Press, 1918.

Chitwood, Lawrence A., Robert A. Jensen, and Edward A. Groh. "The Age of Lava Butte," *The Ore Bin*. Vol. 39, No. 10. October, 1977.

Clark, Ella E. "The Mythology of the Indians in the Pacific Northwest," *Oregon Historical Quarterly*. Portland, Oregon: Vol. 54, No. 3. September, 1953.

Climatological Handbook: Columbia Basin States. Vancouver, Washington: Pacific Northwest River Basin Commission, 1968.

Coleman, Satis N. *Volcanoes New and Old*. New York: The John Day Co., 1946.

Corning, Howard M. (Ed). *Oregon, End of the Trail: American Guide Series*. Portland, Oregon: Binford and Mort, 1951.

Crosby, W. O. *Report on the Benham Falls Project of the Deschutes River Drainage*, Oregon. U.S. Reclamation Service. (no date)

Deschutes Pioneers' Gazette

Deshutes Project, Central Oregon Division, Boise, Idaho: Bureau of Reclamation, 1972.

Dickens, Samuel N. *Oregon Geography*. Ann Arbor, Michigan: Edwards Bros., Inc., 1965.

Dole, Hollis M. (Ed). *Andesite Conference Guidebook*. Portland, Oregon: State of Oregon Department of Geology and Mineral Industries, 1968.

Eaton, Walter P. *Skyline Camps*. Boston, Chicago: W. A. Wilde, Publishers, 1922.

Ekman, Leonard. *Scenic Geology of the Pacific Northwest*. Portland, Oregon: Binfords and Mort, 1962.

Erickson, Sheldon D. *Occupance in the Upper Deschutes Basin, Oregon*. Research Paper No. 32. Chicago, Illinois: The University of Chicago, 1953.

Farnham, J. T. *Life, Adventures and Travels in California and Oregon*. New York: Sheldon, Lamport, and Blakeman, 1855.

Francis, Peter. *Volcanoes*. New York: Penguin Books Ltd., 1976.

Franklin, Jerry F. and C. T. Dyrness. *Natural Vegetation of Oregon and Washington* Portland, Oregon: U.S. Department of Agriculture, 1973.

Fremont, John C. *Report of the Exploring Expedition to the Rocky Mountains in the Year 1842 and to Oregon and North California in the Years 1843-44*. Washington: Gale and Seaton, 1845.

Hall, Don Alan. *On Top of Oregon*. Portland, Oregon: Binford & Mort, 1975.

215

"Hands, Many." *Jefferson County Reminiscences*. Portland, Oregon: Binfords and Mort, 1957.

Harris, Stephen. *Fire and Ice*. Seattle, Washington: The Mountaineers, 1976.

Hastings, Lansford W. *The Emigrants' Guide to Oregon and California*. Cincinnati: George Conclin, 1845.

Hatton, Raymond R. *The Impact of Tourism on Central Oregon*. MA Thesis, University of Oregon, 1969.

Hatton, Raymond R. *Bend in Central Oregon*. Portland: Binford and Mort, 1978.

Hendee, John C., George H. Stankey, Robert C. Lucas. *Wilderness Management*. Washington: Forest Service, U.S. Department of Agriculture, 1978.

Hodge, Edwin T. *Mount Multnomah; Ancient Ancestor of the Three Sisters*. Eugene, Oregon: University of Oregon, 1925.

Horn, Elizabeth. *Wildflowers I*. Beaverton, Oregon: The Touchstone Press, 1972.

Hosmer, Paul. *Now We're Loggin'*. Portland, Oregon: Metropolitan Press, 1930.

Hosmer, Paul. *The Oregon Motorist*. January, 1930.

Jackson, Donald and Mary Lee Spence (Ed.). *The Expeditions of John Charles Fremont*. (Vol I). *Travels from 1838 to 1847*. Urbana, Chicago, and London: University of Illinois Press, 1970.

Juris, Francis. *Old Crook County: the Heart of Oregon*. Prineville, Oregon: The Print Shop, 1975.

Klein, David R. "Wilderness, Evolution of the Concept," *Landscape*. Vol 20, No. 3. Spring 1976.

Land Management Plan: Deschutes National Forest. Portland, Oregon: 1978.

Lowe, Don and Roberta. *60 Hiking Trails Central Oregon Cascades*. Beaverton, Oregon: The Touchstone Press, 1978.

Loy, William G. *Atlas of Oregon*. Eugene: University of Oregon, 1976.

Macdonald, Gordon A. *Volcanoes*. Englewood Cliffs, New Jersey: Prentice-Hall, Inc., 1972.

McArthur, Lewis L. *Oregon Geographic Names*. Portland, Oregon: Oregon Historical Society, 1974.

McClure, A. S. "Diary of a Mining Expedition 1858 of the McClure Family." Unpublished.

McKee, Bates. *Cascadia*. New York, San Francisco: McGraw-Hill Book Co., 1972.

Mimura, Koji. *The Geological Society of America*. Vol. 10, No. 3, February, 1978.

Minto, John. "*Minto Pass: Its History, and an Indian Tradition,*" *Oregon Historical Quarterly*. Portland, Oregon: Vol. 4, No. 3. September, 1903.

Mountain, Keith. "Saga of a Dying Glacier." *Old Oregon*. Vol. 57, No. 3, Spring, 1978.

Murphy, Thomas D. *Oregon the Picturesque*. Boston: The Page Company, 1917.

Newman, Doug and Sally Sharrard. *Oregon Ski Tours*. Beaverton, Oregon: The Touchstone Press, 1973.

Nichols, R. L., and C. E. Stearns. "Fissure Eruptions near Bend, Oregon." (abs.) *Geol. Soc. America Bulletin*. Vol 49, No 12, pt. 2, 1938.

Nolf, Bruce O. (Dr.) "Volcano Watching a Growing Sport," *The Bulletin*. March 15, 1972.

Nolf Bruce. "Broken Top Breaks: Flood Released by Erosion of Glacial Moraine," *The Ore Bin*. Vol. 28, No. 10, October, 1966.

Bibliography

Peattie, Roderick. *The Cascades.* New York: The Vanguard Press, 1949.

Peterson, Norman V., and Edward A. Groh, "Recent Volcanic Landforms in Central Oregon." *The Ore Bin,* Vol. 25, No. 3, March, 1963.

_____, *Lunar Geological Field Conference Guide Book.* Portland, Oregon: Oregon Department of Geology and Mineral Industries Bulletin, No. 57, 1965.

_____, "Geology and Origin of the Metolius Springs, Jefferson County, Oregon." *The Ore Bin.* Vol. 34, No. 3, March, 1972.

Peterson, Norman V., Edward A. Groh, Edward M. Taylor, Donald F. Stensland. *Geology and Mineral Resources of Deschutes County, Oregon.* Portland, Oregon: State of Oregon Department of Geology and Mineral Resources, 1976.

Preston, R. N. *Early Oregon Atlas.* Portland, Oregon: Binford & Mort, 1979.

Purcell, David. *Guide to the Lava Tube Caves of Central Oregon.* (self-published), 1977.

Putnam, George P. *In the Oregon Country.* New York: The Knickerbocker Press, 1915.

_____. *The Smiting of the Rock.* New York: Grosset and Dunlap, 1918.

Russell, Israel. *Geology and Water Resources of Central Oregon.* Washington: Government Printing Office, 1905.

Sawyer, Robert W. "Beginnings of McKenzie Highway, 1862," *Oregon Historical Quarterly,* Vol. 31, No. 3. September 1931.

Smith, Warren D. "A Geological Motorlog." *The Oregon Motorist:* Vol. 10, No. 9, June, 1930.

Stoeser, Douglas B. and Frederick J. Swanson. *Geology of Rock Mesa, Three Sisters Wilderness Area, Oregon.* Eugene: University of Oregon, 1972.

Sutton, Ann and Myron. *The Pacific Crest Trail.* Philadelphia and New York: J. B. Lippincott Co., 1975.

Taylor, Edward M. *Recent Volcanism Between Three Fingered Jack and North Sister Oregon Cascade Range. The Ore Bin.* Vol. 27, No. 7, July, 1965.

Van Vechten III, George W. *The Ecology of the Timberline and Alpine Vegetation of the Three Sisters, Oregon.* Ph.D. dissertation, Oregon State University, 1960.

Volland, Leonard A. *Plant Communities of the Central Oregon Pumice Zone.* Portland, Oregon: U.S. Department of Agriculture, 1976.

Williams, Howel. "Newberry Volcano of Central Oregon." *Geological Society America Bulletin.* Vol. 46, No. 2, 1935.

_____. *Volcanoes of the Three Sisters Region, Oregon Cascades.* Geological Science Bulletin, Vol. 27, 1944.

_____. "Volcanoes." *Scientific American.* November, 1951.

_____. "A Geologic Map of the Bend Quadrangle, Oregon, and a Reconnaissance Geologic Map of the Central Portion of the High Cascade Mountains." Department of Geology and Mineral Industries, 1957.

_____. *Ancient Volcanoes of Oregon.* Eugene, Oregon: University of Oregon Press, 1962.

Williams, Ira A. "Some Little-Known Scenic Pleasure Places in the Cascade Range in Oregon." *The Mineral Resources of Oregon.* Portland: Oregon Bureau of Mines and Geology, May, 1916.

Wilson, Tillie, and Alice Scott. *That was Yesterday.* Redmond, Oregon: Midstate Printing, 1974.

INDEX
(Page numbers of photos in black type)

A

Aasen, Edward J., 163
Abbot, Lieutenant Henry L., 10, 23, 88, 168, 176-177, 188, 194
Abbot Party, 52
Agriculture, 3, 87, 172-173
Ahalapam Cinder Field, 54
Airstrip Burn, 32, 34
Aitken, George, 204
Albany, 31
Allen, C. B. (Ranch), 87
Allen, Joel, 89
Alley, Mr., 195
Allingham, Mrs. Margaret J., 195
Allingham Guard Station, **191**
Allingham Ranch, 189, **191**, 195
Alpine Club (former name of Skyliners), 63
Alworth-Washburn Company, 151-152
Anderson Mill, 66
Anderson Mill Road, 66
Angling (see Fishing)
Appalachian Trail, 14
Applegate, Captain O. C., 168
Archaeology, 80, 89
Army Engineers (see U.S. Army Engineers)
Arnold, William, 146
Arnold Ice Cave, 145-146
Arnold Irrigation District, 78
Aspen Camp, 102
Aspen Flat Fire, **143**
Astronauts, 6, 115
Atkinson Place, 91
Aya, Alfred, 172

B

Bachelor, The (former name of Bachelor Butte), 58
Bachelor Butte, 58 (see also Mt. Bachelor)
Bailey, Maida and Meredith Sheep Ranch, 184
Bailey, Meredith, 196
Barclay Logging Company, 181
Barclay Place, 185
Barlow Lava Cave, 147
Basin and Range Country, 3
Bates Butte, 16
Bechen, Eleanor, 198
Belknap, J. H., 43
Belknap Crater, 41-43
Belknap Springs, 34
Bend, 3, 11, 19-20, 44, 55, 60, 63, 72, 74, 76, 88, 104, 146, 152, **162**-163, 170, 172
Bend Ad Club, **137**
Bend Chamber of Commerce, 50, 63, 67
Bend City Recreation Department (see also Bend Metro Parks and Recreation District), 69
Bend Commercial Club, 60, 111, 148
Bend Company, 152

Bend Elks, **90**
Bend High School, 65, 67, 69, 148
Bend Livery Stable, 103
Bend Metro Parks and Recreation District, 65
Bend Municipal Band, 204
Bend School District, 156, **162**
Bend Ski Club, 61
Bend Timber Company, 152
Bend Water Supply, 55, 65, 88, 96
Benham, J. R., **97**
Benham Falls, 73-74, 89, **97-101**, 144
Benham Falls Dam Project, 98
Benham Falls Reservoir, 170
Berry, Pamelia Ann, 29
Bicycling (see Biking)
Big Lake, 30, 33-34
Big Lava Lake (see Lava Lakes)
Big Meadows (Sunriver), 89, 91
Big Meadows School, 94
Big Obsidian Flow (see Obsidian Flow)
Big Springs, 107
Biking, 85, 93-94, 192
Black Butte, 60, 186, 188, 190-**191**, 193, 200, 202, **209**
Black Butte Land and Livestock Company, 181, 189
Black Butte Ranch, 183, 189-192, 202, 211
Black Butte Ranch Lodge, 192
Black Butte Swamp, 202, 207
Black Crater, 41
Blow Lake, **118**
Blue Lake, 33, 65, 207-210
Blue Lake Resort, **209**-210
Blue River, 35
Boating (see also Canoeing and Sailing), 84, 93, 114, 116, 118, **128**, 208-210
Bonneville Fish Hatchery, 116
Bowerman, Jay, 96
Boy Scouts, 49
Boylen, Bert C., **140**
Bridge Creek, 55, **166**
Brogan, Phil, 21, 49
Broken Top, 2, 39, 41, 48-49, 53-57, 61, 63, 67, 72, **81**, 106-108, 110-111
Brooks, Dr. D. F., 155
Brooks Resources, 183, 189-190
Brooks-Roberts Company, 151
Brooks-Scanlon Company, 13, 146, 152, 154-163, 181, 189, 212
Brooks-Scanlon Logging Camp, 156-159, **162**
Brother Jonathan (former name of Bachelor Butte), 58
Brothers (community), 20
Brown Mountain, 120
Bulletin, The, 13, 38, 55, 61, 63, 74, 77-78, 87, 91, 97, 99, 106, **126**, **140**, 152, 155, 173, 177
Bureau of Land Management, 51, 83

218

Index

Bureau of Reclamation (see U.S. Bureau of Reclamation)
Bureau of Topographical Engineers, 45

C

Cabot Lake, 25
Cabot Lake Trail, 25
Cache Creek, 30
Cache Creek Toll Station, 24, 169
Cache Mountain, 209
Callihan, Vern, 163
Camp Abbot (military camp), 84, **90**-92, 94, 98
Camp Polk (military camp), 30, 36, 180-181, 195
Camp Polk Post Office, 36
Camp Sherman (community), 157, 195, **201**-202, 204
Camp Tamarack (private camp for girls), 210-211
Camping, 9-10, 34, 77, 83-84, 113, 116-120, 124-125, **128**, 194, **199**, 208, 210-211
Canoeing, 83, 94, 113-114, 116-117, 211
Canyon Creek Meadow, 28
Cappy Mountain, 85
Carey Act, 173
Carl Lake, 25
Carver Glacier, 48
Cascade Lakes Highway, 2, 52, 70, 72, 77, 105-121
Cascade National Forest, 150, 172
Cascade Range Forest Reserve, 150
Cascades, 2, 4, 7, 10-11, 13, 15-59, 83, 89, 188, 193, 200
Castellaras (proposed name at Sunriver), 92
Cattle, 81, 87, 92-93, 110-111, 113, 149, 177, 180, 186, 189-190, 195
Cattlemen, 4, 89, 195
Cayuse Indians, 29
Central Oregon Community College, 21
Central Oregon Community College Ski Team, 70
Central Oregon Irrigation District, 78
Century Drive (see also Cascade Lakes Highway), 67, 106
Chambers Lake, 48
Chandler, W. E., 5
Charcoal Cave, 145
Chief Paulina, 129, 168
Chinook Indians, 119
Churches, 157, 202
Cinder Cone, The (Bachelor Butte), 59
Cinder Hill (Newberry Volcano), 125
Circle M-Ranch, 196
Civilian Conservation Corps, 14, 41, 66-67, 79, 208
Clark Van Fleet Trophy, **114**
Clarke, Clinton C., 14
Clarks River (Deschutes River), 76
Clear Lake Cutoff, 39
Cleveland Cave, 146

Cleveland, President Grover, 150
Clyde Skidder (logging equipment), **154**
Cobb, Irvin S., 74
Cold Springs, 61
Cold Springs Campground, 40
Cold Springs Ranch, 196
Coldwell, Ralph, 126
Collier, George H., 47
Collier Cone, 54
Collier Glacier, 47, 54
Collier Glacier Viewpoint, 47, 54
Collier State Park, 155
Columbia River, 17, 76, 150
Columbia River Lava Flows, 51, 124
Columbia Southern Ditch, 55
Condominiums, 94-96, 107-109
Conventions, 90, 94, 96, 107
Cooper, Ross and Ruth, 88
Corbett Ranch, Henry, 196
Corps of Engineers (see U.S. Army Engineers)
Corvallis, 31
Corvallis Valley and Eastern Railroad, 31
Country Mall (Sunriver), 96
Craig, John T., 35-36, 39
Craig Memorial, 43
Craig Memorial Ski Race, 39
Craigs Bride (see McKenzie Bridge)
Cramer, Henry, 20-21
Crane Prairie Meadow, **81**
Crane Prairie Osprey Management Area, 78-79, 119
Crane Prairie Reservoir, 77-79, **81**
Crane Prairie Reservoir Dam, 120
Crane Prairie Resort, 79
Crater Creek, 107
Crater Lake, 46, 58, 66
Crater Springs (see Metolius Springs)
Crescent, 176-178
Crescent District Ranger Office, 178
Crescent Lake, 173
Cressman, Dr. L.S., 80
Crook County, 11
Crooked River, 73-74, 76
Crosby, W.O., 135, 144
Cross Country Skiing (see Skiing, Nordic)
Crystal Springs (see Metolius Springs)
Cultus Creek, 77
Cultus Lake, 117-119
Cultus Lake Resort, **114**
Cultus Mountain, 119
Cultus River, 77, 118

D

Dant and Russell, 150
Dark Lake, 210-211
Davis, "Button", 81
Davis Creek, 80
Davis Lake, 80-82, 120, 173
Davis Mountain, 80
Dead Horse Hill, 35

Dee Wright (see Wright, Dee)
Dee Wright Observatory, 41-42
Derrick, H. F., 147
Derrick Cave, 147
Deschutes Bridge Guard Station, 77
Deschutes County, 11, 21, 77, 85, 172
Deschutes County Historical Society, 126
Deschutes County Library, 157
Deschutes Geology Club, 140
Deschutes National Forest, opp 1, 5, **143**, 150-151, 163, **171**
Deschutes National Forest Service, 76, 79, 130, 138, 206, 211
Deschutes Pioneer Gazette, 146
Deschutes River, 9, **24**, 30, 35, 45, 73-104, 109, 118, 120, 144, 149, 152, 155, **162**, 204-205
Deschutes River Recreation Homesites, 98
Deschutes Valley, **2**, 173
Detroit (Oregon), 19
Devils Garden (Cascade Lakes Highway), 115
Devils Garden (Fort Rock Region), 147-148
Devils Hill, **114**-115
Devils Lake, 9, 50, 52-54, 115-116
Dillman Cave (former name of Lava River Cave), 142
Dillman, James, 142
Dillon Falls, 99-100, 102
Dillon, Leander, 100, 102
Dion, J. P., 155
Dome, The (Cinder Cone), 124
Doris Lake, 118
Douglas, David, 17, 45
Douglas, Kirk, **62**
Drake Lodge, A.M., 76
Dry Hollow Ranch, 189
Dutchman Flat, 57, 69-70, 107-110, **112**
Dwyer (A. J.) Pine Land Company, 151
Dyer, Laurence and Betty, 198

E

East Ice Cave, 146
East Lake, 77, 123-**131**, 173
East Lake Hot Springs, 129, **131**
East Lake Resort, 129, **131**
East Lake Resort Company, 131
Ecology, 96, 111, 115, 121
Economy, 3, 11, 20, 72, 152, 161-**162**, 170, 181-183
Edison Ice Cave, 146
Education, 21, 156, 202
Elk Lake, **2**, 9, 106-107, **114**, 116-**117**
Elk Lake Lodge, **117**
Elk Lake Resort, **117**
Elkhorn Lodge (Sunriver), **90**
Elliot Cut-off Party, 30, 168
Ellis, Judge H. C., 106
Energy (see Geothermal Energy and Hydro-electricity)
Engels, Ralph, 52

Engineers (space), 6
Entrada Lodge, 107
Epworth League Institute, 208
Eugene, 19
Eugene Glacier, 48
Eyerly, Ray, 44

F

Fall Creek, 7, 48-49, 92, 113
Fall Creek Trail, 113
Fall River, 83-84, 87, 121
Fall River Resort, 84
Fall River Trout Hatchery, 84
Far West Mountains (alternate name for Cascades), 17
Farewell Bend Ranch, 111
Farnham, Thomas Jefferson, 17
Felderwood, Dutch John, 110
Ferry, Guy, 20-21
Finley Butte (logging) Camp, 159
Fire Lookouts, 59, 133-134, **137**-138, 188
Fires, Forest, **8**, 10, 12, **32**, **143**, 166
Fish Hatcheries, 84, 204-205
Fish Trap (Pringle Falls), 82
Fishing, 74-**75**, 77-84, 88, 91, 94, 106, 113-**114**, 116-118, 120, 124, 127-129, 173, 193, 198-**199**, 208
Forest Park (Sunriver), 93
Forked Butte, 25
Fort Dalles, 168
Fort Klamath—Crater Lake Ski Race, 61
Fort Laramie (movie set), **101**
Fort Rock (landmark), 89, 124
Fort Rock Valley, 146-147
Fox, Mayor R. H., 50
Fremont, Captain John, 17, 85, 97, 149, 168, 194
Fremont Highway (Highway 31), 12, 159
Fremont Land Company, 152
Fremont National Forest, 150, **171**
Fremont Trail, 2
Fur Trading, 74

G

Gallois, John and Elizabeth, 198
Garrison Butte, 16
Gaspé Bay, Quebec, 205
Gates, George "Lem", 26
Geology, 3, 15-16, 26-28, 40-43, 46-**56**, 58-59, 73-76, 80, 83, 87-89, 97-98, 103, **114**-115, 120, 122-125, 134-147, 192-193, 200, 202, 205, 207, **209**-210
General Patch Bridge, 84-85, 92, 121
Geothermal Energy, 6, 125
Gidley, Dr. J. W., 144-145
Gilchrist, 11, **171**, 175-176
Gilchrist Timber Company, **171**, 175-176, 212
Gilchrist, Frank R., 176
Gilchrist, R. E., 151
Gill, Miss Donna E., 211

Index

Glaciation, 6-8, 16, 26-28, 40-41, 43, 46-48, 51, **53-56**, 200, 207
Glaciers, 6, 8, 16, **24-26**, 46-48, 54, **56**, 200
Glaze Meadow, 189, 202
Glaze, Till, 189
Gleason, James, 172
Gold, 40-41, 55, 57
Golf, 94, **191**-192
Government Camp (pass), 29
Gray, John, 92
Great Hall (Sunriver), **90**, 94
Green Lakes, 14, 48-50, 113
Green Ridge, 192-193, 200, 202
Greenhow, Robert, 17

H
Hansen, Martin (resort), 196
Happy Valley, 107
Harper (townsite), 87
Harper Bridge, 87
Harper Hotel, 87
Hatfield, Senator Mark, 50
Hayden Glacier, 8
Hayrick Butte, **32**, 33
Head of Jack Creek, 205-206
Head of the Metolius (see Metolius Springs)
Hein, C. E. "Slim", 50, 198
Heising, Dan (resort), 196, 198
Hells Creek, 115-116
Hidden Valley, 33
High Cascades (see also Cascades), 15-16, 200
High Desert, 20, 44, 89, 123-125, 149, 168, 173
High Wheels (logging equipment), **53**, 155
Highway 20, 12, 39, 72, 189, 207
Highway 58, 120
Highway 97, 168-179
Hiking, 9, 14, 16, 25, 28-29, 34, 39, 41, 43, 48, 52-54, 65, 110, 116, 118-119, 130, 188, 211
Hill, James J., 173, 181
Hill, Louis W., 65
Hindman, Samuel M. W., 180
Historical Markers, 31, 40
Hixon, Frank P., 152
Hodge, Dr. Edwin T., 45-47, 52
Hogg, Col. T. Egenton, 31
Hogg Pass, 31
Hogg Rock, 30-31, **32**
Hole-in-the-Ground, 120
Hole-in-the-Wall Park, 25
Holt, A. W., 145
Homesteaders, **86**-87, 100, 145-146, 149
Homesteading, 85-87, 97, 100, 149, 173, 186
Hoodoo Butte, 33
Hoodoo Ski Area, 32-33, **66**-**68**
Hoover, President Herbert, 74, 120
Horseback Riding, 94, **108**-109, 130, 186, 189, **191**-192, 210-211

Horton, F. V. (Jack), 126
Hosmer Lake, 2, 59, **117**
Hosmer, Paul, 63, 66, 116-117
Hot Springs, 128-129, 131, 173
House on the Metolius, 197-198
Hudspeth Land and Livestock Co., 92
Hudson Bay Co., 30
Hunting, **81**, 88, 106
Husband, The (mountain), 45
Hydroelectricity, 76, 82, 88, 97-98, 173

I
Ice Caves, 145-146, 157
Ice Skating, 60, 64-65, **108**-109
Immigrant Trains, 74
Indian Fighters, The (movie), **101**
Indian Ford Creek, 185, 190, 202
Indian Ford Meadow, 185, 207
Indian Ford Ranch, 183, 185-**187**, 212
Indian Government, 159
Indian, 17, 23, 29-30, 34, 76, 79-80, 82, 89, 113, 115, 119, 126, 129, 142, 145, 147, 168, 180, 186, 194, 211
Inn of the Seventh Mountain, 103, 107-109
Inyo National Forest, 50
Irrigation, 3, 11, **24**, 49-50, 74, 77-78, 80, 82, 97-98, 126, 173-174, 195, 207-208
Irwin, Astronaut James R., 115

J
Jack Creek, 205-206
Jack Lake, 29
Jefferson, President Thomas, 23
Jefferson County, 11
Jefferson Creek, 25
Jefferson Park, 14, 26,
Jefferson Park Glacier, 26
John Muir Trail, 14
Johnson, S. Orie, **199**
Johnson, S. S., 151
Johnson, Sam and Becky, **199**
Jordan, J. W., 30

K
Kelley, Hall J., 17
Kiluea, Hawaiian Islands, 122
Kinzua Lumber Plant, 175
Klamath Indians, 17, 76, 89, 115
Klamath Indian Reservation, 168
Kolamkeni Koke (Klamath Indians name for Deschutes River), 76
Korrish, Wayne, 202
Kostol, Chris, 20, 60, 69
KTVZ (television station), 4
Kwolh Butte, 58

L
Lake Bend (proposed name for Todd Lake), 111
Lake Billy Chinook, **199**
Lake Creek, 195, 207-208, 210

High Country

Lake Creek Lodge, 196
Lake La Pine, 84
Lake Shevlin (proposed name for Todd Lake), 111
Lakes, 2, 9, 14, 16, 25, 29-30, 33-35, 41-43, 46, 48-50, 52-54, **56**, 58-59, 65-67, 70, 72, 74-77, **80-81**, 111-120, 123-**131**, 173, 206-210
La Follette, Captain Charles, 180
Lammi, Mrs. J. O., 145
Langille, H. D., 210
La Pine, 11, 44, 82, 170-175, 178
La Pine Intermountain (newspaper), 174
La Pine State Recreation Area, 83
La Pine Townsite Company, 87, 173
Lassen Peak, 15-16
Latta, John, 35
Laurel, Mississippi, 175
Lava Bear, 147-148
Lava Butte, 16, 60, 67, 89, 93, 97, 100, 130-139, 144
Lava Butte Logging Camp, 156
Lava Butte Observation Building, 133-134, **137-138**
Lava Camp, 52
Lava Camp Lake, 41
Lava Cast Forest, 131, 138-141
Lava Caves, 141-147, 157
Lava Island, 98, 103
Lava Island Falls, 103
Lava Lake, 76, 118
Lava Lake Murder, 118
Lava Lakes, 59, 118
Lava Lands Visitor Center, 133, 136, 138-**139**
Lava River Cave, 98, 131, 141-144
Lava River Cave State Park, 142, 170
Lava Tubes, (see Lava Caves)
Lavacicle Cave, **143**
Lechner, Pearl and Burdette, 174
Le Conte, Joseph, 51
Le Conte Crater, 51, **53**
Legislation (Oregon), 74
Leithauser, Frank, 195
Lewis and Clark (explorers), 16, 23, 76
Lewis Glacier, 48
Link Creek, 210
Linn Glacier, 46
Linton Creek, 54
Linton Lake, 43, 54
Lions Club (Bend), 144
Little Belknap Crater, **42-43**
Little Brother (mountain), 45
Little Crater, 124
Little Cultus Lake, 119
Little Deschutes River, 65, 75, 83, 85-87, 168, **171**, 174, 176-177
Little Ice Age, 16
Little Lava Lake, **75-77**, 118
Livestock, 4, 110, 177, 180-181, 186, 189-190, 195

Logging, 11, 100, 149-167
Logging Camps, 99, 155-159
Lolah Butte, 58
Lone Pine Irrigation District, 78
Lost Creek Canyon, 35
Lost Lake (former name of Todd Lake), 111
Lower Bridge, 49
Lowery, Stewart S., 189
Lumber Mills, 8, 11, 104, 149-150, 152, 155, 161-163, **171**, 175-176, 179, 181
Lumbermen, 104, 150
Lumrun Butte, 58

M

Macy Party, 30
Madison (proposed name for Three Sisters), 17
Mahoney, J. N., 163
Marion and Wasco Stock and Wagon Road, 29
Marion Creek, 29
Matoles (post office), 195
Matthieu, Francis Xavier, 52
Matthieu Lakes, 34, 41, 52
Mauna Loa, 122
Mazamas, 26
McArthur, Lewis L., 17, 27, 33, 45, 87, 110
McCure, A. S., 134
McHarg, Ian, 190
McKay Butte, **164**
McKenzie Bridge, 35-36
McKenzie Highway, 22, 34-43, 53, **62**, 65-66, 180
McKenzie Pass, 6, 29, 34-43, 52, 60-61, 65-66, 72
McKenzie River, 34, 38
McKenzie Salt Springs and Deschutes Wagon Road Company, 35
McKenzie Valley and Deschutes Wagon Road Company, 35
McKenzie Wagon Road, **42**, 169
McKenzie Wagon Road Company, 35
McKinney Butte, 185
McMullin, Hays, 196, 202
Meadow Village (Sunriver), 93
Melvin Butte, 125
Mennonites, 79
Mesa Creek, 54
Methodist Mission (Salem), 45
Methodist Youth Camp, 208
Metolius Meadows (subdivision), 194, 196-197
Metolius River, 9, 76, 192-200, 202, 204
Metolius River Valley, 192-205
Metolius Springs, 198-200, 202
Metolo (proposed development), 197
Michigan, 175
Middle Sister, 8, 20, 45, 47, 54
Midstate Electric Cooperative, 174
Midwest, 150
Mining, 5, 50-51

Index

Mink Lake Basin, 118-119
Minnesota, 150
Minnie Scott Springs, 52
Minto, John, 29
Minto Pass, 29
Minto Trail, 29
Mirror Pond (Bend), 76, 204
Mitchum, Robert, 62
Modoc Indians, 89
Mollala Indians, 29
Moraine Lake, 48, 116
Morgan, Mr. and Mrs. Howard, 189
Morson (irrigation) Project, 173-174
Morton, Superintendent K. E., 204
Mount Charity (South Sister), 45
Mount Etna, Sicily, 122
Mount Faith (North Sister), 45
Mount Hope (Middle Sister), 45
Mount Marion (former name of Three Fingered Jack), 27
Mountain Climbing, 26, 28, 39, 43, 48, 54, 59, 65, 116, 211
Mountain Village (Sunriver), 93
Mpto-ly-as (Indian name for Metolius River), 195
Mt. Bachelor, 16, 56-59, 62, 67-71, 76, 81, 90, 109-111
Mt. Baker, 16-17
Mt. Hood, 2, 15, 23-24, 41, 47
Mt. Jefferson, 2, 15, 17, 23-27, 32, 40, 45, 193, 197, 199-200
Mt. Jefferson Wilderness Area, 24-26, 29, 32
Mt. Mazama, 58, 80
Mt. Rainier, 17, 47
Mt. Washington, 15-16, 28, 33-34, 39-41, 43-44, 203, 207, 209
Mt. Washington Wilderness Area, 34, 39, 43
Mud Lake (former name for Hosmer Lake), 117
Mueller Land and Timber Company, 151-152
Murphy, Lucille, 211
Murphy, Thomas, 117

N

National Parks Service, 14
National Trails System Act, 14
National Wilderness Preservation System, 52
New England, 150
Newberry, Dr. John S., 78, 123
Newberry Crater, 6, 9, 72, 77, 83, 122-130
Newberry Lava Flow, 48
Newberry Volcano, 10, 44, 89, 122-148
Newberry Volcano National Park, 131
Nichols, Dr. R. L., 131
Nordeen, Emil, 20, 60-61, 140, 163
North Matthieu Lake, 52
North Paulina Peak, 126, 129
North Santiam River, 29
North Sister, 8, 15, 39, 45-47, 54
North Twin Lake, 120

North Unit Canal Company, 78
North Unit Irrigation District, 80
Northern Pacific Railroad, 31, 100, 102
Northwest Rift Zone, 135

O

Oak Springs Hatchery, 204
Obsidian Falls, 54
Obsidian Flow, 124-126, 130
Ochoco National Forest, 151
Odell (community), 177
Odell Lake, 82, 173, 177
Officers Club (Camp Abbot), 90
Ogden, Peter Skene, 30, 126
Ogden Trail, Peter Skene, 126
Old Baldy (former name of Bachelor Butte), 58
Old Homestead (Vandevert Ranch), 86-87
Olson, Carrie, 100
Olympic Skiers (see U.S. Olympic Skiers)
Oppie Dildock Pass, 52
Oregon and Western Colonization Company, 33
Oregon Department of Environmental Quality, 51
Oregon Fish and Wildlife Department, 84, 196, 204
Oregon Game Commission, 127
Oregon Geographical Names Board, 58, 80
Oregon Highway Department, 5, 65
Oregon Rural Mail Carriers, 36
Oregon Skyline Trail (see also Pacific Crest National Trail), 14
Oregon Stages, 38
Oregon State Parks System, 83
OSPIRG (Oregon Students Public Interest Research Group), 51
Osprey (see Crane Prairie Osprey Management Area)
Outdoor Club (former name of Skyliners), 63
Overlook Park (Sunriver), 93

P

Pacific Crest National Trail, 14, 34, 41, 43, 52-54
Pacific Crest National Trail System Conference, 14
Pacific Northwest, 150
Pacific Railroad Survey (see also Abbot, Lieutenant Henry L.), 10, 23, 52, 78, 88, 113, 123, 176, 186, 194
Packwood, Senator Bob, 50
Paleontology, 144-146
Pamelia Lake, 29
Panner, Owen, 50
Parker, Ed, 134
Parks Service (see National Parks Service)
Patch, Lieutenant General Alexander M., 84, 92
Patsy Lake, 25
Patterson, Dick and Kay, 184

Patterson Arabian Horse and Llama Ranch, 39, 184, **187**
Paulina Creek, 127
Paulina Falls, 127
Paulina Lake, 66, 123-131
Paulina Lake Hot Springs, 129
Paulina Lake Lodge, 127-**128**
Paulina Lake Resort, **128**
Paulina Mountain, 123
Paulina Mountains, 126, 140
Paulina Peak, 93, 122-123, 127, 129-**131**
Pelton Dam, 97
Pelton Place, 91
Pengra, B. J., 172
Perry, Walter J., 138, 146
Peterson and Groh (geologists), 200
Pilot Butte (Bend), 5, 44, 60
Pilot Butte Development Company, 149
Pine Echoes (Brooks-Scanlon Magazine), **117**
Pioneer Park (Bend), 168
Pivot Mountain (former name for Black Butte), 186
Plainview, 49
Plainview Project, 208
Pleistocene Epoch (geological time period), 15, 58, 80, 124, 145
Pliocene Age, 200
Plot Cave (former name of Lavacicle Cave), **143**
Pole Creek, 50, 181
Polk County, 180
Pollution, Water, 74
Polo, 94
Poly Top Butte, 16
Pope and Talbot, 150
Population, 4, 170-171, 174, 183
Portland, 31
Portland State University, 70
Post Offices, 36, 116, **158**-159, 172-173, 176, 180, **191**, 195, 201-202
Presidents Range (former name of Cascades), 17
Prineville, 11
Pringle, Octavius M., 82
Pringle Falls, 82-83, **86**, 121, 173
Pringle Falls (townsite), 82, **86**
Pringle Falls Electric Power Company, 82
Pringle Falls Experimental Forest, 121
Prouty, Harley H., 54
Prouty Glacier, 47-48
Prouty Memorial, 54
Proxy Falls, 43
Puget Sound, 150
Pumice (mining), 5, 50-51
Pumice Butte, 124
Pumice Cone, 124-125
Puyallup Flood, 17

Q

Que-y-ee (Indian for Indian Ford Creek), 186

Quimper, Manuel, 16
Quinn Meadows, 116
Quinn River, 77
Quinn River Campground, 79

R

Railroads, 31, 99-102, 150, 152, **154**-161, 163, 173-174, 181, 194, 199
Ranchers (see Stockmen)
Ranches, 39, 65, **86**-87, 111, 181, 183-**187**, 189-192, 195-196, 202, 211, 212
Ranyard, Mr. and Mrs., 84
Recreation (also see individual activities), 3, 74, 89, 94, 105-107, 115-117, 119, 174, **191**-192, 208
Red Hill (Bachelor Butte), 59
Redmond, 11, 19
Register Guard (Eugene), 38
Resorts, 79, 84, 88-97, 107-109, **114**, 118-120, 123, **128**, 194, 196, **203**, 208-210
Riley, Bill, 172
Riley Hotel, 174
Riviere des Chutes (former name of Deschutes River), 74, 76
Roaring River Station (fish hatchery), 204
Rock Mesa, 50-51, **53**-54, 116
Ronalds, Mrs. Bertha Perry, 196-197
Rosland, 10, 87, 121, 172
Round Butte Dam, 97
Russell, Israel C., 73, 97-98, 123, 134
Russell Glacier, 26
Ryan, John, 100
Ryan Ranch Meadow, 100

S

Sailing, **114**, 116, 211
Salishan, 92
Salt Springs (Belknap Springs), 34
San Francisco, 31
Sand Mountain, 30
Santiam Highway, **32**, 34, 180
Santiam Pass, 7, 19-20, 22, 29-34, 65-66, **68**, 72
Santiam Wagon Road, **24**, 30-31, 33, 181
Scandinavians, 3, 60-61, 66, 72
Scanlon-Gipson Lumber Company, 151
Schatz, Mrs. A. L., 134
Schools, 156, 177, 179, 202
Scott, Felix and Marion, 34-35, **42**, 52
Scott Lake, 34-35, **42**-43
Scott Mountain, **42**
Scott Pass, 52
Scott Trail, 35
Scout Lake, 210-211
Settle, John, 207
Sheep, 110, **112**, 149, 177, 180-181, 195
Sheepherders, 4, 195
Sherars Bridge, 111, 169
Sheridan, Lieutenant Phil, 78
Sheridan Mountain, 58
Sherman County, 195

Index

Sherman Crater (Mt. Baker), 16
Shevlin (logging Camp), 155, 157-159, 163
Shevlin, T. H., 152
Shevlin-Hixon Company, 65, 99-102, 138, 140, 142, 152, 155, 157-159, 161-163
Shevlin-Hixon Company Band, 113
Shevlin-Hixon Company Picnic, 99, 101
Shevlin Park, 60, 65
Shintaffer, Fred, 131
Shirley Lake, 25
Shoemaker, Phil, 134
Shonquest, Fred A., 91
Shotts, Charles, 176
Sierras Nevadas de S. Antonio (former name of Cascades), 16
Siah Butte, 58
Simer Brothers, 89
Sisters, 7, 10, 19, 39, 158, 162, 179-184
Sisters Chamber of Commerce, 183
Sisters Ranger Station, 195
Skeleton Cave, 144-145
Ski Carnival, 66, 69-70
Ski Club (former name of Skyliners), 63
Ski Jumping, 62, 66, 70
Skidmore, Owings, and Merrill, 92
Skiing, Alpine, 4, 56-61, 65-72, 136
Skiing, Nordic, 4, 8, 39, 48, 56-57, 62, 66-68, 70, 72, 95, 108, 110, 113, 123
Skjersaa, Nels, 20, 60-61, 163
Skjersaa, Olaf, 65, 67
Skyliners (ski organization), 4, 26, 62-67, 69, 136
Skyliners Hill, 66-67, 69-70
Skyliners Lodge, 66-67, 70
Slagsvold, Hans, 69
Sledding, 62
Smith, Alex and Robert, 179
Smith, Harold E., 127
Snake Indians, 129, 168
Snow Creek, 77
Snow Mountain (former name of Bachelor Butte), 58
Snowmobiling, 72, 123-124, 128
Snowshoeing, 60
Snowy Range (former name of Cascade Range), 16
Soda Creek, 7, 56, 92, 113
Soda Springs, 106
South, Perry A., 195
South Ice Cave, 146
South Matthieu Lake, 35
South Santiam River, 30
South Sister, 45, 47-50, 81, 111, 113-114, 116
South Twin Lake, 74, 120
South Twin Resort, 120
Southern Pacific Railroad, 31
Sparks Lake, 2, 9, 49, 56, 58-59, 106-107, 110, 113-114
Sparks, Lige, 113
Spring River, 87-88

Spring River Land Corporation, 88
Spring River Resort, 88
Squaw Creek, 7, 50, 180-181
Squaw Creek Canal, 208
Squaw Creek Irrigation District, 207
Squaw Valley Olympics, 63
Stage Stop Meadows, 85
Steidl, Steve, 119
Steidl and Reid Mill, 149
Stockmen, 74, 79, 110-111, 113, 149, 181
Stone and Timber Claims, 82
Summit Stage Station, 159
Sun River, 95
Sunriver, 76, 83, 88-97, 107, 212
Sunriver Lodge, 94-95
Sunshine Shelter, 54
Suttle Lake, 16, 33, 203, 205-210
Suttle Lake Improvement Company, 207
Suttle Lake Irrigation District, 207
Suttle Lake Resort, 203
Swampy Lakes, 67, 70
Swedish Ski Association, 61
Swimming, 80, 94, 108-109, 114, 119, 191-192, 211

T

Table, The (mountain), 25
Table Lake, 25
Tam McArthur Rim, 39, 72
Tam McArthur Volcano, 53
Taylor, Dr. Ed., 210
Tennis, 85, 94, 108-109, 191-192, 211
Tetherow Bridge, 30
Tetherow Crossing, 35, 180
Tetherow Log Jam, 83
Thayer Glacier, 46
The Dalles-California Highway, 142, 161, 163, 168, 169
Three Creeks Lake, 72
Three Fingered Jack, 15, 27-29, 32, 67, 193, 197
Three Sisters, 2, 15, 17, 24, 39, 41-52, 68, 108, 110, 113, 179
Three Sisters Wilderness Area, 14, 39, 43-57
Three Trappers Butte, 58
Timber and Stone Act, 150
Timbers (The), 159
Tobogganing, 60
Todd, John Y., 89, 111
Todd Lake, 70, 110-113
Toll Roads, 24, 30, 33, 35, 169-170
Tollgate, 185
Tomes, Frank W., 174
Tot Mountain, 58
Tourism, 72, 107, 138, 182-184, 202
Towornehiooks (Indian word for Deschutes River), 76
Traffic Counts, 170
Trails (see Hiking Trails)
Trout Creek, 35
Tuff Ring, 124

Tules, The (see also Ryan Ranch), 100
Tumalo Creek, 55, 66-67, 160
Tumalo Creek Lodge, 65
Tumalo Falls, 8, 55, 67, 70
Tumalo Fish Hatchery, 65
Tumalo Lake, 67
Tumalo Mountain, 58, 109-110
Tumalo Ranger Station, 63
Tumalo Reservoir, 64
Tumalo Ski Area, 66
Twin Lakes, 119-120
Tyee Creek, 115

U
Union Pacific Railroad, 69
United Artists (Hollywood), 101
U.S. Army Engineers, 84, 91, 94, 123
U.S. Bureau of Public Roads, 38
U.S. Bureau of Reclamation, 78, 80, 98
U.S. Forest Service, 4-5, 14, 29, 33, 51, 58-59, 66, 69, 101-102, 106, 116, 140-141, 144, 181, 194-195, 199, 205, 212
U.S. Forest Service Nursery, 167
U.S. Forest Service Silviculture Laboratory, 121
U.S. Geographical Board, 111
U.S. Government, 97
U.S. Olympic Skiers, 69-70
U.S. Pumice Company, 50-51

V
Vancouver, George, 16
Vandevert, Claude, 86
Vandevert Ranch, William, 65, 86-87
Vegetation, 3, 8, 11-13, 18, 22, 25-26, 28, 40, 43, 49, 102, 109, 139, 153, 164, 185, 188, 192, 205-207
Volcanism, 3, 5-6, 15-16, 27, 40-43, 46, 48, 50-55, 58-59, 74, 80-81, 83, 88-89, 97-98, 114-115, 120, 122-125, 134-136, 138-144, 147, 200, 205, 209-210
Volcanoes, 2-3, 5-6, 15-16, 24-28, 32-33, 41-48, 52-59, 80, 91, 122-125, 130-138, 186, 188, 191, 209

W
Wagon Trail, 185
Waldo Glacier, 25
Walking Race, 65
Warm Springs Indians, 101, 115, 126, 168
Wasco Lake, 29
Water Skiing, 114, 119
Water Sports, 34, 114, 119
Water Supply, 5, 50, 55, 65, 88, 96
Way West, The (movie), 62
Weather and Climate, 2-4, 7-11, 13, 18-22, 38, 42, 45, 47, 57, 59, 74-77, 95-96, 102, 110, 122-123, 134-135, 169, 172-173, 178, 188
West Lake (proposed name for Crane Prairie), 77
West, Oswald (Governor), 77-78
Western Cascades, 15
Western Mountains, 17
Weyerhauser, 150
White Branch Creek, 54
Whitewater Glacier, 26
Why-Chus (Indian name for Squaw Creek), 180, 186
Wickiup Plains, 50-54, 116
Wickiup Reservoir, 75, 79-82, 120
Widmark, Richard, 62
Wiest, L. D., 207
Wife, The (mountain), 45
Wild River (subdivision), 82
Wilderness Areas, 2, 13-15, 23-27, 32, 34, 39, 43-57
Wildlife, 57, 83, 100, 133, 142
Wiley, Andrew, 30
Wilkes, George, 17
Willamette Hatchery, 204
Willamette Pass, 29-30
Willamette Valley and Cascade Mountain Company, 30
Willamette Valley and Cascade Mountain Road Project, 207
Williams, Howel, 46, 51, 58, 124, 135
Williamson, Lieutenant R. L., 52, 78
Williamson Railroad Survey Party (see Pacific Railroad Survey)
Willow Creek, 149
Willow Ranch, 186
Windy Point, 36, 40-41
Winema National Forest, 171
Winopee Lake, 119
Winter Carnival (see Ski Carnival)
Winter Sports, 3, 4, 60-72, 136
Wisconsin, 175
Wizard Falls Fish Hatchery, 193, 203-205
Wright, Dee, 41, 52
Wulfsberg, Nels, 20, 60-61, 63
Wyeth, Nathaniel J., 17, 168

Y
Yamakiasham Yaima (Indian name for Cascade Range), 17
Yaquina Bay, 31
Yapoah Crater, 34-35, 41, 52-53

Z
Zig Zag Glacier, 47